"Touching . . . I believed in the dilemma itself and felt its force and dignity."
—*Saturday Review*

"Painfully familiar to anyone who has had a love affair disintegrate, passions extinguished like a candle . . . leaving only the memory of light. The prose is agonizing, each detail is recorded." —*NewsWest*

Also by Kate Millett
Published by Ballantine Books:

THE PROSTITUTION PAPERS
FLYING

SITA

by Kate Millett

BALLANTINE BOOKS · NEW YORK

A portion of this book appeared, in somewhat different form, in *Christopher Street*.

Library of Congress Catalog Card Number: 77-2267

ISBN 0-345-27362-1

This edition published by arrangement with
Farrar, Straus and Giroux

Title-page drawing by Kate Millett

Manufactured in the United States of America

First Ballantine Books Edition: June 1978

For Herself

I fall back on the bed. The nightmare change of it all. "You haven't seen the house since the gypsies took over," she'd said in Sausalito. All that, of course. Hit me in the first few minutes: the bits of fabric on the walls where Sherman's drawings had been, the bedspread draped over what was once the breakfast nook, now little Emily's bedroom, the rumpled rugs, the hodgepodge of bureaus and tables in hallways. Each like a slap against what had once been our house, the house the two of us had taken together, furnished, loved.

"But you've rented a loft in New York; you've been away for months. Remember we had Paul and Valerie move in for the summer when we went to Europe? Well, when you stopped off in New York and I came back here, I just let them stay on." My bedspread in her son Paul's room, the front room he shares with his girlfriend Valerie, my towels on everyone's rack in the bathroom. "Then Pia moved in. I was down with bronchitis and she took care of me. She and Dan had gone on the methadone program and they needed to be here." Of course it was good, good that she have her children with her, the commune she used to dream about. When she called me and said that Pia had moved in and I needn't worry about the rent for a few months, it seemed a good solution. She didn't mention Dan, she didn't mention Emily. It was all temporary, till the kids got on their feet. I love Sita's two grown children, but I don't want to live with them. "Listen, Kate, I will not throw them out," she shouted when she came to New York at Christmas. And she nearly didn't

1

come. Days of evasions on the phone, lies at the office
and at home, Pia telling me she was out, fibbing outrageously when I telephoned time after time. And then
she did come. Sita in the great white light of the loft,
Sita for Christmas. Four days of lovemaking and wine
and quarrels over the house. But it was good, all the
old power. If our thing had gone shaky, those four days
brought it all together again. I would come back for
sure, stay the winter as we'd planned, teach a course at
the university. I would live half the year in each place.
Since the loft was cheap, I could still have the excitement of New York and the stability of my life with her.
Both. All. Everything. Even hold on to New York, my
old town, my old life. All as we'd planned.

But there was so much I'd never guessed at, so many
changes. She had made a new life without me, a life
from which I was eliminated. I might have done that in
New York, too. But I kept the old schedule, the old
plans. Had returned to them now. Had come back to
Berkeley and our house in the hills. To find it gone.
Vanished into another existence, into a commune, a
crowd. Well, adjust then, be flexible. Of course it was
good she should have them with her, we have been
over that a hundred times. When she came to New
York at Christmas, it began to dawn on me that she
had given our house over to her children, that I had
been dispossessed. But I hadn't *seen* it yet.

Memories of the old life, the few things left, the bedspreads, in Paul's room and the one here in this room
too, the drawings on the wall behind me, the three
nudes I'd done of her that hang over my head. Evenings in a hotel room in Mexico City, her brown and
lovely body, the quiet luxury of drawing her while we
sipped tequila, while the traffic in the Zócalo grew still
outside the windows. Mexico, the night before we left.
I had just got well enough to come home. Knew the
very shrimp that poisoned me, knew it as I put it in
my mouth, could see it hadn't been cleaned, wonderful
night we had dinner on the roof of the hotel, looking
out over the cathedral and the square, the black line of
poison sliding down my throat. Then the hell of it, even
crapping on the rug, impossible to get to the toilet, shit-

ting and throwing up all at once. The intravenous feeding, the diplomatic English-speaking doctor, miraculous recovery. But that night it hit her, leaving me to run like a maniac to check us out, pay the bills, tip and bully porters into getting medicine at four in the morning, inventing Spanish. Cajoling the doctor's office by phone, struggling with the nurse who couldn't find her vein, haranguing her in gibberish and English while Sita, who is our Spanish, lies gray, eyes closed, her veins collapsing. And this ox jabbing her without pity. Until I bellow enough to bring another nurse, one with wiser hands. Wondering while I wait how I can get hold of a thousand dollars, pay for a hospital, my mind screaming at the thought of a funeral. Urging the next nurse with sheer force of will to find that vein, begin the intravenous feeding, save her. My Sita so nearly gone, the whole journey, which had started in such luxury, ending in a bad dream. Even the luxury of the first afternoon, making love in a cheap room that reminded both of us of all the existential wonder we had known in third-class hotels when we were students. Then moving to the grand place on the Zócalo, the sheer arrogance of it, our dinners on the roof, our sumptuous room, the whimsy of changing from one double bed to another, the long afternoons turning to evening while I drew her naked in the evening calm. That same body dying on the bed unless I can make this creature find a vein. Sita an ashen thing that can hardly cry out now when they stab her. But somehow I saved her life.

And last spring, living here together after we got the house, the two of us. How it hurts even to summon that time, how it stings the eyes. Now the place full of other people, their things, their paraphernalia. Sherman's big yellow painting should be on the wall before me, but it's gone. In its place a Mucha poster advertising Monte Carlo, probably something of Pia's. She stares at it too. "You won't believe me, maybe"—her voice hesitant, then definite—"but I like that better. Yes, a lot better. I guess I'm a gypsy too." She has taken sides, taken a stand. I lie back on the bed and close my eyes. My things are foreign here now, unwanted. My paintings and drawings and photographs are taken down. The room, once our bedroom, simple and stark and lovely, the yellow canvas, the Greek bedspread, the white walls—now crowded with random furniture and posters and lamps. Funky—the kid's taste. And it's her thing too; it was all along.

Well, this is endurable somehow. Mustn't get hung up on aesthetics, objects, possessions. Why not share, have a commune? In New York it had sounded vaguely romantic, a relief from the loneliness of trying to write there, the terrible solitude I'd grown to hate and be afraid of after she'd been with me at Christmas. All these changes, well, really to be expected, so many people living here. But what murders me is the sight of another room just glimpsed while climbing the stairs. Crowded and unfamiliar now. Stuffed with others, stuffed. "Pia's room," that's what it's called now. That was where I worked. My "study," she'd called it. The room where I wrote, my big lovely table before the two windows and the bay. All of San Francisco and the Golden Gate at my disposal. The hills of Berkeley at a glance, and then the water, the city, and beyond it to the west the great orange bridge. I look again. Pia's big bed, table, bureaus, Dan's armchair. "It's a house full of love," she keeps saying. I lie back and close my eyes. "There's nowhere for me to work, my room's gone, nowhere to put a table." "Maybe you can rent a little studio some place. Pia has a friend who's just moving out of one."

"Just set up your table in a corner of the bedroom," she'd said in New York. As if it were a trivial problem about furniture. "I can't sleep and work cooped up in the same little room all day and night," I protested, looking up and down the magnificent space of the loft. Why should I leave this for California? Why indeed. And she'd never urged it. Was punctilious about that, keeps reminding me how she never insisted I come. But I came anyway. Unable to forget or be away from her after those four high days at Christmas, the loft suddenly turning sour after she left, lonely. Life in New York, the new independence of it all, living alone after the wreck of a ten-year marriage, the man gone, even the studio where we lived torn down by the city. And

starting out on my own again in the town, my own
studio, but it had somehow lost its effervescence after
she left. New York, my New York; all those mellow
bohemian years grown cold as an empty plate. After
Christmas, after the joy of her, the rest was solitude.
And Christmas had been bed and champagne and fighting. Holding her that first afternoon, listening to
Bohème, the album I'd given her as a present, routinely
listened to—I did not realize it would affect me. We
had heard it once together at the farm, but it only reminded me of Zoe and our early days on the Bowery.
Sita had tried to translate it and to sing it for me, but
I was angry and impossible and berated her for not
being an artist, for not being Zoe. Regretting that time
so as I listened then, both of us going back to that crazy
little rehearsal we'd watched in the square at San
Gimignano when we'd first come together over that
music. Holding her that first afternoon in New York,
sitting on the sofa in the winter dark, all the poignant
grasp of her, listening, the two of us sitting on the sofa,
and suddenly it is here, the great wrenching lyric speaking as direct as the knowledge of death, the flesh of her
arm in my hand, the months, the years of loving her.
And came to her now in January, knowing that I was
helpless—couldn't get away.

Following that dream back to California. But already it was wrong. Even before we got to the house.
The weekend. Coming down the ramp I saw her, coming to meet my plane. Sita standing patiently behind
the barrier. The shock, as it is always a shock, to
realize I am in love with a middle-aged woman. A
plain, rather intimidating face, off-putting behind her
hard shell-like glasses. Her armor. Only when she takes
them off do you realize she is beautiful. It is only when
you know her. And the manner too, the stance, an attitude that warns away the Anglo world, America,
vulnerable as her touch of lameness, withdrawn, slightly
arrogant. The foreigner's defensiveness, hauteur. It
always takes a moment. Then sliding again into her
beauty, her spell. Her wit, her tenderness. The perfume
of her exoticism.

We would have the weekend in Sausalito and then

go back to the house in Berkeley. There would be some
little transition before the new reality. But the weekend
was a downer. Disparate, fragmented. Making love was
not what it had been in New York, the great shuddering need to come together, weeping in her arms as after
a terrible absence. There had been no great swell or
volume. We had even been afraid to start. Both of us
were. Rushed out and bought a bottle of champagne,
postponing it. Her passion for champagne. As if that
would begin things, make it possible, that talisman. She
must have been just as conscious as I how the need did
not transcend the shyness, the awkwardness, the uncertainty. Both of us seeing it: how we could wait,
how we didn't have to have each other. I reminded
myself there was time now, less pressure; this time it
would be no mere four days. But I saw it like a crack
in a bowl. We who had once been such lovers, so hot,
so intemperate.

And the thing perfunctory almost when it happened.
I had wanted to make love all afternoon; that had been
my fantasy, one whole long slow afternoon, every var-
iation and possibility explored, savored, every sensation lingered over. Yet the room seemed defenseless;
noises in the hall and next door. And the room so
small, without even a bathroom, one we'd never had
before in all our visits; this old hotel our rendezvous
how many times. Sausalito, the great nights of our love
ago, the fire burning in the big room, our bodies spread
out before it on a rug, nights once, or afternoons, long
late mornings of being every experiment in the great
mahogany bed. General Grant's own hand-carved bed
in the plushest room of all. A room I remember, can
conjure by. Every moment in it precious, irretrievable,
the hurt of its very pastness as certain as burial. Even
how she wept and shivered before the fire that one
night, lovely in the naked brown skin of her body, crying because she had an interview in Los Angeles the
next day and was afraid of the job, afraid they'd hire
her, afraid they wouldn't. Wanting Berkeley more, but
the other paid better. And was she old? Would they
sniff at her credentials? And could she go on standing
on her own after a lifetime of marriages, and was it

worth it, these jobs you killed yourself to get and then hated? And would they see all that right there at the interview and humiliate her? Her body shaking in my arms. Another Sita out of my thousand Sitas. I had never seen her scared, only the serene competence of the absolute campus politician, the administrator, the fighter for civil rights, the feminist, the subtle and magnificent bringer of change, my Machiavel. Her womanliness, her intelligence, her courage. Latin diplomacy, finesse, the loveliest manner, the charm of her age and her breeding saying the same things as the radical toughs, but saying them smoothly, reasonably, concisely; better yet, getting it done. For an hour this lost and terrified woman rocking naked before a fire. I comforted her, I listened, I reassured. The look and the feel of her in that room that night, a room just down at the end of the hall but a million years ago. I remember its bow windows, her wicker traveling case, the scent of her perfume in a scarf as she stood before the windows in the morning. It echoes in the mind like the feel of silk. Like the soft flesh of her name, Sita. Formally Innocenza, stately, nearly pompous; the humor and irony of it—*Innocenza di che?* In Italy and in Brazil, where she grew up, other children playfully softened the name, reshaped it to Sensita and then, to make it handy, cut it down to Sita, the most private of names, the dearest and most secret. Pronouncing it is like a kiss, the sound in the mouth like the lips grazing over soft flesh.

Now this disappointing little room. The hurry of it, the confinement. There was a dismaying absence of romance this weekend. Like the fear you have of sex sometimes, looking forward to it but afraid you will not be able, not be open, not reach orgasm. Lying in bed watching her prepare to dress on Sunday morning, realizing she is already wanting to dress, to leave. While I had been waiting for her to finish her coffee, come back to bed, begin some delicious or leisurely exploration of one kind or another in the two fine hours before noon and check-out time. She stands before the mirror brushing her hair. The silver of the mirror, its strange empty light. The mercury gray of her hair. The feeling she gives off is impatience, irritation. Yet how beautiful she is, poised before the watery space of the mirror—the dark skin of her face, her lovely hair, the brush. A loveliness at odds with her exasperated, "Why did you wait till now to suggest it? I've long since lost interest. I'm ready to go." Seeing her pack, the neat efficient little gestures, a sinking feeling. It's all over. Suddenly all over. Almost as if it were already Monday. The weekend collapses into the prosaic sidewalks and concrete of a weekday. A workday.

It was wrong even when we went to visit Sherman. A visit lifeless, almost ceremonial. After visits made so many times, visits hilarious or tragic or inebriated. But this one almost silent, formal. Sherman, this old painter recluse, my friend for twenty years, strange dyke saint of art, in a new studio, cramped, broke, her canvases spread in new rooms now, smaller, shrunken. Yet somehow the old flair there still, her gift for turning any ordinary room into a work of art, a place of rest. But even then something was off somehow, anticlimactic. Though Sherman is my friend, it was Sita who talked to her. I said nothing. Had nothing to say, astonished to discover I had nothing to say, feeling estranged, distracted, removed from myself and the two of them. Sherman's face turned toward Sita. I am observing their friendship, moved by the sight of it, feeling an affection for it. Yet the displacement remains; it is as if I am not there, have evaporated, vanished. Listening to Sita's news: "Danny's leaving. He's moving out of the house. Such a relief. Now maybe Pia can get it together and do her own thing, she'll be free of his influence. Dan holds her back." Sherman nods. Behind it is Pia's long addiction to heroin, discovered again after five years when we thought she was clean, the five years since she had kicked the first time, alone with Sita in the old house in Sacramento. And then last year it turned out she had been using all along. Came to light only when she began the methadone program with Dan. The two of them would be cured together. Then maybe they could do something in music, in life. They are through it now and have come out whole and triumphant. But Dan just drives his truck. He will never go back to his drums. Years and years in a basement, he'd told me, living only at night. No life at all, he said. So he drives a truck in the produce market. "I want to devote myself entirely to my family now," he says solemnly.

I search for something to say, anything, anything, any sign I am alive, feel, exist. Nothing comes. I had looked forward to this, yet I feel nothing but emptiness, unease. They go on talking. What am I doing here? It is all a rerun of the past, California last time, the time before. But with all the sensation gone. Weekends in Sausalito with a stop at Sherman's on the way home— how magical they used to be, how euphoric those early weekends, how every moment with Sita glistened, whatever we did: driving or shopping or lunching. Long wineglasses and fruit and the lights of the bay through mellow dinners at the Trident. At dinner there last night there was not enough conversation to fill the hour. Our silence embarrassed me, made us conspicuous. And now at Sherman's, watching the two of them gossip. Sita has plenty to say, and I look on and relish her vitality. But it is not for me. With me she is silent. Sherman's weathered face and denims, such a contrast to Sita's beringed fingers, her supple and elegant leather boots, her gloves and her bag. Sita goes on about her job, how her provost is an ass, a pompous fool, how they pay her one salary to do two jobs, how they thwart her at every turn, how overworked she is, how there is not one weekend free till April. I watch the two of them, everything closing in, becoming trivial. Are we old?

Finally Sherman questions me perfunctorily about New York. Fumio. How is he? The muscles of my stomach tighten and then turn liquid. How long will people go on torturing me with this question? How long will I go on with my pat answers—that he is busy working for his next show, that we see each other often, that we are great friends, that he sends his regards. "How about your place?" Another nerve. The house I lived in fifteen years, grew up in, the dear old Bowery house where I lived with Fumio ten of those years, crazy wonderful 1806 Dutch masterpiece of zigzags and leaking roofs, condemned now and torn down by the city. Everything ends at once. Fumio, the house. Our eviction the signal for his escape. "So what are you going to do?" "I got another loft. My friend Ruth badgered the city until they came through with relocation." "You're lucky." "Yeah. Yeah."

"How long will you be out here?" Awkwardness. "Maybe two weeks, maybe the semester. I might be teaching a writing course for Sita's program." "You don't know yet?" A pause, Sita laughs to cover this and looks away. "Well, we'll kind of see how it goes." I still have no idea. Two weeks or four months—there's a difference. And I simply didn't know when I left, Ruth promising to forward the mail, water the plants. It would depend on how things went, it would depend in fact on the commune. And Sita. Everything depends.

They go on talking together. I go on being apart. What am I doing out here? What a fool I must look, not even knowing my own plans. A beautiful studio in New York and I'm hungering around out here where I have a table in the corner of a bedroom in a menagerie of hippies and children. I dread seeing the house again, I dread the weekend being over, cheerless thing that it was. I dread the visit with Sherman coming to an end, terrified of my own silence, my vacuity. Surely they must notice it. Sita, who decides everything, decides we must leave. A spiritless ride back to Berkeley, the sight of San Francisco, the great bridge, the bay— all curiously without effect. The Queen City, I always called it in my mind, used to worship the sight of it coming into view as you cross the bay; now only distant, unlovely, pointless. Even beloved landmarks like the Hills Brothers Coffee sign, an old friend now regarded with indifference. A mistake, the whole thing a mistake. Shouldn't have come.

I fall back on the bed. Thank God, they're not all here, the bunch of them looking on at my dismay. It will be just between the two of us. Or just within myself. I knew what I was getting into, or should have. This many people in the place, of course it has to change. She stirs beside me. "Shall I drive you to the airport?" I look at her, a long terrified look, realizing that if I were to say yes, she would simply do it. Calmly and easily do it. She will not budge an inch. Now even more than at Christmas, when she shouted she would not kick them out. "Who says kick them out?" I had argued. "Surely they know I'm coming back, they're there just temporarily, you say Paul's moving over to Marin soon anyway. Wouldn't this be a good time for them to find their own place?" It had seemed so reasonable then. They were taking my place in the house, substituting, but now I was home. They were taking advantage of my absence, but now I would be coming back. The rent was my obligation and I paid my half through the summer and part of the fall until Sita told me, *fait accompli,* that Pia had moved in. Paul and Valerie pay no rent, never have. But Pia and Dan would pay my half for a few months and this would solve the problem through the fall. And now I was back, only to discover it was no longer my house at all but theirs, hers, and in some mysterious way, her brood's. Sita melting into them as she did, the group of them merged and standing away and at odds with me, the outsider, the stranger. They are her family, I am merely her lover. A family, and I the interloper. It has taken me so long to understand.

When Hatsie came back from California in November, she'd warned me about this, but I was in no mood to listen. "Sita's really into this motherhood thing now. She says she hasn't had all her children together with her for years." "But they're grown up, they're not even children any more." Pia's twenty-six, Paul's finished high school now and has lived away from home for years. "Don't ask me, but she says being together with her whole family this Christmas will be the most beautiful thing in the world." "No, she's coming *here* for Christmas, to New York." "Oh, really?"

And then of course she almost didn't come. Crisis with her job, she said. Canceled and then let me persuade her to make the trip for just four days. The four days that brought me back. Because when she canceled her trip at Christmas I was ready to give up. There had been the months apart, the telephone tricks, the terrible memory of the summer in Italy, the great five-thousand-dollar catastrophe I had treated her to. "Two glorious months in Italy and Ireland," but we never got to Ireland, spent the summer in her brother Paolo's villa under family guard and in separate beds, a summer when she was with me not at all, hardly bothered to speak to me, a summer during which she openly despised me. Then the parting in September, she to California, I to build my loft in New York.

But the four days at Christmas when it all came back, came together again, all the months and years, the two, nearly three years of this impossibly lovely and exasperating affair reasserting itself, the old passion, the old sweep of it. And I'm here again, here in the house where we set up housekeeping together last spring, my marriage over, a breakdown and the suicide months that followed. Over, everything of the past over. New York behind me—or almost, and I came to the house here where we began our pseudo-marriage last spring, the two of us. Until I got another loft in New York. And then it was to be half and half, here and there six months each year. Back again now to find the house as I knew it gone. And the life we had there utterly erased. Throw in the towel and give up entirely? Go home to New York and the bare empty loft, tough it out? Wanting her, even as we lie here, even in this anger and despair, wanting her.

The sound of the front door. An odd sound. Never before while we lived here did anyone ever turn a key in that door while we listened. But now there are so many, so many keys, so many footsteps on the stairs. And now Pia's voice—"Hi, you guys." Pia on the stairs. And Dan. I am as surprised to see him as Sita is. But it is Dan who hugs me hello in the hall, Dan who is warm and friendly. The other loner, interloper, outsider. Pia is her usual breezy delight. But not after a moment or so. Sita is cold to her, annoyed that Dan is still with her, still in the house. Suddenly Pia is furious and shouting, "Mom, where *are* you, I look at you and I don't see you, where'd you go, what's with you?"

We follow them down to the kitchen where Pia has started cooking chicken. We had planned to go out for dinner; a little more privacy, more time of our own. Pia

is obviously cooking for us too, demanding we stay. I
am not committed to this chicken and don't want to be,
but there is no time to confer. Pia before the stove,
brutally angry. "Dan's my old man, and he's staying if
he wants to stay. He's my man and he can be here if
he feels like it. He's my person, he's my friend, he's my
lover. I can have him here." I lean against the cup-
board, embarrassed. Envious. How I wish Sita would
say this of me, stick up for me. Because I am under
attack too. "You said this was our house, Mom. Didn't
you, didn't you promise us that? Didn't you say it was
ours?" And I am not one of ours. Odd that if Pia is
entitled to her husband in my house, my own standing
should be so precarious. Or rather, putting it the new
way, if Pia is entitled to a husband in her mother's
house (since everyone sees it as Sita's house now),
why should I as her mother's lover find it so hard to
justify my existence while leaning against a counter?
Noncombatively. Because I answer Pia's assault with
silence, terrified of her shouts. It will all be over in ten
minutes. The children will drive me out. Paul and
Valerie have arrived by now, Paul not even shaking
my hand. How I used to love these kids, their chatter
and pot, their parties and music and good times, but
especially their music. Now they are strangers. Paul,
who used to hug me against the bare chest of his
gawky, six foot four, affectionate late adolescence. And
now nothing. His Valerie beautiful and distant. But
then I hardly know her, met her only once. They go off
to their room together in the casual alienated way life
seems to take here. Dan has also disappeared. I remain in the kitchen with Pia. With Sita, who is also
silent. Waiting out the yelling. The chicken goes on siz-
zling through Pia's recriminations. "This was *our*
house." I listen, fighting my tears and humiliation.
"And by God, it's *staying* that way." If only I had her
fight, if only I could fight for my place. Is this some
pecking-order savage society? If only Sita would speak
out for me, settle it, say anything at all. Pia's voice is
terrible. The commune is hell, a jungle. And it could
have been fun. I never meant to quarrel with these
people. We used to be friends till we had to live to-

gether. Pia wheels around from her chicken and toward me. "What's the matter with you?" "I have no place to work." "Tough shit." "Do you know what it means to me? Do you have any idea?" "Too fucking bad. Look, Mom—you promised, you fucking promised. And we're staying. This is *our* place." "No one questions that, Pia." "We belong here, see?" "Sure." "And Dan can be here till it suits him. Yes, he's going. We are splitting up. But it's going to take him some time to get his stuff together, to get himself together, and he can have just as long as he wants. See?" Sita never answers, but her very silence is a humbling acquiescence. The chicken sputters contentedly, its aroma a mocking invitation to dinner, celebration, conviviality.

Pia slams together the contents of a salad, Valerie assists. They refuse my help, Valerie's movements stiff and angry. I watch them, two very beautiful young women. Pia's fragility, Valerie's blond virago type. I am outclassed. They are younger, prettier, tougher. I hear Sita in conference with the two men. Then the sound of my table being carried up from the garage and installed in our bedroom. The chicken purrs on: we are stuck with it, the joyless family dinner. My fantasies of communal delight wither at the crowded table. The awkwardness of people feeding an unwelcome guest, the silences and broken jokes. Only little Emily is glad to see me. At eight she can ignore the opinions of the others. My old friend of dress-up games, my solemn fellow artist who shows me each new drawing. Pia's Emily, this strange grown-up child who has survived her mother's odyssey into drugs, hip, the music world, the white high of heroin. Sita's treasure, this granddaughter, the only one to remind her of Italy. Pia and Paul are fair and repeat their American fathers. But Emily has the darkness in her eyes.

"Whatsa matter with all you guys?" Emily's face examines us one by one. No one answers her. Dinner marches on. I do not even look at Sita any more; appeal is futile, the numbers between us cancel our relationship. You are on your own here. The others are couples, but we are not a couple. Sita is the matriarch, it is her house, she is the center, the authority, the

power. Pia and Dan, Valerie and Paul, the pairs, each
guarding the other, backing them up in the fierce battle
for space and prerogative. Emily and I the extras, but
Emily has the privilege of childhood, is owned by and
appended to Pia. I have none of these claims of mate
or kin. As the bizarre meal progresses like a mechani-
cal farce, a movie parody—the communal act, tedious,
empty, hostile, surreal—an amazement comes over me,
trying to remember that I used to live here. As if it
were a lie.

She is already asleep, and I next to her, smoking one
last cigarette—the first day is over. Survived it. Go on
surviving? This is not life. This is masochism. Get out
of here. The suitcases still unpacked, shapes in the dark
of the room. Leave? Leave her? Call it quits, the
whole thing? Behind me in the dark those drawings,
and beyond the room where I used to work, and Paul's
room, which used to be our library, so rich we were in
space; the dining room downstairs, scene of our candle-
lit steaks and artichokes, the yard where we would read
or lie in the sun, the garden and the gardener, only a
matter of bills to pay now. The life that was. And isn't
any more. Your own fault for leaving, for wanting New
York too, for needing a loft and a sculpture studio, for
the extravagance of that independence, for feeling con-
fined by last spring's "marriage." Last spring, when the
place was your hospital after you lost the studio in New
York, after you lost Fumio, after you lost your mind
for the last and final time, the suicide trip. And then,
well and recovered a bit, first thing you do is get another place in New York, set up shop, and do a couple
hundred drawings and try to write . . . And nothing
comes, and the manuscript you drag around with you
now will never be finished. Bits in notebooks, pages
here and there out of the chaos of a life wrecked: your
madness, your separation, your attempts to die. How
would you ever put that together? Nerve endings,
blood, hunks of flesh. Tomorrow you have to pull the
pages, file, put in order, begin to type. The room spins
at the hopelessness of it.

Write? Here? Are you crazy? The table in the corner, huge, obstructing the room. Write in a goddamn bedroom? 'Cause that's all they've left you—when you have that great big loft in New York? Or pack? Give up one more time, one more person, love, hope, chance —run one more time? Leave here and there is nothing left. Nothing but the loft. Empty, still unfinished. Loneliness. Distilled loneliness. The solitude of years. Being an old woman eating alone. No one to call. Friends too busy. You need an appointment a week ahead, can't just call up and say, Let's eat together. If it were not for the eating. Sleeping alone is almost easy. But the nights after she left. Wanting her every night. Holding back, trying not to, despising it; masturbation, secondrate, still somewhere ashamed, ashamed that it is such a substitute, saying her name, almost weeping it, saying her name, talking to her, the sweet obscenities, touch me fuck me take me from behind yes baby yes cries weeping to remember the taste of her cunt in my mouth as I came, all illusion more bitter afterward than the fact.

Lying next to her now, bitter too. Bitter even the touch of her hand on that part of me which waits for her in such heat and need. Always that I want her. And she does not always want me. That, just that, that inequality; the lever, that fulcrum of power and loss and defeat even before battle; conquest operable in any area of life from money to ideas. That dependency, that humiliation of need and desire. Because it has occurred to her, perhaps in compensation, compassion, pity, who knows the mind of the ruler—it has occurred to her to take me now. Here in this bed surrounded by others, here where one cannot make a noise. I had been afraid we would never make love, since the presence of her children had always made it impossible before—after a visit to them in San Rafael, she was always frigid when we returned to be alone in our hotel or at the house.

But it is her making love to me. She will not have me, I may not touch her. Even this, even this I take, accept, taking all I can get, beggarly, without pride, taking the heat of her hand on me, in me, taking the slim affection it betrays, the sense, if nothing else, of

power. Of remembrance. Remembering, always remembering the power of her fingers inside my body,
their absolute strength, I had never been fucked. I
realized it the first time with her. I had never been
fucked by a woman, hard, thorough, entire as by a
man. Never by a woman, never before. And I discovered it the first time, coming upon the knowledge like
a hallway mysteriously entered, taking me to where I
imagined I could not bear the pain and then beyond
to where there was no pain at all. But always the
breathless force of her blows, how they caught in my
throat like an elevator falling, the near terror of this
new place, this new force. And to realize afterward in
her gentleness that it was passion, that she could fuck
that hard, be that ferocious, because of tenderness.

Sacramento—in her bedroom there with the great
tree painted over the ceiling and along the windows
of the morning. I had come to teach out there; she was
the "welcoming committee." We will never stop being
amused at having stumbled into love in this banal way,
fulfilling our friends' cynical expectations, astonishing
ourselves. When I saw her in the airport I saw a
homely woman in a raincoat and glasses, a being not
very interesting, a little scary, "Third World," taller,
politically tougher. And as for the "Third World" business—more like a Puerto Rican who's made it, I
grinned to myself: establishment, administration rather
than faculty, an official person, a bureaucrat to my
bohemian and artist. And then her tacky little house
full of madras bedspreads across the windows, like a
hippie pad. Over a good steak I discovered her sense
of humor and began to call her Chiquita Banana to
tease her about her recent flight from expensive sub-
urbia and the way she'd embraced this funky place.

Over dinner she told me her tribulations in the land
of the Anglos: demeaning jobs, and how the D.A.R.
had handed out soap to the immigrants at her naturali-
zation ceremony and she was given a paper to sign that
demanded foreigners give up their foreign titles. I
looked at her over my wineglass, high; growing to like
her, challenging the whole thing, an outrageous joke.
"And did you tell them you were the Pope?" "In Italy

I am a countess. With that and fifteen cents you can buy yourself a cup of coffee." Chiquita Banana indeed, I thought, astounded, a little ashamed; suddenly I wanted to apologize for America, for the snobbery of every lesser soul (the D.A.R. ladies stopped handing out soap and began to curtsy), for all her poverty and humiliations, raising two children alone in a stony country. Because I am growing fascinated with this woman, her courage and her sufferings, her wit and now her beauty. Which is coming to life as a paper flower opens in water. She does not wear it in the street. There it's the trenchcoat and the opaque steel glasses.

The first night I wanted her. And could not understand why. And feared it. Was I merely adventuring? Consider her age, she is older than you. Is it honest to seduce her (assuming you could, she has two children and is probably straight, though she mentioned an affair with another woman)—but still, seduce her and then just trip off to your professorship and your new apartment and meet the other prospects here and that be the end of it? No. Lighting cigarette after cigarette. Wishing that she would turn on the light in the living room, invite me to have another joint, any excuse to make contact, at least see her. But I do see her, from my room at the end of the hall I see her going back and forth to the bathroom. Naked. Her habit to go around the house nude, she had said. Disturbing habit.

And the next day I met the others and they made no impression on me at all. I only wanted her. I knew it now, had tested it, waited, decided. Wanted her seriously and not merely to trifle. Loving her, sliding deeper and deeper into loving her, the improbable choice, her age, her looks new to me and at first unattractive, her life, her history so different, a life of marriages, wifehood, being rich, being broke too, but utterly unlike my life, my friends' lives, the art world downtown. And when the others had left, we sat on the couch and smoked a joint and talked the movement and understood each other in a mere sentence on this or that personality or issue. I mentioned rape, and she told me, in mere phrases, of being raped, how she had run out of gas one night in the desert. A car stopped and six men got out. "And all I could think of was how happy I was to see them." The help that turned into nightmare and mutilation. How they had had to sew her up, the clitoris nearly torn clean off and replaced imperfectly. I remembered this at odd times all through the next day, mixed in surreal apposition to the sheer delight I felt in my nipples that she had touched them, that they were like new flowers, changed, changed utterly for the rest of my life. Then my anger would return, this new and overwhelming rage that anyone could have harmed her, a livid desire to kill them. A pacifist and I wanted to kill. Avenge this. I had never heard anything before that had made me hate men. This fury coming back like an electric shock at stoplights, and then the memory, the equally improbable memory of her hands on my body. I had loved her for her suffering. And now for her passion. The whole day drunk on these bits of recollection, lost at stop signs, how her fingers felt inside me fucking me, fucking me into a whole new apprehension of fucking—exploring Sacramento, giggling as I noticed a sign in a seedy part of this little town proclaiming FIFTH AVENUE, getting lost, finding my way to my new apartment, to campus, buying furniture, remembering this new miracle. At first I thought I could not endure it, completely unused to that force, imagined it was pain, would leave me ragged and torn. I did not understand that a woman could even be that strong. That fierce, that passionate. But she was, and her long, slender, her most beautiful hands. After that I was hooked. After that there was no going back. There is none now.

Remembering now as she enters me, remembering everything, two years of the thing between us, a thousand occasions. Remembering, in her hasty and perhaps even indifferent touch, other times, times like hallucination, times when all time stopped as she held me, her fingers at the core and the center of consciousness, places within me I knew not, bends, wrinkles, plateaus, mountains and hillsides, and sunrises, caves

and secret recesses, time hanging still above us as I
asked her to be perfectly still within me, not to move
at all while the silence held like a species of medita-
tion. And all so that when she moved, were it the
slightest tremor, it would be felt the more, a tremor
would be like an earthquake. And then the whirlwind
of her sudden and strongest gesture, her hardest fucking. Dizzy and hardly able to bear it, seized, forced to
cry out, to gasp, to wonder if I would faint or die with
pleasure. The lovely terror of it.

How she knows me, rules me, masters me, plays
me, pleasures me. How I am always there for her;
ready, open, writhing with desire. Knowing all this and
against her new indifference, hating it, hating her
power, the lever of control, the abuses of domination
I am subject to. All love becomes vulnerability, the
doorway to cruelty, the stairway to contempt. The
very passion and adoration is now our undoing, the
means of our evil, I in despising myself for loving, she
in despising the one she had loved. Love turning back
on itself, becoming its opposite.

All that had made us lovers now unmakes us. We
are the end of the cycle, the bottom of the lie. The
process draws to its conclusion as her hand finds me in
the despairing dark. Still the fire, still the desire building. To stay or to go? The suitcases' shadows in the
corner of the bedroom like crouching dogs. And her
hand finding me, stroking a thigh, like the heat of
music or death on the matted hair at the pubis, the
soft flesh beyond calling her. Liquid like sparks or
snow, the touch of her fingertips on the wet smooth
flesh. Wet to receive her. And then a blow a storm a
convulsion, she enters me. Hard and at once, fierceness
and power like some creature beyond the mere human
who trembles to receive her. Energy and indifference
of the divine. Churned over and over in the force of
her thrusts to fall spent on the shore of bliss, saying in
the last place of the mind, I will stay. I will stay. I
will stay. I will endure it, outlast everything that stands
between us, not only will I stay, I would never leave
you. And in the lonely moment before sleep, now

without any certainty whatsoever, whispering to myself in secret: Not only will I stay, I'll beat this.

I watch her dress. She is at home in her body. Her perfect and lovely body. Marvelous that a woman nearly fifty should possess such a body. The luscious curve of her breast, the great brown Indio nipples, the place where she is neither Italian nor aristocrat but Brazilian aborigine. Nothing about her is so poignant, so moving, so "of herself" and individual as those nipples. Wonderful brown aureoles, I would know them beyond death. The line of her flanks as she moves, tracing it with my morning eyes. The ripples of her spine as she bends over to pull on her stockings. The flesh supple, delectable; I lust for it, watching.

"Lady," we always call each other, partly a joke, partly in earnest, using still the old word, in its full flavor a kind of exorcism against "saleslady," "old lady," "ladylike." Relishing the anachronism, even the formality a type of aphrodisiac, a contrast to our delight in the horny, the vulgar, the vernacular which we cultivate just as ardently. Lady, because the distant courtliness of the term, her idea after all, has a necessary charm, is maybe the last memory of her beginnings. She fastens her belt and pulls on a sweater. Gestures definite, complete. The mother of a son and daughter, the grandmother of a granddaughter. That most of all I loved. How can I resist a grandmother? I used to laugh to myself, falling in love against all expectation.

Let me celebrate this, this perfection in age, this ripeness and fullness. The fig-like fall of her breast, the mellow coffee of the flesh on her long legs and slender buttocks, the easy slimness of her waist. Even her little hint of lameness, an injury from a fall years ago that occasionally gives her movements a childlike vulnerability, and which, like her accent, makes a special appeal to my tenderness and to the world's kindness and forbearance, now even this seems absent as she moves about. It is seven in the morning, she is dressing for work, moving quietly, smoothly, intending not to wake me. Knowing what she does, who she is, how she will spend her day. I remember my manuscript and wish I hadn't. It yawns in wait for me like the mouth of suicide. Today I was supposed to put it in order, begin. She zips up her beautiful leather boots. Fitted and glovelike and perfect. How I envy her everything.

At home in her body, its supple strength, the spring of her step. Once I was youth and thought she fed upon me as I fed upon her, love making me still younger, forever young. Far otherwise now. Watching her, I am old. Yet I am younger, Sita is nearly ten years older than I. But this ten years I am her junior is nothing, only my own emptiness. She is a being made for living, I am not. She goes to rule, administer, put in order. I stay only to fight confusion and lose. It is easier, being her. Not only easier than being an artist, it is being art, which is better. Beyond that, she lives in the real world, with adult cares, mature responsibilities; things I partly despise and partly revere. There, she is at home, capable, majestic. Even in a job she frequently loathes, where she is consistently underpaid and overworked and threatened with layoff. A job that begins at the ungodly hour of eight in the morning. And yet she is ready, eager, I feel her eagerness. I even resent it. Envy it. Wish it were eagerness toward me, for whom she now has so little eagerness, so little enthusiasm: I who was once such a paragon in her eyes. She never tired of telling me I was pretty when she first knew me, my long, brown hair soft under her caresses, my long, brown hair endlessly laundered for her enjoyment. Once when she came to visit me at my farm during my breakdown and I was busy being crazy and had neglected to wash my hair, she hit upon that as the most visible proof of my madness. Wrote a nasty letter to all my friends and family bringing my deplorable condition to their notice on this account. I was already a damaged product. But not at the outset. At the outset I was a catch. I was a sculptor who had written a book which made me a minor heroine for a few months, a momentary genius. And I was pretty, she thought, quietly purring under it as a cat sits carefully when being stroked. Small and dark and almost demure I was, and so pleased with this taller and older woman's flattery. "Pretty," how rarely she says this to me now. And how enormous my sense of physical inferiority as I lie watching her. At home in her body, both plant and machine, this tool of flesh for the consummation of her will. Content inside it, the mellow light brown of her flesh, creamy yellow, smooth, graceful, the corporeal extension of her intelligence.

Who is she finally, this brisk and efficient woman; slim, elegant, off to administer her university programs in the gray January morning? Yet sensual, always, even at this hour in the morning, always there is this perfume of sensuality about her, in the brown of her skin, in the glow of her face and hair, in the sinuous movements of her long legs, in her delicate and lovely breasts, in her hands as she ties a scarf. And her history, how it fascinates me, how I retell it to myself. Born in Milan, daughter of a literary Italian count and a Brazilian opera singer, raised in convents, older sister to an adored little brother, the heir. A childhood severed in the middle as her mother's affinity for artists, for Jews, and for smuggling them to Brazil began to come to light. Sita's father was arrested by the Fascists, her mother fled back to Brazil with the two children. Being poor there, not nobility any more, poor relations to her mother's rich and indifferent tribe. To improve their fortunes it was decided Sita should marry, should be sold to a rich American. She was just out of school, he was fifty-five. After a child was born she escaped, divorced. Set out on her own with Pia in this new country. Until she fell into another marriage, even worse. Paul was born. Another divorce, another marriage; better, but still unsatisfactory. And then freedom. Now, near the end of her life, its ripe maturity to be her own, her own woman.

One night she showed me a box of old photographs of herself, the years of her young womanhood: Sita with babies, Sita with husbands, with Ben, who loved to take pictures, Sita the wife of his bungalow and his madonna with a dainty Pia, and pudgy Paul, her face a set smile, so strained it belied her good looks. Even her hair rigid in its forties and fifties hairdos, artificial, bent on pleasing and conforming, answering other demands. And that frozen wistful grimace in picture after picture, the look of someone completely ill at ease with life itself, with captivity within her own body.

But there was one picture, grand and glamorous and large, that denied all the others. Professional and on fine matte paper in contrast to all the little glossies of the candid home product. It was Sita one summer day before her second marriage. John Ford had come to the little Southern town and called for movie extras. She applied with her roommate and they got the parts. They'd be in the movies, they'd earn a hundred dollars a day for one bewitching week and wear long, old-fashioned dresses and big hats and walk across the lawn of illusion. A photographer had captured her doing this. And she was grand. And she was beautiful. Tall and stately, lady and aristocrat, her head fine under the great hat, her long neck, her benign carriage. Ebullient and quickening as she walks toward you. The mouth entirely sensual in its smile, perhaps even a little cruel. But confident, regal, utterly sure of itself. It was the only picture where she was alive, of herself. The only moment where she could be what she could be. This illusion was more real than her real life had ever been.

I am ten years younger, but I am not my own self. May never be. Am lost still nearly two years after a breakdown and a separation, lost in my work and my writing and my self. I have none of her assurance, can only envy it. And hate it—where it pushes me away. Coming here, I have lost myself utterly, relinquished the little world constructed with such effort in New York. The new beginning, shored up from the ruins of the ten years I lived there married. Fumio. All the agony of that severance fresh as a dismembered limb. Going back to New York, alone, the last time, and in those few months I was away from her, putting together a new studio, fixing up a loft. But in this time she had started over alone. Instead I kept to our plan, leaning toward her, always living three thousand miles away in part of my mind. And in returning to her now I lose my work and my studio and my self; ego and identity. Nowhere to paint or sculpt, nowhere even to write. Coming back only for love then. And the love is gone.

Artists who hazard their work for love commit a terrible sin. And for me she hazards nothing, would hazard nothing at all. She has never even considered living in New York. Her job is here, her life is here. New York is loathsome, she says, California the only place to live. She risks nothing, wouldn't think of it. Indeed, she scarcely considers inconveniencing herself on my behalf. The children, for example, are here to stay, they must not be disturbed, their welfare and happiness come before mine. If I mention that I have come far to be with her, been to time or expense, gambled my plans or work, ambitions or intentions—she only says that it was my own decision, she cannot take any responsibility. And I must not remind her; she will have no "guilt" imposed upon her. "You must come to California for yourself, not for me. Not on my account." Since nothing in the world would drag me to California except her, this leaves me nothing to say. So the proof of my affection is only another count against me. Time after time trying to explain to her that I am uprooted here, bereft of my friends, my work, my whole system of support and familiarity. Trying to make her understand. And she will not. Finding, even as I explain, that it becomes a fault. Why don't I have friends in Berkeley and San Francisco? Why do I cling and have no plans of my own, no calendar, no busy schedule to fill all the days and nights she will find it necessary to be gone from me, "busy," otherwise committed, and so forth. Because she is very busy now. This will be a crowded semester. She is even booked on weekends, every weekend until April she'd said at Sherman's. So ominous it sounded. Why did I come? I will be marginal in her time and her life, just as I am marginal in the house, an extra body tucked away in a bedroom typing, a fringe person without a room or space of her own. In a house where I was once mistress the whole day through.

I must speak to her. I must communicate, connect
where we have ceased to be connected. My eyes find
her like hunger. And are turned away. There is no
chance to speak at breakfast, so thoroughly does the
presence of others murder privacy, stifle, prevent intimacy. Her car is being fixed today, I can drive her to
the garage and then to work. Sitting through the grim
boiled egg, Valerie's impatient gestures. "Valerie's one
of those people who don't speak in the morning for
fear of an explosion," Sita warns me. I try to pour
Valerie's coffee when I pour ours. I use a cup and
saucer. Without speaking Valerie forbids my hand and
presents a mug, taking the pot and pouring it herself.
The coffee I had poured her grows cold as an insult.
I can't do anything to please, it seems. The hell with
it. Yet I'm sorry, too, the commune fantasy still tug-
ging at me, my admiration for Valerie's remarkable
beauty, the terrible vitality of her youth. Sita and I
are silent through breakfast.

In the car, still silence. Searching frantically for an
entrance, a way to begin. Finally, just for anything to
say, anything at all, Berkeley going by, the road down
from the hills and Indian Rock, the Marin Circle,
Shattuck. Each bit remembered with a greater sense
of loss. Last year. When this was all ours and there
was no one else but the two of us. How she protected
me then, how carefully she would give instructions so
that I would not lose my way in the town, how endlessly kind and considerate, how careful of my time,
how she watched over me, treasured me. Once. And
now I am merely a convenience, or rather an incon-
venience who can occasionally be put to some use. Of
course she didn't urge me this morning; Pia could drive
her if I didn't want to. But I grabbed for it—a chance
to be alone with her. The poverty of this situation,
the cheap irony—that I would scramble up at seven
in the morning just to have ten minutes alone with
her. A woman I used to live with, share a house and
life with. And having the chance—the last one I would
have for twelve hours or so, until we are in our room
after dinner tonight—and having the chance, the
precious privacy—I have nothing to say at all, am in

too much pain and confusion to talk. Too blank and desolate to have any topic to embark on, even any words.

Coming upon a piece of notepaper engraved with her matron's name and address, Mrs. Martin Richter: one of her former lives. When she was married to Martin and lived in the suburbs, the sprawling successful businessman's house he built for her. She used to have a picture of it in the hall, together with those strange and magical photos of the house in which she grew up in Italy. Palace rather than a house, its walls painted like Fragonards, its stiff ornate chairs, its monumental sideboards and lacy sofas. Photographs of rooms empty of people. All but one. Sita, in one touching picture, sitting primly on a silken chair. Staring out at the world from immense unhappy eyes, prisoner of this place she always describes as a penitentiary of unease. And yet she keeps the pictures. They have hung in the entranceway of every place we've lived. All the houses of her past as well, these last talismans of who she was born. The old Milanese house was destroyed in the war, I saw only its shadow down an empty alleyway last summer. It exists now only in these photographs, only in the unhappy eyes of its child.

And this piece of notepaper, before me, fit only for grocery lists. Echo of still another life. All the former lives, so many of them, her many selves. It was for this perhaps that I fell in love with her, captivated by her multiple personae, the sinuous change from one woman to another. In Sacramento once she went to lunch with me wearing a wig. Great silly blond thing of curls and peroxide. I did not know her. Excusing myself in confusion, I went into the bathroom and leaned against a wall, appalled to realize I was already involved, hell, in love, with someone who could look so grotesque, so different from my world and its values, aesthetics, its snobbery of scholar and artist. And came out, risking it, only to be overcome by a woman in a pants suit with vast bell-bottom trousers and that out-

rageous abominable wig, a woman of a kind and appearance I had probably never spoken to before in
my life. And found her enchanting.

It was a "test," she told me. A test to see how much
of who she was or had been I could absorb. And all
that she has been, it bewilders me still, after three
years. There was a certain photograph on the wall near
the phone in my place in Sacramento just to remind
myself of what constitutes efficacy: Sita with the determination of Il Duce on her face and a huge improbable Louis XIV hairdo, steel platinum mounted over
a flowered dress, receiving an award for being the most
enterprising woman in her housing development.
"Woman of the Year." Sita in her suburban self,
woman of the year. Before her independence, before
her amicable divorce from Martin, before her present
political and administrative eminence.

In three marriages you are many women. First a
rich officer's wife, then the victim of a drunk, then
finally sheltered by Martin's stability and kindness,
which could pay for Pia's polio and the operations on
her back and save Sita from the line of menial office
jobs, the tired battle to raise two children, one of them
dangerously ill. Martin saved them and then Martin
became too small, his world too confining. Then Hank
beckoned, a hippie painter from the commune Pia
had taken off to live in. Only a few years older than
her daughter—hairy mountain of a man, rough and
crude as an early settler—yet he must have been like
sunlight to her, his youth, his shaggy virility. Hank
was the way out, but after a year or two she struck
off on her own, beginning again alone after forty.
Brave, new, both courageous and afraid. It was that
that I loved, both the determination and the vacillation.
Because I knew she would always come through it,
because I sensed that this sort of woman was something new in the world.

All my Sitas: countess, courtesan, matron, flirt,
mother, wife, lover, gossip playing with blouses or
jewelry, administrator, coquette. Years of her, of her
moods and troubles and gaieties and ardor. And now
only this dead sensation, this hostile screen about her

and between us, forbidding me even to speak. For my silence comes from her as well as from my own bafflement.

Her face. Watching her face as the desperate need to recover her comes on again, wanting to grab after her, the realization that I've lost her, that she is relinquishing me, putting me aside as she might slip off a sweater or a glove. The face I have loved so long. The fine aristocratic profile. Watching her so often in profile, preferring it even, because the front view is less perfect, too rounded perhaps—surprising myself that I should prefer even the distance of profile, its objectivity, its near indifference—all for the marvelous pure line running from brow to chin and throat, a line I covet, would draw, would capture, would possess. And the treasured dent just at the throat, how soft the skin there, how delicious to kiss, holding her very life in my lips. The gray of her hair, the brown of it going to gray. But that still doesn't satisfy her— my God, the very contrariness of tinting one's hair gray, confronting age and pushing it along, is characteristic of her. She insists on it despite my remonstrance. I was aghast when she did it first—to make yourself old, how perverse it seemed, but she laughed and refused to listen.

The gray lines of her hair about her face. Like silverpoint in an old engraving. The gray of her hair against the fine soft brown of her skin, how tender and inescapably sensuous, warm with that earthly warmth she has always, gives off continually like kindness. How that face shone on me once, adored and worshipped and cherished me like a living miracle. Even now, when I see its indifference or hostility, the old glow blocks my perception for a moment and delays me in registering the change, even crueler when the recognition comes. It had seemed a permanent state, her love. Absolute and entire, a great passion clung to with the patient tenacity of Latin womanhood. The way she forgave me for missing the plane that first time into Sacramento. I had been organizing a women's prison strike in Iowa, living in continual excitement and what even appeared to be some danger—

and just as we were winning I remembered a flight
landing in Sacramento. I had just plain missed it.
Called and apologized desperately, her terrible incon-
venience, she would never forgive me. But she only
laughed. "You don't know anything about Latin
women," she said. And forgave me. As she forgave the
madness and the breakdown. But she forgave it less.
And she never did forgive me for taking a loft in New
York after we had rented the house here and begun to
live that curious little marriage she now so bitterly despises. Now that she's her own single self again, matriarch of a commune, administrator in a university,
a woman available to men. And there are some about,
strangers at the edges of her life. She told me about
one at Christmas. Chuckling, confiding, women chattering, half-deprecatory. Lovers too, snuggled in our
pillows sipping wine.

He was young, she said, she'd met him at a conference in Virginia City. Everyone went off to a meeting and they stayed in the bar and had a few drinks.
She told him women were better lovers than men. He
was challenged. She took him up on it. An adventure.
Told after the story of another adventure, her deplorable behavior at Emily's birthday party. Got utterly
sloshed and took on some handsome fellow and even
another lady. "I never called him back, but the lady
was a bit more interesting." "You're terrible." I
laughed. "We were worse than that. Imagine the garden party and the eight-year-olds and there we were
getting it on in the upstairs bedroom. Even Pia and
Paul didn't know how to deal with it all." "And you a
grandmother." We are helpless with laughter while
she invents and embroiders, they were "hanging moons"
from the upstairs window. "You're making it up. You
got it from Chaucer." "Or Boccaccio. But what are
you going to do if you're two stories up and you need
more wine or marijuana or want to tell someone down
in the yard they have a telephone call?" "Shameless.
Blessing you didn't get arrested." "It was the back
window." I kiss her, laughing. Not knowing what to
think. Not even quite believing. Like the stories she
used to tell of how she celebrated her divorce from

Martin by screwing some total stranger at the end of
a party on her hands and knees under the dining-room
table, the rug burns on her shins a joke between us for
years. That there is somewhere a wilder self within
her—promiscuous, a hussy—is only a probability,
never a certainty. And piquant, teasing my own lust
for her. Somewhere it is also terrifying, a hidden and
dreadful threat. Amused as I am, admiring even, when
I hear these stories I am also, at the very back of
my stomach and near the spine, in panic, poised over
a trapdoor that could open.

But the danger now is the very shut quality, the
closed and decided set of her face lately. An expression I had never known before. Or seen only as something she gave to others, all the others she excluded
from her beauty and herself. Whereas for me she was
always open, my mystery, my good fortune and treasure—what for the whole world she would somehow
shut like a shopkeeper's metal front rolled down. The
reason other people often had no inkling of how beautiful she was, no notion of her stunning good looks.
The face that opened and shone for me like the sun,
warm, reassuring, protective. Permanently and definitely loving. How fatuous I was to believe, to imagine that. Nothing of love is permanent, ever. Yet I
believed it; so passionate she was, so ardent, so entire
in her promises, so Indian in her patience, so Latin in
her attentions, so tender, so elaborately considerate.
The package of cigarettes she kept in her purse. In
case I should run out. She who doesn't smoke but was
never without fresh Marlboros. When I landed I remember her mentioning that she had matches in
case I needed them. I smiled a wry smile inside, registering the difference.

I am a spy in the house of love. A figure on stair-
cases thrust into the role of eavesdropper. In what was
once my own house. Populated now with hundreds.
Emily is finally off to school. Valerie has stormed her
way out the door and into the old black truck she
and Paul own but still haven't paid for. As usual it will

not start. This requires running it down a steep hill and hoping. Paul gets up to help her. The truck has a broom attached to the back of the cab, erect as a tin soldier; it would do well in a musical or a nostalgia film about the fifties. It has all the goofy charm of youth, just as they do, the childlike helplessness, the day-saving final ingenuity, the sense of adventure, the fantasy, that their life is grim and difficult. I find myself trampled and annihilated by their beauty, their youth, their carefree indifference. Pia rouses herself from bed, eats breakfast, and settles down with a book. She is supposed to be looking for a job, but there will be no pretense of that today. She glides around in a nightshirt, tall, slim, delicately and remarkably beautiful. Coming on the fragile and childlike perfection of her face, its utter innocence, you would never believe she was a junkie. Years in hip-pad filth, a filth imposed on Emily in neglect and abuse, the child's hair hopelessly matted, Sita said, when they showed up in Sacramento for cold turkey. Years of Janis and her crowd at the Trident in Sausalito, years singing and not going anywhere with it, not really working very hard, "laid back" and easy with dope and wine and the white song in the veins. "The greatest high in the world," she always described it to Sita. And now it's over. But the methadone is depleting. Pia and Dan slept most of the day for the first two months of withdrawal. Now that it's over, Dan's back at work driving his truck. Pia is free to do whatever she wishes: get a job, sing, study music, go to school, leave Dan, strike out on her own, join a band, make the contacts with musicians that her friend Michael is providing, wait for the mood or the moment to strike. Beginning life all over again.

We sit at the table drinking coffee, making small talk. Very small, because we are uncomfortable together and have nothing to say. I am uneasy with her. I would love to help, encourage, exert some benign influence. Sita always says I have influence with Pia, that she respects me and looks up to me. The teacher takes over and yearns as toward an undergraduate, a younger artist. If I could bring her along, sustain.

And part of Pia lingers at the table for this. But part is distant with a new distance. Closed toward me as her mother is, taking her cue. She doesn't want me here. And she doesn't want what I offer. Or wants it only a little. I feel her teeter on the brink between an old life and a new. I must be very careful not to push, diplomatically pursuing her with questions about bands, this or that contact in San Francisco, the new women's groups. She has leads, but they are all vague, and you can never put your hand around what she says. It seems she has to get to know a few more people. There's a real tough lady in the city who could put her on to some good things. She'll be getting around to meeting her pretty soon. Nothing's hurried. Is she practicing, rehearsing? Well, a little bit with Paul. But it seems you really have to have a band, know what kind of material they do, there's the right stuff and the wrong stuff, and a lot of that rock 'n' roll shit she "just can't get into." Everything is pushed away, ideas and events and activities seem swept off to arm's length, floated away from the dining-room table and out to the living room. I see reality dismissed in the wave of her hand toward the living-room sofa. I must be very careful not to push.

Paul comes home and disappears into his room. Sleeping. It is terrible that there is no connection between us any more. There had been such a fondness. The parties and visits in San Rafael when the kids lived there together and Sita and I visited them on weekends. But they were always parties, visits, special occasions, celebrations. And Sita there to mediate our shyness, transmit her great affection for me then, show me off, even. For they had been impressed at the beginning. The nervous breakdown settled that. I was scarcely impressive after that. After that I was an embarrassment, a broken instrument, an uncertainty. I had caused their mother pain, and that was unforgivable. Their loyalty to her, how I had loved and admired it even then, their fierce devotion. How they would stand against anyone who hurt her. Pia in her loyalty lying to me

over the telephone last fall, probably hating what
she did as she did it, and her own friendliness for
me making her hate it still more. But she did it for
her mother. They are blood together. And always
I am not. My fortunes rising or falling on precisely
whatever quotient of interest or disinterest Sita sig-
nals. They have no real relationship to me at all.
Valerie passes me on the stairs, brusque, almost
bullying in her size and her haste. Only Emily holds
out. But even Emily picks it up. This morning when
I bundled her off to school she was cross and tyran-
nical, dying to get away, to go off fifteen minutes
earlier than she needed to and superior about what
coat to choose, disdainful of my notion of red tights
to set off her dark blue dress, and suspicious I wouldn't
really be in touch with the correct time.

I am letting myself grow paranoid. It is hard to
be one in a household of seven. I must buy Emily
a little present, I must connect again. I must buy
the rest of us some feasts, a carload of groceries.
There is endless talk of poverty. Paul's job as a dish-
washer hardly runs his pickup truck. Valerie teaches
a class or two, but that only pays her tuition. Paul
doesn't want college, talks vaguely of repairing guitars, and does a little inlay work in the basement,
bits of ivory fitted into the top of a jewelry box, the
neck of a guitar, the handle of a knife. His mother
is proud: her son the artist. As if Paul were still so
much a child his hobbies could pass for a profession.
It used to be her son the rock 'n' roll star. And at
seventeen it seemed that Paul might make music his
life; he had his little band, his little gigs at pizza par-
lors. But since Valerie he has grown shadowy and
stands behind her radiant energy in some contented
nonentity that may satisfy him a long time. Valerie
is determined; she will survive beautifully. She studies
now to be a schoolteacher. Later she may take over
the world. But I worry about Paul.

Paul will be fine, Sita says, Valerie will see to that.
In being a male, he is already complete in her eyes,
she has named him after her brother, Paolo, she has
even given him her father's ring, the signet of the

count, which Paolo had gallantly given to her. After a moment's annoyance had passed when I heard this, I realized I had wanted Sita still to wear it. Or Emily. Or Pia. But one doesn't hope for Pia; Sita has passed her by utterly. Yet oddly, for all the approval she showers on Paul, all the calm and assured affection, the easy and obvious favoritism, it is with the woman-child Pia that she has the stronger, more passionate relationship, even in its disappointment, its long, probably lifelong disapproval, even in this it is fuller and more fierce and more wonderful. To watch them together, to feel all the waves of energy and emotion, whether they are playing at lady friends comparing jewelry or whispering about men, or whether squaring off for battle, for chilly refusals or grief-filled embraces—it is always a matter of equals. Paul is a raw young page sitting on the rug at his lady mother's feet: but Pia is a queen and rival, they sit side by side.

Misplaced, I think, I am simply misplaced in life, incompetent, unable to cope, as lately I have been unable to speak, to make conversation, chitchat, jokes, any sound at all. As if tongue-tied, becoming a moron, a cretin, an idiot. Does the withdrawal of love produce all these symptoms of degeneracy? Remove every vestige of confidence, ability, intelligence?

Upstairs each object menaces. Remnants. I have so many clothes here, having meant to return, to stay, to arrive each year, to have my life here. So many books, feeling ashamed of the extravagance that bought them, a whole library of politics, thinking I would write and study. Shoved now, all of them, into the hall closet. We used to have them lining the floor in what is Paul's room, and I was going to build bookshelves when I got around to it. Now they tumble out of the closet at me. They have been displaced, as have all my other things that I come upon in corners, closets, the garage.

How would I ever bring it all home, assuming New York were home, all that's left? Boxes, clothes, files of papers, dressers, rugs, Sherman's paintings. Even a car. The car most problematic of all. Too much stuff to pile everything in and drive cross-country—an old car, might not even make it. And the long, lonely trip. I clench my jaws thinking of it. Giving up. Admitting it didn't work, is over, Sita a part of the past like other lovers gone. Leaving a car here was a guarantee always. Taking it away marks the end. Absurd, of course. Mere material objects, how they structure life. But having a car in a place, even a used and leaky Dodge convertible, is some sign and assurance you actually live there.

And I came back to find it gone, the place vanished, invaded, transformed by others. Sita, just one now among a horde of persons, and herself changed, preoccupied with them, absent from me, chilly when I recall her, her resolute new expression of face and shoulders, hostile under the surface politeness, waiting finally to snap, call it off, tell me to go. Impossible therefore even to complain or confront—it would only bring about disaster. I cannot afford confrontation.

The sounds of the commune go on relentlessly—Emily comes home from school and sits before her idol the television, Paul's dog pads up and down the stairs. The day is almost over, concentrate. Try to get a few letters written, anyway. Remember New York details, the mail, the bills, the plants. Ruth watering the plants. Her very expensive favors. Meant to ask Linda, who lives downstairs, to look after them, but Ruth offered, insisted she would enjoy it.

A mistake to become lovers again with Ruth. The night they tore down the old house, or rather that dawning—fifteen years of my life and a marriage, a good so good existence made there, loved it as I loved him, not loved, adored—all down under a wrecking ball. The night before, late so late, did I intuit it?—that it would be that very dawn when I would wake and the old studio would be gone—only a hole in the street. Fifteen years. Rubble. Bricks. Friends I kept running into for months confided after the usual condolences, while I grimaced or kept my face like starch, that walking by they'd picked up a brick and saved it. Relics. Even of their own

good times, the high fine drinking talk those rooms
had known, my sculptures, Fumio's mobiles floating
against the ceilings. Did I intuit it all by calling up
Ruth—Come on over here. It's four in the morning.
And I'm asking her to come over and fuck me. Must
have even said that. Dead drunk I was. Dinner
with Hatsie and for some inconceivable reason got
blasted. Outrageous, raucous, even made a fool of
myself at a club where Esther Phillips was singing,
almost got us thrown out. And came home blind and
called Ruth. Did I know it would happen, that they'd
blow the house that bleak top of the morning? Months
of the props and beams against the old walls and
wrecking crews who wouldn't even let me in to say
it goodbye. To gather the few last tidbits, the shut-
ters from the front windows, the other ones in my
studio, the ones with paper windows that I'd made
by hand. Big gruff men who wouldn't bend. Not even
the foreman. Sure to collapse, look at that crack in the
wall, are you crazy, lady? And crazy and drunk and
alone on a foam mattress on the floor of the new place,
not even a bed yet, and called Ruth, pleading with her
to fuck me. And she came. Unspeakably kind, patient,
generous.

Bad faith, it was all bad faith. Never should have
started. Bad faith when she's in love and you're
not. Sexual friendship sort of nonsense doesn't work,
not against her adoring obsession. She said it would,
of course, sex not important to her really, only another dimension of friendship. Our real bond being
sculpture. And so forth. Came and was kind. Healed
something broken that night. Hatsie, her report on
visiting California. The news that Sita's children
snickered and ridiculed me, criticized my housework,
said that I was selfish, I ought to have a maid, and
so on. And Sita was cold. That came across. That
she might not bother to come at Christmas. That
there would "be a lot of changes," that if I came
back it would "certainly never be like last time." All
mysterious and hesitant. Hatsie dense as smoke, all
hints, portents. Dreading even to hear the report,
sounded so ominous when she first came back to town

and telephoned. Was it disloyal of me even to listen?
Put her off for two days. And then I had to know.
Spent the dinner getting lush, proclaiming how I loved
Sita, her charm her fascination her beauty her passion.
Hatsie benign, gossipy, full of intrigue—pumping me:
"Really shouldn't ask, but I'm so curious, how did Sita
afford that trip to Europe with you last summer; did
you pay for it?" Point-blank like that, I admitted it,
hating myself for admitting the truth. Off my guard,
swept away with my romantic rant.

Building all evening, Hatsie's little gestures, crab-
like movements toward letting me know the truth.
That I was in trouble, that I couldn't trust either
Sita or the kids, that they'd changed. Nothing there
to count on. And if I'd sinned in counting on Sita
too much in the past, it was all over now, the group
of them, only sand shifting. Blowing another way.
No. It can't be, just can't be. It's got to be Hatsie.
Merely Hatsie, Hatsie the trifler, the meddler, she's
famous for it. And she landed on them, an unwelcome house guest, of course they'd all thoroughly
disliked one another. Dismiss it. Keep believing. No,
you can't dismiss it, the bug of unease, the germ of
doubt is set now. To grow.

Slamming down on the mattress, I called Ruth.
The call of an orphan, a sick call. And she came.
New York. Ruth. Fumio and Ruth. And Dobie.
Dobie the casual buddy. Fumio the rigid force that
shuts me out. Ruth. Don't want to go back to Ruth.
I want it to be over. Again and again, against her
infatuation, insisting it isn't fair, can't return it,
merely be friends. A much better thing. When I go
back I'll break off, no more sex—remembering a
lover saying that to me once—punitive, it seemed,
perverse. To separate sex from love from life from
the rest of a friendship. But with Ruth I can't keep it
up, the pretense of romance. A sexual friendship,
as the phrase used to go. Ruth. Enormous sensuality.
The great lush body I've drawn thousands and thousands of times. Fine. But not the obscene presence
of her worship, that almost religious dependence on
the magic object. For that's what I am. From that

first speech at Columbia probably. And all my efforts to prod her along in art, make her believe in herself as a sculptor, all never fill the maw of her fixation. A thing she's done all her life. Crush on Greta Garbo when she was eight. Every day after school roaming the Upper West Side just to bump into her. And she did. Same terrible awesome child-radar still. Does it to me, can locate me anywhere on the Lower East Side within thirty minutes.

I can't be responsible for this. And being with Sita now only confirms it. And I can't respond either. The body makes its own decisions. All the ripe sensuality in the world, all the languorous drawing sessions when Ruth poses for me, all our naughty afternoons when the paintbrushes end up in bed, all nothing to the terrible tenderness that first time when Sita came at Christmas, choking almost, the absolute necessity of tears.

Stupid to choose. Sensuality's a fine thing too. But the choice falls elsewhere. In that Ruth's in love and I'm not. And won't be. Gratification is not the same. But Sita's not in love and I am. She was once. Once, once is the past. You don't get it back. Even sitting here and hoping. Even hanging on. Quit and go home. Even if you go home to nothing.

I sit next to her on the rocks. She is tired. When she came home I rubbed her shoulders. When she came home, the sound of the front door I had waited to hear for hours. And then she was upstairs at the door of our room. "Her room," in the commune. Though it seems ours again these first moments. Sita spreads out upon the bed, exhausted. Lady, I will take off your boots. Managing the first, its long, blue body of glove leather, its elegant shape, its sinuous zipper. Pia comes up the stairs. We will be seen. I will be caught in the strange erotic posture of taking off a boot. Sita feels it too and springs up to sit, doing the second boot herself. Then lies down again on the bed. I lie next to her. More noises in the hall. I shut the door, making the gesture, shutting the door, shutting out the world and the commune. But the moment is past.

And the sun is setting. Heroic across the bay, the city beyond. It pulls me as it always does here, the one spectacular moment for which the whole day is prelude, the drama building already at four o'clock, that special golden light beginning to filter into consciousness. And from there you are always aware the rest is coming, preparing yourself for it, wondering if you will be in the right spot when the moment comes, if your work will be finished, if you'll be in sight of the water. Because the moment is coming, the climax is approaching with one light and then another and then all. Memory, the memory of these sunsets last year. How well we are placed to see them; my old study had a superb view, so does this bedroom. But a better place is outside on the rocks at the crest of the hill. "Shall we go out and watch it from the rocks?" I ask. Neutral, not an invitation to the Marina and drinks at Grundy's, the best place of all, heeding the warnings that she would be too tired for this worldliness, effort, expense.

And she is companionable on the rocks. We perch next to each other, I knead her shoulders, trying to take away the day's tiredness, the frustrations of the job. "I had my secretary send out letters to your students today, canceling your class." I'm thunderstruck. Last night, having dinner at Grundy's, she had asked me what I wanted to do about the class. I still didn't know, but was doubtful if we could order the books in time. And she had simply canceled it. "I thought that's what you wanted, I thought you wanted to write while you were here." I hardly know what to say, embarrassed by my own malingering over the class, my inability to decide whether to do it or not, even my fear of the project, the responsibility, the way it would tie and compel me to stay here for ten weeks. When part of me wants so desperately to run. The class would commit me by contract to stay. But if she's canceled it, perhaps the inference is that I should go. I sit confused and humiliated next to her. "If I don't do the class, may

I stay on anyway?" "Of course, you should do whatever you like. I just didn't want you to be under any pressure." Not to be under any pressure, not to be doing the class as a favor to her, not to be under any obligation to go to California—this has been her line since Christmas. I am as confused as ever about my fate. The future is impossible but also mandatory: the course required me to decide. And now she has decided for me. I am both relieved and disappointed. Had dreaded the class but also looked forward to it; in my unproductive time it would be work, something to do, the pretense and perhaps even the actuality of activity, meaningful activity, any activity at all. And now it is gone. I watch the sky, thinking of the class, thinking of her, thinking of the past. All the things lost. I don't speak because I don't dare. There is so much to tell her, but if I told her she would withdraw, grow angry, distant. And I would lose what little I have, this pretense of intimacy, two persons sitting high on a rock formation watching the sun set over a bay. The air growing chilly, the extinction of light and color a prefiguration of death.

In a little while we will have to go back and join the others. A few hours and then the few moments before sleep. All there is in a day. Last night at Grundy's we reminisced over the way we first became lovers that long wakeful night in Sacramento when I lit cigarette after cigarette and she made innumerable trips to the bathroom, both of us appalled at our own desire. It was not hospitality, it was not correct, laughing at ourselves, but the laughter a bit automatic perhaps, a bit too polite, perfunctory. I felt more like tears than laughter, the remembrance of our good times only makes the present more hateful, and to watch her playing at being a lover is more humiliating than outright rejection. Yet I am such a coward, I prefer it, would have even that, am greedy for whatever moment, whatever absentminded smile. Even the stolid companionship of her body here upon this stone looking to sea, the little lights of Berkeley's houses coming into the darkness, the sweep of

San Francisco's skyline, the melancholy shadow of the
bridges as the air grows blue and cold. Once I thought
I would grow old with this woman, our love going on
for years. I have been here three days. How many
days have I left?

I read the paper. The *San Francisco Chronicle,* de-
livered each morning to the house. My solace, my
sedative, my shame. Idleness and the terror of idleness. I have no work here, why am I staying? The
class is canceled. She has canceled it. And my own
work only a void; dry, sterile, hopeless. She works
of course. Was off before eight in the morning. And
I merely read the paper, my fear of death in every
murder, in every high-placed heart attack, my worry
worries at the layoffs, the depression. Every item finds
my soft gray spot of vulnerability, locates my dread,
I suffer with all the losers in obscure places, cringe
with corrupt officials exposed and indicted, experience
a vast amorphous despair over a planeload of Japanese
tourists poisoned by their scrambled eggs. Two days
later the official in charge commits the inevitable suicide of responsibility. I've tried that too, but it didn't
work.
    As soon as she leaves in the morning, I am seized
with anxiety, heart-pounding, throat-closing panic,
pacing the floor. For what? I ask myself. Because my
life means nothing, is essentially over, is useless, in-
active, unemployed. That I age and grow ugly and
reach the end of love. That I love her and am not
loved, love and am no longer loved. But if I were,
would I stay here? Hungering for New York, yearning back after it, the little beginnings I had made
there, my own loft, the scraggly little circle of old
friends. Who were never enough. Knowing I was
bored there too. And what is boredom? Perhaps the
inability to find meaning, to complete a perception, to
arrive at an understanding: partly grasped, but forever
just out of reach. It is not lack of interest, but interest
frustrated, cut off, imperfectly held. So says the *Chronicle* today. But for me it is the fear of emptiness.

I see her life and realize that my own is shallow, improvised, empty of the things she is rich in—family, children, grandchild—the young; and even the respectable: position, employment, colleagues, community. Would I ever have noticed if I hadn't come here, or gone on imagining my fringe bohemia was an existence without comparison? Asking myself now, Do I envy this here? Yes. Do I want it myself? No. Then why the flurry, the terrible grief this house inspires? The past haunting me, last spring when it was only the two of us and the house a kind of music. Yet I didn't want to stay, limit myself entirely, so I went off to outfit a loft in the city. Meaning of course to live both lives, one here, one there, half a year in turn.

You can't live in two places, of course it's impossible. No one is so vain, so full of hubris, so full of illusion to imagine such a thing. It isn't done. The world isn't constructed that way. You live in one place or another, but not two; one world or another, but not both. You stick with town, the Big Apple, where it all happens, the artists and the dealers and the publishers and the machine that rules the earth —or you follow a will-of-the-wisp and decide on sunny California, lie back and settle for nature and landscape and an easier way of life. You don't say to a confirmed and unswerving Californian, Look, I have personal and professional reasons to need New York: it's my home these fifteen years, my friends and my known world are there. She is not an artist, the art world and the necessity for its dubious oxygen mean nothing to her. And without her I began to be stifled there. So here I am.

Reading the paper. Saving the funnies for last. Dreading the moment when they run out, when I get to Herb Caen, the second section with its two frivolous columnists, then Caen fronting the obituaries and the want ads, the three of them "witty" in that sophomoric manner of daily journalism, even that spark rebuking my lassitude. Surely this morbid sloth is only self-pity: reasonless and gigantic terror of life, hollow, vacuous, and inexcusable angst. But it comes down to this: that I don't know what to do today. Have nothing to do. Now or ever. Write, work, but I cannot work, loathe the aging dried manuscript upstairs. The first day after I arrived I was determined, forced myself, tore out all the old handwritten entries from their notebooks and filed them in order. A week of blood, the sight of that old stuff, the time and memories it evokes, nearly nauseating. Time of the separation, the breakdown, the suicide trips. The idea was to type it up, fill in the holes, mold it into a book. But I doubt now it can be a book. And I can't work here in this madhouse, this uncertainty, this emotional whirlpool. If I went home, back to New York . . . remembering how it paled after her visit, how the well-made little plan, the fresh growth of the new life wilted, how I longed to leave and then just started packing, keeping the appointed time. "I'm not trying to talk you into coming back, things are very different now," she'd said. How different I never guessed. "Come only of your own free will. Don't come unless you really want to."

To be this age and have so little direction in one's life. The emptiness of my freedom. She cannot go to this coast or the other, there is always her job. So it is for most people. Never having choices, they don't bump up against the strange gray limits. Or do I trot out these vague generalities only to try to obscure my disappointment in her, the knowledge of love dying, another place of safety closing? No, it's my own dissatisfaction with myself. My disappearing self, which had lived in my work and is now homeless. Other people live without work, would love to be unemployed, can think of nothing better. But the artist, staring and impotent, unable to work, deprived of the saving and sustaining art. Hideous that experience, that knowledge of failure.

And so I drug myself with Cypriot warfare, pop stars, the price of crude oil, new ideas in home decoration, the machinations of the C.I.A., shake-ups in the prison hierarchy. And the comics. So delicious, over so soon. If life resembles the newspaper, so huge, so various, so dull, it is love which resembles the comics, so charming and so brief. When the comics are over, you have, wherever you may have begun, even if you began with the comics, you have finished the *San Francisco Chronicle*. The only dependable part of my day.

Hating myself for the triviality of this crutch, because when the paper is over I have to face working, trying to work, deciding to leave, deciding to stay. And how smug and alone with themselves the others are—Sita, her competence, her matriarchal and managing power throughout the house; Valerie in her long red skirt and her Cossack boots off to school in her definiteness; Paul lying lazily in bed; Pia slopping around looking lovely in the most bedraggled nightgown, chatting on the phone or prone across her bed reading a book. They are certain, they know who they are. I know nothing, only this crippling fear. In a week I have lost all my bearings, utterly at sea among these people, strangers. Lost in life. And in a few moments I will have run out of train wrecks, the heroics of firemen, the arrests of extortionists, the opinions of editors. It is all merely how to spend the day while she is gone—all of it's just time waiting for her.

Our commune is invaded by new faces. Friends of Pia. Yesterday there were Jeff and Tina who were supposed to be arriving with good music. The music never happened, but they stayed two days. Today it is Hedy and her little boy, Jon-Jon, and an Englishman of indeterminate status named Pete. They sleep in the living room, and when you come down for breakfast you inevitably wake them all. Pete yawns and approaches the dining-room table with his shirt off. Jon-Jon cries and will not be comforted. Hedy and Pia discuss long-lost friends from Beech Street, their first commune ten years ago. We are polite and uncomfortable. The arrival of Hedy, Jon-Jon, and Pete brings our total to ten persons, plus Limbo the dog. Presently in heat. No one can open a door without the danger of Limbo's escape. This is her first heat. She is Paul and Valerie's dog, but we are all responsible twenty-four hours a day to prevent her impregnation. There are bells attached to the handle of the front door and I must leave my work and run

downstairs and stand guard over Limbo each time they
sound. Pia can't be depended upon, the solemn duty
rests largely on me. Life becomes more and more
unbearable. The presence of the visitors limits me to
the bedroom without respite for the entire day, since
I cannot walk through the downstairs without disturbing them. Writing, the solitary art, grows more
and more impossible. Sita takes no notice at all, she
is only here in the evening and by then they have
usually gone out. And perhaps she relishes the in-
trusions of young persons who treat her with elaborate respect; how "groovy" this grandmother must
appear to them, how fond she is of their awed def-
erence which understands that this is ultimately her
house, no one else's. And perhaps she welcomes anything that will drive me away, convince me finally
to leave, to surrender my hopes of reclaiming the
place. And herself. Sita, who is now so distant and
disagreeable to me, who forbids any complaint whatever. This is the way the place is, if you don't like it
you can leave. She keeps suggesting I look at Michael's
studio apartment. He's moving out this weekend. "I
didn't come three thousand miles to live in Michael's
apartment." She regards this remark as unreasonable.
She is not responsible for me, she will not be made
to feel guilty.

Pete talks of nothing but his passport, the need
to get his visa extended, his troubles with the officials. Hedy dreams aloud about a trip to New Orleans
they have planned. Got to get the car in shape first.
Long disquisitions on the car and its condition. They
have no money, everything seems dangerously vague.
Hedy calls it being on the road. She transports two
curious little sculptures with her. Pia and I admire
them on the living-room rug. Pia asks if I will show
them photographs of my sculptures. I would like to,
but in the confusion of my effects I cannot locate
the albums. No one notices. I spend two hours searching and give up. Hedy and Pia are still chattering
on the rug. I am worried that I cannot find these
valuable pictures, unique copies most of them, annoyed at the waste of time, the presence of strangers.

Finding myself irate and hostile toward these gentle and innocent people, good souls wandering around the country meaning no harm. Hating myself for meandering through the day without purpose, for joining in the aimless drift of all those around me, their lunches, their snacks, their telephone calls. Endlessly conveying messages for Pia from employment agencies, suitors, creditors, gentlemen who might need a typist, the insurance company against which Paul and Valerie have laid a claim for a dent in their truck. The insurance money is their El Dorado, it might even pay for the truck. If not that, then the utility bills. They have spent the money a hundred times over, like lovable children. The company is slow and unwilling. Innumerable calls are necessary. Paul's earnest young voice playing man over the phone, nearly crumbling into tears when the check arrives with a stipulation that it cannot be cashed for a month. Who will cover it, meanwhile? They want to spend it right now, and they do not have enough in the bank to cover it themselves. Sita is uninterested in advancing two hundred dollars, so am I. I have made bad loans to the kids in the past and the job of making them solvent would never end. I listen to the mounting hysteria from the bedroom, sticking to my desk. First Pia negotiates with the bureaucrats, then Paul. A call to Valerie in Marin. The inevitable calls to Sita for advice. Further calls to lawyer friends of Pia's. Explanations of the delay. Paul again on the line to the company, brother and sister between calls furious and bellicose, but admirably patient when dealing with official stupidity. A call to the bank. How well I know that outrage, that sense of insult before pointless obstacle. I listen with painful empathy below my amusement, but they have used up three hours of my time with their emergency. The phonograph blares. Emily is home from school and has turned on the television. It's already four o'clock. Sita will be home in an hour. Hedy has decided to stay another day.

When we come in, the usual funky furniture from some improbable long-ago living room, the pictures rotting in junk stores twenty years. Camp. Kind of stuff Pia loves. The eternal dress-up of old satin, ankle straps, moldy ballads. Lampshades with fringes, pink overstuffed chairs, ponderous frieze sofas. Oleg's has expanded, taken over the adjoining storefronts, leaked its funk over two more rooms. Acres of depressing memorabilia in which to wait for lunch. Arrogant young man playing maître d'. He will call our table when he gets around to it. Signed us up as "Sita." Refused to bother with a last name. She permitted him. Will we drink? She won't. I will. A Bloody Mary at noon, despite the manuscript, the typing. Celebrate life, enjoy the time—a voice I locate as sanity. Death, the emptiness of time ahead. Fight it off, think of something to say. Since I am silence. This most of all, that I have nothing to say, am hollow—this most of all will drive her away.

"Did you take a look at Michael's place?" It is long and hard even to get out the word—yes. "Well, what do you think of it?" "It's a nice place." Hovering, holding fire. We look at each other through the silence. Palpable, almost visible. Visible surely in the slight annoyance on her face, the eyes blinking, the chin line hardening in impatience. I sympathize, I agree it's tedious. But what is there to say? Nothing or too much. Start out bravely, the truth—or some of it. "I think I'd be too alone there." I stop and then risk it: "I'm afraid I'd spend all my time waiting." She shifts at the end of her sofa, flicks back her hair. Gesture I love, seeing it now in fear. The wave of hair that falls across her forehead, always the same piece, always the same way. Throwing it off her face, perfect dip of the wrist, pat of the long competent fingers. My fingers.

She had expected a more satisfactory report, is still waiting for one. But how can I tell her that I took one look at the place and foresaw the most desperate future? One room, a nice-enough room, view of a nice little garden behind, fashionable neighborhood. Perfect bachelor apartment for someone like Michael, a young lawyer-about-town. Behind me at that moment, nuzzling Pia, with whom it is transparent he's having a thing that totally engages them both, leaving me, ostensibly the purpose of the visit, an awkward intruder. Pleasant little place, we all agree. They expect me to love it and take it on the spot. I look around the room and imagine life here; table by the window, fireplace, kitchen, shower—a life of waiting. Waiting all day until she finishes work. Waiting each evening until she tears herself away from the commune on the evenings she comes. And the evenings she doesn't come? Telephoning the house. Being told she's out. Being told she's at a meeting. But no, I'm only supposed to work here daytimes, stay at the house otherwise. How do I pay both rents? And I know already that if I took it I would be exiled here finally; it would come to be regarded as considerate or convenient. And here I would lead no other life but waiting. The life of Victor Hugo's mistress comes to mind. Here in this little room with its partial view I would learn all there was to know of waiting, exasperation, hope deferred, sad patience, the doglike expectation of a sound in the driveway, a step on the path. No, damn it, no. It would be hell to live it, hell to live like that. The most slavish conditions, the most insufferable circumstances. Accepting the last defeat, becoming her occasional visit, the creature she has stored away in a room in the hills, visited only when the mood strikes her. Marginal before, I would now be completely expendable.

Meanwhile, she goes on persuading me from the

sofa at my side. The place needn't be seen as a penitentiary or a punishment, after all. It might be a great convenience to both of us; I would have a place to work and we would both have a place to be together, to be alone together. "A love nest?" I challenge her. "Sure, why not?" she agrees, seeing that's a good line to follow. And I follow it, despite the irony of our paying three hundred fifty dollars' rent to have a house together which she has so filled with people that I should now be expected to pay another hundred seventy-five so that we can have a little privacy. In addition to paying rent in New York. Perhaps I should. Maybe I'm being cheap, maybe I should just go ahead even if I can't afford it, go for broke. Love doesn't go by money, after all. A love nest, how charming; a place of assignation, a rendezvous. Delightful. Then I see the room and remember its true scent: waiting, merely waiting. Hours at the whim of her caprice, a life on tenterhooks. The terrible loneliness the place gave off predicted, even warned me, of itself. She expects me to have agreed by now. I haven't. Her name is called and we go in to lunch.

Oleg's garden is all under Plexiglas, the light generous and easy, the sensation of air and sky and plants is carefree and Californian and beguiling. I had forgotten there's nothing I like on the menu. There is no time to study it anyway, because she is lecturing me. I am pressing too close, take up too much of her time and energy. She wants and needs and insists upon a greater independence. I look on, helpless to argue or interrupt, not really understanding what she is talking about. She is talking about her own individual life, which had flowered and developed in my absence and which she is now in no mood to relinquish. "I don't want you to relinquish anything," I sputter, forgetting even to consider how much I relinquish. There is no way to parry her when she attacks. It seems there are a great many friends she has not seen since my arrival. "I've only been here a few days," I say weakly. There are a number of people dear to her, she goes on, her voice getting hard, building to its crisis, and she has no intention, absolutely none, of giving them up. "Who

would ask you to?" I say innocently. "Men friends."
"Really?" "People very dear to me." "I see." "Neal."
"Who's Neal?" "I told you about Neal at Christmas."
Neal, whom she seduced by telling him women were
better lovers than men; Neal, who seems to owe his
success to her particularly cruel use of me as a challenge. Neal. "He was a very good lover," she'd said.
"Gentle, really very good." I'd winced for a second at
the recommendation, but it was frivolous talk, giggling in bed. "Men don't really count, after all." She'd
chuckled. And I'd weakened and told her about my
friend Dobie. Whatever Neal was, Dobie is really only
a friend, impossible to mistake our two abortive efforts at sex as being lovers. "What's Dobie like?"
"He's black and was an actor a long time with the
Living Theatre. He wants to practice their anarchist
philosophy, so now he's running a bunch of food co-
ops in Harlem, he's decided to devote two years to it.
Very nice guy, he's helped me a lot with my loft,
lives in the neighborhood. He's a buddy, we eat together a lot." "Men don't really count"—it seemed an
awfully smug thing to say, however reassuring, and
now I find that Neal does count, a great deal. Over
and over she reiterates that Neal is part of her life,
being free to see him is indispensable. "I'll be here
only a short time, couldn't he be sort of—in
abeyance?" It would never occur to me to impose
Ruth or Dobie upon her. The time I am with her I
am only with her. No, she doesn't see it that way at
all. "Of course when we're apart it's understood we
might have other lovers, but when we're together . . ."
"Look, I live here all year round. I have to make a
life for myself here. Just here. Nowhere else. And
there are people in that life who matter to me." "I
see." "You don't see. I insist upon having complete
independence." "But you _have_ it, whereas I don't. You
have remarkable independence and I have none at all."

Now you want more: complete, total, totalitarian—
all things I might say but don't. Can't, don't dare.
Instead, I sit before her playing with my food, growing a little sick, my forehead hot with shame. No one
hears us, the waiter approaches and withdraws at her

commands, and yet I have an enormous feeling of shame, as if everyone there were party to my humiliation. Which proceeds. She taunts me: Wasn't I the great advocate of sexual liberation, where was all my nonsense jargon of "multiple relationships" and so forth now? I don't know. I know only that I feel the most craven fear, insecurity, even jealousy at the prospect of sharing her with Neal. She will go on seeing Neal, that is for sure, that's settled, she tells me. "Why should you possibly object?" "Of course not, how could I? I had only thought the thing could wait until I left." The inference seems to be that Neal has no interest in waiting. At Christmas she had mentioned telling him about me—"Neal understands, knows how much I love you"—but at Christmas Neal seemed a one-shot affair, nearly a joke, no rival at all. And now he is someone who makes demands, takes precedence, will be fought for. For the worst thing of all is that she makes this a fight, her fight for independence against my brutal and possessive ways. And her rhetoric is precisely the rhetoric of the woman's movement. I have somehow become "the enemy." This on the day I inspected a place where I was supposed to take up residence as the little woman, spending eons of lonely afternoons and evenings waiting for her to arrive like a masterful seigneur. The whole thing is too confusing. And I don't want to fight, lose even in peacetime, have fallen already, here in the sun and the hanging fuchsias and potted greenery, have fallen into a nightmare. The thought of going back to New York occurs only like further mortification. Lunch is over.

When I reach my car, I have to search for the keys. Have I lost them? Frantic for a second till they swim into view at the bottom of my purse. When I hold them in my hand I realize this is really all I have in California.

Lunch today. The No Name. They would not let us sit in the garden. "It's winter." When will winter stop? I wondered. "Too chilly to serve you out there." The

garden shining beyond the window in the sun. We used
to have such lovely afternoons there. Squeezed into a
disappointing little booth, and she touched my knee.
It is what I remember afterward. My trophy. With the
long wait ahead I examine it and weigh it against my
losses. The winning and losing of love, the balance of
points, the quick little slide into failure.

"I found that whatever the relationship, I kept turning it into marriage," Sita announces. The poet nods.
She is taking a woman poet to lunch and has invited
me along. "Man or woman, that was all I knew, that
tight little . . ." Sita cups her hands illustrating
her point. The poet nods again. I munch, agreeing and
nodding, my compliance at odds with the knowledge
inside me—she is talking about me. Last spring she
had "married" me. Now she is all vehemence against
it. My leaving for the city again, my needing it, wanting it still, taking the loft there, that was defection and
betrayal.

Now Sita has seen her errors, she finds them con-
temptible. Marriage in any form (and it's a chame-
leon) is the enemy. She goes on attacking it, how it
keeps cropping up. The poet nods. They agree
perfectly. The poet's divorce. Her book of poems
which chronicle it staring at me from the tabletop. "My
daughter's going through a divorce right now." Dan, the
lonely figure in cut-off dungarees I ran into in the
kitchen last night, his lovely body defeated in its flesh,
the naked legs, the bare vulnerable chest—Dan a divorce Pia is going through. His long, yellow hair hag-
gard on either side of a face trying to be brave, keeping
his dignity. Before me even. Dan pouring a glass of
milk, his voice gently saying hello in the middle of the
night. And this morning he was gone.

Only last night Dan was expelled. Martin was
brought in to deliver the final blow of dislodgment, the
whole execution taking place with disarming subtlety
and discretion backstage in kitchen and dining room
while Sita's inane committee babbled on in the living
room. And when Dan balked, upstairs in the bedroom
he shared with Pia, and seemed unwilling to leave,
Martin, a domestic Kissinger, was forced to shuttle

from whispered conference with Pia at the dining-room table, where she was being promised schooling and a secondhand car, up to Dan's den, where he suffered unknown humiliations as Martin came with kindly reasonableness to tell him he really must pack. And the whole thing going on side by side with a committee meeting, Sita's committee on male and female relationships. The committee busily eating a spaghetti dinner while planning their coming weekend in the mountains. They went on earnestly about opening a new dialogue between the sexes, bringing a new respect to interpersonal relationships across sex lines. Bizarre, dreadful evening, the conjunction of their abstract jargon with the actual manipulations going on elsewhere in the house.

But even the committee had one reality: Percy. When I came into the kitchen to give a hand and make the salad, I met Percy. Black. Magnificent. Beautiful and arrogant and spoiled. The whole evening passed in an alarm of danger at the way he appropriated Sita, appropriated even the space of kitchen she stood in. And then at the Chinese table in the living room, each and every member of the committee deferring clownishly to his self-importance, to the cruel humor of his story of how he forced two young girls hitchhiking to get out of his car and walk the road again when he found one of them insufficiently docile. Pia watched him fascinated, later compared notes with Sita. "I've always been afraid we might flash on the same dude . . ."

"Pia will be a little blue." Sita guiding, directing, supervising at breakfast. Not all that blue either. Michael was leaving the house as I came home from the dentist midmorning. The employment agency called four times while Pia was in the shower. The radio plays. The phonograph. Pia, her long, luxurious teenage mornings. I try to type the mess I have sorted, hating it, waiting for lunch. For her body at the corner of the parking lot, the arm waving. The body I dream of seeing all day long, her body at the corner before an office, in the parking lot, or leaving her car at the curb and approaching the house in the evening. Wav-

ing now as I find a parking spot. Catching sight of this
poet she has brought along to lunch. Her book of poems
with photographs to match. Published it herself, a story
I encourage her to tell as I consume my meal. Her
friend Nancy who did the layout. Her best friend. Sita
touches my knee. Her hand along the outside of my
thigh. Sweet confusion. I do not move. Dare not even
reciprocate by an inch. The poet breaks off with a
commercial publisher, chooses her paper, takes bids
from printers. Sita's hand is lovely where it is. I must
make some slight move, some infinitely subtle gesture
of gratitude. The hand deserts me, hesitates, returns.
"What sort of paper?" "It's called Patina." I nod.
"Picking out a paper could take forever, couldn't it?"
"We ended up using this kind called Patina. It has to
be sixty- or seventy-pound stock or the photographs
come through to the other side." Knowledgeable nod.
The hand on my knee as warm as a bank account.
"And Nancy did all the layouts." "How did you set
the type?" "We had a typesetter right here in
Berkeley." Sita has decided we will have all three
kinds of pie. Having coaxed me into the chocolate
fudge. "Well, just to help you out," I tease. Her smile
warming me like a hand.

Then in the street. Suddenly. Announcing, casually
as if it were to both of us, that she is going to Davis
overnight. The provost, his television film, his ego, her
schedule. It's a bore but the provost is her boss. She'll
stay at her friend Maud's. Just a few of them are going
up from the office and the men will stay at a hotel.
Neal? The poet says the street looks like New York.
This is Shattuck Avenue and it has never looked like
New York. Can it be Neal? Yesterday's announcement, ultimatum. Oleg's. Can she be lying to me?
Would she do that, telling herself it's kinder? Accepting
the ease of it, that it brings no confrontation. For
I was bold, protested yesterday. The poet gurgling about
this street and New York. Sita breezy about Davis,
the provost, his folly. I can hardly see to walk. This
street and New York, she goes on. Never in a million years, I mumble. The provost and his television
film, the provost's magnificent goitered ego, chuckling

in Sita's voice. They need it for a conference, preparations laid days ago, the better deal she got for them in San Francisco, the packaged crew, the provost's complete inability to judge time in media, the way he intended to drone on for thirty minutes all alone, this ham performer.

I had thought she might perhaps be late tonight, some meeting or other, was hoping for dinner out together at eight. Now instead this all-night vacancy. Immediately I try to improvise: I'll read, later go to a film. The sun on the pavement is hard and grim. "This friend of mine took me all over New York, I even rode the subway." The voice irrelevant at my side. Her cover. The reason why Sita invited her. The whole crashing news done so casually, three ladies striding along Shattuck Avenue and one happens to say, "I'll be out of town overnight and I'll go straight to work in the morning." Not even the sad ten minutes in the early dark, snuggling, the poached egg, the newspaper fragments, Emily's nightie bouncing at its place at the table, Valerie's definitive tread, Pia's wavering coffee cup. The silent ride to her office, driving her in order to have those few fruitless moments alone. None of these. Till lunch then tomorrow. Twenty-four hours. And will she even take lunch tomorrow? So hard to believe she will not be home at five this evening. The hour I wait for. This evening there will be a five o'clock and it will bring nothing at all. To endure dinner with the kids. Escaping to the movies. Reading magazines on the bed in our room upstairs, the only place I have title to.

Other times force themselves back: making love in Sacramento, my perfect little garden apartment there, the fuchsias hanging from the eaves so you could see them from the bed, even her old house on Fordham Way. This morning a woman telephoning for a lecture bureau said that she had sent me a wire at Fordham Way, the name almost buried, stinging as it bounced back from under those years. Those days, those first nights and days, the sight of our two coffee cups in the morning, the two of us standing together before a table naked, her nakedness and mine, hers brown as syrup, beautiful large brown nipples, the smoothness of her skin was sense itself. The other times here, even here in Berkeley last spring. Indian Rock, our house here on Indian Rock, her fortress made to treasure me against the world. Gone, invaded.

No, I am merely inflexible. Foolish. Possessive. Every vice I used to castigate in others. She's gone overnight on business, so what? Why the panic, the suspicion, the unreasoning terror? This is just a simple matter, friendship understands, takes it in stride. Can't be helped anyway, these are her responsibilities. You knew she was a very busy person. Even if you are here only a short time and get to see her rarely and under the most absurd and crowded circumstances, take it philosophically. You're in California only on a visit, it seems. A friendly visit. Enjoy it, the better climate. Pretend you're a jet-setter avoiding the New York winter or something. Take advantage of the landscape, the sunset from the Indian rocks, that sort of thing. And understand that this trip of hers is just part of her job; obligatory, boring. She is staying with Maud to avoid having to spend the night in a hotel in Sacramento. Where the men are staying. She used the plural. What men? The provost, yes. The other one? Neal? Were I to call, would Maud cover? Is she instructed? But I would never call. Not my sort of thing, despicable. Time stretches ahead.

I sit outside and write on the picnic table. Beginning this notebook. Or rather, acknowledging that I begin it. Begin? Begin what? "Begin" is inappropriate. All I'm doing is hanging on to the edge during a dizzy spell. Like that ride at Coney Island I went on a few Saturdays before I came out here. Innocent-looking thing. "Crack the Whip" or something. Round disks with cars mounted, a bench inside for two or three. And the whole car would spin about as it advanced along the larger circle, the motion itself making the light car whirl on its platform. So you'd be propelled by two forces, and the thing, which seemed matter-of-fact enough from the ground, actually built up a formidable momentum. You were whirled until your neck cracked and your stomach protested in nausea and terror. I had been insanely afraid, which delighted and amused my friends. Shut my eyes and prayed for life: just to get out of this alive.

Moments out here have the same panic. To come and find the house full of strangers and hostility and indifference. To find her changed past knowing, hardened past caring. I am lost here. Go back to New York or stay and go on suffering, experiencing whatever is to be experienced here? Maybe that's it, maybe the lure of the experience itself, painful as it might be, the experience in its learning and its sensations. If I leave I will not have had it. If I stay I can study it, even record, possess it. I hold on to the notebook and the ballpoint. As I held on to the bar in the carnival car. I am doing this, setting down words, just to survive, to fight off panic.

And the picnic table is warm. If I scribble something, I am writing rather than falling apart. Though it comes to nothing, is wasted time, doesn't even qualify as exercise or practice, it is still activity, some rag of work or doing to satisfy self-respect. Not merely pretense. "I'll be outside at the picnic table," I say as I go down the basement stairs and out into the yard, a face or two seeing me through the window, respectfully imagining that I work. When I only fiddle. Fiddle a forbidden tune: what would they think if they knew I recorded today's lunch, this morning's breakfast, this very four o'clock on a wooden picnic table, the little daisies in the grass, the rose tree still blighted with winter, or what passes for winter here? What would they think? Like a spy in the house of love, the house she claims is so full of love. Pia appears, opening a window to air a room, for a second as powerful as the appearance of a ghost. I saw her at the window of my study. Then it became her bedroom again. Not until the window is open do I realize it is another room, catching sight of her plants and her bed. There was no bed, there was my table once.

The thing was a surprise. I love carnival rides. Never been on the roller coaster, but I had negotiated almost every other offering. And had not felt this horror since I was a child, when it was pleasurable and one courted it. So when this bit of silliness, experiment, bravado with friends turned into a nightmare, I was astonished. I felt old. It is how I feel all the time now. I turned forty last summer and it scared me. Since being here I am obsessed with death. Not the imminent death of my suicidal time, not a death you steel yourself to impose, but the "natural" and inevitable death that begins when the sense of age begins. If I was forty I was no longer young; when you are no longer young you are old. Old age is only the tedious and debilitating prelude to death, being dead while still being minimally alive. It is odd that I should feel so much older than Sita— ten years older than I, but she seems youthful and vital and alive. While I seem pale and gray and old. Losing her makes me old. It was the last love, the last conquest and romance, and losing it is losing the last chance. Having lost so much already, a marriage and a man and a home and a way of life. And now losing her, the last lover, the last resort or hope, and the time to come stretching away, so many empty years to kill before death.

I am aware that this is morbid. Desperation comes easy here. Like the old saying about running out of continent when you get to California; it's the edge, you fall off into the sea. Under the greenery and the complacency there is a lot of desperation. Everywhere people doing nothing with their lives. Pia gives off the scent of it below her studied cool, her beauty, her idleness, her outrageous camp clothes, the stockings with individual toes, each one a different color, the ridiculous six-inch wedgies she totters around on, the old silk gowns turned into afternoon dresses, the feather boas. I give it off in an old shirt and corduroys spotted with paint, pants I used to paint in at the loft, each spot a rebuke against the life I lead now. The manuscript abandoned upstairs while I fritter down here with a notebook. Scribbling because the compulsion is so great, because it might ease the pain, because like a primitive and magical gesture it might lance a wound, give me some control over what happens to me, upon

me, beyond my control. If I could close my hand over
this experience, capture it like a caterpillar or a grass-
hopper in a bottle, preserve it in its reality; useless to
change it, one does not aspire to govern life, only to
convey it accurately—accurately, but that's the problem, I will get nothing accurate, the picture blurred,
lifeless. How to garner up events and persons and atmosphere I do not myself understand, am overpowered
by?

And then I see her in the window. She has come
back. She has come home. Finally she has returned
after Davis, the night away. Her face shining on me,
her arm waving. But she is not alone, some hairy hulk
of a man in a denim jacket and Levi's, a beard, disheveled hair. Like another edition of Hank. But it's Mark.

"You mustn't be afraid of Mark. He's an old friend
I've loved for years. Like one of my kids." "Yes, of
course." I have heard all the descriptions of Mark, how
they worked on the paper together when he was a
journalism student and she was a housewife moving
back into the job market. Then Mark's absorption into
a commune of religious fanatics and LSD for the last
three years, his efforts to recover his mind and his
profession. "We were rookies together. You see, we're
both hack journalists, it's our great bond. That we can
yak away about our ratty prose. Something you'd never
understand." A dig that stung more than all the endearments heaped up whenever he's mentioned.

Mark was the seventh and final personality laid on
me when she came at Christmas. Not only that there
were Pia and Dan and Emily, Valerie and Paul and
Limbo the dog—but even someone I'd never heard of,
all living in the house. This Mark Thorne person. All
of them living at the house. Is he permanent or temporary? Permanent he seemed then. But he was gone
when I arrived. Temporary then? All the arrangements
of her life so fluid, so elusive, so provisional. And now
he's back. Permanent or temporary? No one bothers
to tell me.

And how he makes himself at home here. How free
and easy he is, his great weight complacently settled
in the fragile rocker. "I'll be taking the Toyota up to

Sacramento tomorrow," he says with a coolness that appalls me. Telling her, not asking her, that he is borrowing her car. Dan destroyed her Mercedes, totaled it, but not until after Hank had damaged it to the extent of a thousand dollars' worth of repairs. When will she ever learn about lending her car to young men? Fortunately, her new little sports car is in the shop, Mark can't have it. Pia passes us on her way to an audition, a real band, a real job. She needs twenty dollars, she announces. No one moves. Sita hasn't been to the bank. Mark has no money. "Give her the twenty dollars," Sita orders me.

Later Sita handed me a letter. "This is not going to set you up quite like your mother's letter did." We sit politely in the living room opening the day's mail. Mark rocks in the rocking chair. Mother's letter with its dear, almost inexplicable last sentence—how happy she was to have Sita as a member of the family. Inconceivable once, and now finally, at this late date, approval, acceptance. The mother's gratitude reserved for someone who truly loves her daughter. Coming now when that love is running out. I unfold the letter Sita has handed me. Jaycee, under a neat letterhead and a new address, complaining in a letter which Sita has now casually passed along, Jaycee complaining that her new Karen has "turned out to be like your Kate, a nine-year-old tyrant." I catch my breath. Why did she bother to show me this? Why did Jaycee say it? Where would she get this attitude but from Sita herself? Is this what I am to Sita, this caricature reflected back through an old lover who should have known better, whose docile young follower I was once for four years. How persuasive Sita must have been. I swallow and say nothing. Mark in his rocker, witness to all of this. "Mark showed up at my office today so I came home early." Would she have done that for me? "We're going to walk down the hill to pick up some photographs. Do you want to come?" This long I have waited. To be invited along for a walk with Mark. Time with her so impossibly precious, so rare in this house. He will want her time as much as I do. She will

want him along. The invitation mere courtesy and to
be treated as such. With stoicism I decline.

When she comes back, she's buoyant. I have waited
in the bedroom. Her smiles, her glances, her voice
planning dinner, dispensing gaiety, relief, well-being.
Should I mention Jaycee's phrase, confront her, annoy
her, spoil her mood? I wait, savoring all the kindness,
the charm, gobbling up the rare good humor, the warm
moments. She moves to go downstairs. "I was very
hurt by that phrase in Jaycee's letter." "Were you?"
"Where would she get such a notion but from you?" "I
can assure you, she arrived at it by herself." "I never
did anything to deserve that description." "People remember things differently. But I promise you, I am
not going to feel guilty for Jaycee's remarks." I know
she is lying, yet I have to pretend to believe her. Either
that or fight. Sita, her energy like a wall before me.
She always attacks now, never stoops to defend. And
this formula "not going to feel guilty," how frequent
and emphatic she is with it. In New York she resorted
to it whenever the summer in Italy came up. Cheerfully admitting she spent two months treating me like
dirt, but it was just something she was not going to feel
"guilty" over. Either something is past and we should
simply forget about it, or else it is something she does
not intend to feel guilty about—these two approaches:
it is over or I don't care, or, better yet, I don't care and
anyway it's over. She does not intend to "feel guilty."
How popular this phrase, how often you hear it from
friends, the moral back scratching of pop psychology.
And Sita uses it like a gun. Her universal justification.
Or rather, a negation of responsibility altogether, a
refusal to discuss it. Yet what strict lines of conduct I
am held to. For what offense am I a nine-year-old
tyrant? What does one do to undo such a reputation?

After she leaves I try to imagine this view of myself.
Is it true? Am I wrong at every juncture, and the two
of them right? Or rather Sita's view of me as passed on
to Jaycee, who wouldn't have thought of it herself but
is delighted to apply it to her own friend when the affair begins to give way under her. Because Jaycee
wants to come West and Karen, upon whom she has

pinned all her hopes, is backing out. To be malicious, she compares her to me. To me, as Sita sees me and describes me to her friends? Maybe this is who I really am. I don't know myself any more, have no self to know, am only someone with two suitcases ready to pack who seems not to know when she's unwelcome.

And Mark making himself very at home downstairs. I don't think I can face that just now. Take a little walk up to the rocks and watch the sun go down. Meeting little Emily on the stairs. "Do you want to go with me?" "No, I want to watch television." Just as well, I prefer to be alone. I can't cope any more, don't understand, have lost my way and sense of direction. In every contest between us she wins. Since she has nothing to lose, is in no way anxious to keep me, has all the power base in herself, in the others, her own children, her own guests. It is impossible to quarrel. Impossible also to disagree.

I will be quiet then. Well-mannered. Faultless. Live down my past. I have put on the long dress she admired the other night. As I pass the kitchen, the sound of an ice tray being opened in the sink. For Mark's drink. I will be self-sufficient, entertain myself, walking to the rocks in a long dress, this absurd marginal figure staying on inexplicably in a house full of people with whom I have nothing in common, in distant California, asking myself as I go along what on earth I am doing here. Trying to remember I used to live here. Or trying instead to pretend this is a vacation, a short visit with a friend, part of an ongoing connection, a love affair that mellows for years on into middle age. Or— see it one day at a time, the alcoholic's slogan.

It's not that I like sunsets, I assure myself. The banal, tomato-paste sentiment of them. Only that the end of the day, its death in the sea, the explosion of color—is something against which I have no resistance. Even on days when it's forbidden by pressing activities, the disinclination of companions, the lack of a view, even on those days I can feel it coming, sense it in the light each moment through the afternoon, know its arrival, the gold of its imminence, the rose of the act like a vulva, the red aftermath. I watch on, stolid

through the chill. The usual crew of rock-climbing en-
thusiasts. The six-year-olds, the lovers. I in my solitude, my outlandish dress.

And walking back I am astounded to see her coming
toward me on the opposite sidewalk. If I had only
waited, she might have joined me. I have committed
another blunder. "I have made you a martini." "You
did? How wonderful." And it is wonderful. That she
has done this for me. Like a thousand-year plenary
indulgence, Sita hating martinis and making one; martinis, the vice of a New Yorker, a drink I had no idea
she even knew how to compose. "When you came
downstairs I looked around and couldn't find you."
"I'm sorry." How sorry—if I had only known, for in
my treachery I had imagined that it was Mark's ice I
heard in the kitchen. What folly, it was mine. My
martini. "Let's hope it's still all right. I summoned all
my bartending skills and you know what they are."
Her laugh, her arm comfortably tucked in mine. The
warmth of her body coming blissfully through my
dress.

At breakfast Pia laughs and tells me she blew it.
"You'll never believe what happened. You know I
left here early. So first I went by to visit a few friends.
Nobody home. So I went to this favorite bar of mine.
Bartender says, This is your big night, honey. Buys me
a corsage. Then this guy comes in that I really like.
We start to split a bottle of mescal. Mescal . . . whee."
She is lost, remembering it in the cigarette smoke she
exhales in revery. I sit off to her side, she doesn't see
me. "Never tasted mescal before. First thing I know,
I'm throwing up in the john. Never got to the audition
at all. Called up the band, drunk as a louse, gave them
some fool excuse. Blew the whole damn thing. Can
you believe it?" Now she turns toward me, she'll
give it to me in the face. I mustn't wince. "Blew the
whole damn thing. Can you believe it?"

I can. All too easily. Even the smell of mescal. The
toilet and the air in the toilet and Pia's special fragile
beauty humiliated there. The other night it was just the

two of us at dinner, and Emily. Dan was gone, Sita in Davis. Pia her most delightful self, pleasing, pretty, all the talk of Janis, Pia having been one of her set, how she lived, how she died. Billie Holiday records. The biography of Bessie Smith Pia loaned me to take to bed. Making dinner together, talking, enjoying her imitations of Billie, her love of the blues. I could read all the jazz-singer signs, the hypnotic fascination with danger, the blaze, and then the sinking out of sight. Booze. Drugs. Assorted suicides. The tradition solid enough now to demand self-immolation. And the thing expected somehow by all those who stand near, manipulating, participating, making it ready. "Those people around Janis, they needed her, needed her to give 'em dope. They needed everything she did, who she was. They thought *they* were Janis—yeah, that's what it came to, they were what she was. But she's the one who crashed. They didn't. They got out. Even that chick Sunshine, and I'll tell you, she's one strung-out chick."

After dinner she got out her high-school yearbooks and showed them to Emily. "This is what your mommy looked like." Pia in teased hair, bobby socks, cheerleader, American-girl pretty. The child fascinated, entranced by the myth of her mother as I have seen Pia entranced by Sita's baby book issued by Queen Elena, royal arms commemorating the beginnings of a new crop of nobles, pictures of an Italian childhood, summers at Lake Como, the count her father looking distinguished and appropriate, her mother florid and diva-like, Sita dark and homely yet somehow haunting, compelling, posing in absurd ballet postures, tutus, the long legs, the anguished face of self-conscious childhood imposed upon in some grotesque way by the world, yet half believing, more than half believing the fantasy of her silk roses, her magical shoes, her voile skirts, believing so earnestly perhaps that the betrayal on her face is not that they make her do it but that she cannot live there always. How different the stolid American face of Pia, grinning from out of a cluster of her classmates' smug Southern Californian crew cuts. "To a swell gal," "To a dreamy

date," "To a girl with a great future," "To a gal with
real talent." "Is this you, Mommy, is this really you?"
"I sure look different, don't I?" "Is this you, Mommy?"
"Yes, Emily, I just told you so." The child loving the
mystery of it, that the almost plump, almost woman,
almost child blur of the photograph is her own slender
beautiful wonderful mother.

The mysteries of mothers and daughters. Hard to
believe that Pia is Sita's daughter, so fair she is, so
Anglo. "They are both Wasps," she always says; "only
Emily is like me." Emily with her dark eyes. Strange
deep child eyes searching the glossy pages of meaning as she searches everything and everyone. Already
orphaned. It is part of Pia's new regime of "doing her
thing" to send Emily away to her father's mother, "the
other grandmother," as she's called. Emily's father,
Pia's first husband, was a musician on drugs, long
since disappeared. "I never put him down in front of
Emily, and Margaret's a good woman." Pia calling
long distance, asking permission, making the arrangements. "You're gonna go on a trip, Emily, up to
Gramma Margaret's, aren't you excited?" The child
uncertain, already afraid, half in love with the adventure, half terrified of leaving her mother, Dan
whom she calls Daddy, Sita, her world here. "Who'd
ever believe that Joe and Louise would ever break
up?" Pia crows, "Just goes to show." Margaret has
told her that her other son and daughter-in-law are
getting a divorce and she has both their children with
her too. Seems like a lot for an older woman to
handle, Pia speculates, but nothing will discourage or
deter her now; it will give Emily two playmates and
Oregon's a healthy place—"They have snow there
now, Emily."

Hedy comes for breakfast. Pia repeats her story, a
joke almost, a triumph. "Pia just plain bombed out
last night. She just never got there," talking of herself
in the third person. "Pia's your all-time fuck-up. Missing in action." Hedy has to laugh, so do I. The sporting
and total admission, the absolute vulnerability, the
summary judgment. We are left with nothing to say,
she disarms criticism. And the whole performance,

even its reenactment, is so classic, so steeped in tradition. I urge her to call back. She says they'll let her try again. Call them, I say, get another chance at it, you'll do fine. She says she'll call them, but she doesn't move. Pete comes in. Jon-Jon wakes up on the living-room floor. I escape upstairs. What am I doing here?

I put down one bag of groceries and go back for the rest. Valerie springs to help me. "My God, what did you spend?" I grin and she hugs me. I have shopped up a storm, feeling proud and a little silly as she marvels over the steaks, the Chateaubriands, the roasts, the chickens, the vegetables, the fruit. "I'm so glad to have you here," she says, "and not just for the food. It's good you're with us, I'm glad you came." It's not the first time she's said it. The other day, up in our bedroom, I came upon her chatting with Sita on our bed, mother- and daughter-in-law, or since Paul and Valerie aren't married, Sita invented the term "daughter-in-love." I remember a second's jealousy, seeing Sita sprawled on the bed talking with this beautiful blond young amazon. I went to the closet to search for something, perhaps to undress before bed. Sita got up to answer the phone. And Valerie lay on the bed and talked to me, saying it was so good I was there, how glad of it she was. I was astonished, over-come with gratitude, humbled before her goodness and generosity. So as her healthy size and big child's vitality shrieks and marvels at this vast windfall of groceries, I believe her. Somehow Valerie has accepted me. And Emily. I will keep trying, I will win them all.

The numbers rise and fall. Hedy, Pete, Jon-Jon, et al. have finally departed. But the next day another of Pia's friends, Pigtail, arrives. Days and nights of giggles and stories and reminiscences, the first mythical commune on Beech Street, the perfection of its chaos, the fate of each of its members. Pia ignores the employment agencies, they call to no effect, she is busy. And besides, she did go to one interview and the guy made her spend several hours typing his briefs "to try her out" and then never paid her. She has figured out that the salary he was offering was only three dollars more than unemployment. "Throw in the carfare and it's just the same thing." She gestures, droll, pathetic, vulnerable. "The whole thing's a rip-off. Life's a rip-off." Pigtail chuckles and they go back to entertaining each other, waiting for Michael, discussing last night's party, admiring a new pair of shoes. From time to time Pia wanders in to interrupt me and smoke a cigarette. "Art's very tough. You just gotta do it," she sighs. I encourage, buoy, prop up her confidence, remind her to call the band. She's going to, she'll get around to it soon. I must be subtle, patient.

Paul is removed. Stumbling in the round of his sleep and his toil and his inlay puttering and guitar tinkering. But he practices very little now, seems shadowy, a figure forever leaving for or being retrieved from work. He and Valerie spend most of their time going to and from Marin County, where his job is, where she goes to school. His conversation consists of jokes about his coming promotion to busboy, an elevation he takes very seriously. And fond, phony male-chauvinist jokes at Valerie's expense. There is no reaching Paul, this big gawky boy in long hair and glasses. But with all the others I will keep on trying, the trying an effort to bring back Sita herself. Through all those that she has put between us. I must survive in her. And if I win I have her again.

She snuggles my leg under hers. Solomon Grundy's with its great windows onto the sea. The old feeling. The old place. Like the night last week we had dinner here, talked about the first time in Sacramento, becoming lovers. That long night, lighting one cigarette after another. She was awake too. Her trips to the bathroom. Seeing her body in and out of the corridor, looking down the dark hall afraid to stir, to turn on the light. Hoping she'd ask me back into the living room, roll another joint, make it possible to come together. The barest sheen of her back floating away into the gloom, returning to her bedroom. What was I, crazy? Arrive here in the afternoon and already full of designs on my hostess. She laughed, remembering it. "Hospitality, you know, can't seduce the visiting faculty member on the first night." So we waited for the second. Waiting to be sure that I wanted her, was not acting out of some mere impulse toward a stranger, some perverse pity for her age, that she was older, waiting till I knew certainly it was just her age that I wanted, that this stranger was the very ripe and intriguing experience I chose. Sober, awake, with the whole day to think about it, to be sure. That I did not wrong her with philandering, curiosity. So we waited till the second night. And then it happened as if by accident, each of us ready on her side, happened in the middle of a sentence, sitting on the sofa talking politics a mile a minute. Suddenly our mouths kissing. I remember her voice telling me to come to bed. Like fate. Sent, knowing it was a finality like some sort of seal. Went anyway, wanting it. Then the astonishment of her lovemaking, the force of it. Nearly begging off, sure I couldn't bear it. But then I could, could just barely hold on through the terrible force of her hands, the power inside me nearly pain, at the brink of fainting, coming far ahead of will or realization, catching my breath only to drown again. Utterly commanded. Overwhelmed. The mastery of those hands—and yet her tenderness, the woman's passion of her. Falling asleep bewildered. No woman had ever fucked me before. The force of a man. I was hooked.

A sailboat goes by through the big windows of night. Ghostly gray in the black. I have never seen one in the dark. Daytime's serene shape, the white sails that flock around Grundy's in the sun are phantoms now. Her leg nestles next to mine, our knees warm and knowledgeable with each other. A mood perfect at the end of day, a day described, discussed, even the office settled. Even Pia's audition. Sita is disappointed, disgusted; all the times Pia has let her down. Even a pretense of hardness—she'll wash her hands of it. I break my rule of absolute detachment (it is none of my business and very dangerous to intervene) and make one suggestion —that the emphasis stay right on the issue, the audition, that Pia make another try and carry through. The point is not to hassle her but to get her started with a band. The knee squeezes me, I am content. Beloved as

I used to be, cherished even. Because she is so anxious that I like the little Japanese restaurant she has picked for us tonight. "Finish your drink, I'm so excited to see what you think of the place." As I turn around to get my sweater, I see the sailboat again. Like a ghost in the pitch. Grim somehow, some strange and unexpected warning.

Pia slouches into breakfast. Emily fidgets over her food. Valerie storms in on us as she always does, the swirl of her red skirt, the definite strokes of the Cossack boots. Emily grumbles. Valerie scolds. "Keep out of this, Valerie," Pia shouts. "The kid is spoiled, she's got to learn," Valerie says and goes on scolding. Suddenly something is flying through the air. Valerie ducks, the cream pitcher hits the door frame and falls to the floor. We are all astonished. I cannot recognize Pia, know only her vagueness, her prettiness, her "cool," her vulnerability, her teen aura and idleness, her slippery promises. But never her temper. Raging now and still shouting at Valerie to leave the child alone, it's her child, don't you dare interfere. "Peace, peace," I say, trying to laugh, trying to make it a joke. Paul begins shouting on Valerie's side. Sita goes off to work.

That day I drove to Sacramento to see one of the prisoners in Folsom. There was still quarreling when I left. And when I came back home, there was no one. Until the phone rang—Pia from a bar explaining in her circular way that Paul and Valerie had left. There had been another fight in the afternoon. Pia hit Valerie, slugged her. "And I'm not sorry either." Though she sounds sorry and more than a little worried. "Don't tell Mom, or tell her just a little bit, make it easy for her." "Sure." The familiar "don't tell," when she borrows money from me, when she's late, when things go wrong and Pia can't "get it together," as she puts it. "Where are you?" "Emily and I are in a bar. Mom had to make a quick trip to L.A. and she wants you to pick her up at Oakland Airport at seven instead of eight. Do you know the way?" "She wrote down the instructions. Pia, what happened?" "So she kept going on about

Emily and I couldn't take it, so I let her have it. Then Paul gets into it, my own brother, and he starts hitting me. And then they left. It was just crazy." "Where did they go?" "To Marin, Valerie's brother's got a place out there. I guess that's where they'll stay till they get a place of their own."

Paul and Valerie's closed bedroom door. Once another room, once a library. One of Emily's innumerable paintings decorates it. "I love Paul and Valerie," herself portrayed as a princess of the sun, bestowing blessings. Now there is war. Driving Sita home, I mention the thing offhandedly, gently, as if it were trivia. Just a spat between the kids. And fail to get the point across, though I break the fall. Pia does it, sitting disconsolately on the sofa as we come in. Crying. Weeping her daughter's tears while Sita strokes and comforts. I am in the way. I make a drink and sit in the kitchen alone, giving them time and place. An hour later they are still rapt in their own sorrow, Sita not even remonstrating, Pia contrite, remorseful, the sadness of years in them. I will cook them a good chicken dinner, roasting and basting the bird while reading in the kitchen on a little stool. They protest they are not hungry. I am chagrined, but go on, since I have started. And at dinner they are hungry and revived and Pia stops weeping to eat. I am useful, my patience is rewarded.

The rest is confusion. Our commune is over, ended suddenly in one afternoon. Confusing how I regret Paul and Valerie's leaving, much as I had wanted them gone, much as I had never wanted to live in a commune at all. Yet there's a little sorrow in its passing. Sita's sorrow not least of all. It had meant so much to her, living with her children. Yet it seemed to mean so little to them. And the irony of it all vanishing the one afternoon I was not there to intervene, perhaps to save it. Though I had wanted them gone—no wish of mine, no preference or claim had ever had any effect on them—yet what a relief that I had nothing to do with it.

The commune is over. Foolishly, I remember all the food. All the food I bought that we will never eat, all the dinners, the guitars, the music. Little Emily goes north soon. Dan is long gone. I feel Sita's grief as she gets ready for bed, her exhaustion, her tears. "Maybe they will come back." Though I want them away, I would have them come back for her. She looks old, beaten. I feel an enormous pity, and enormous tenderness. And am helpless to help. Tomorrow I go to Texas for a speech. "I'll call Martin," she says. As she always does, Martin still somehow the husband and father even after four years of divorce. Martin, lately her financial agent, who writes her checks since she has decided she will give up trying to handle money at all. My beloved administrator cannot balance her checkbook and is heavily in debt. Martin will bank her checks, pay all the bills, get her out of debt, and begin to force her to save. She will pay me back for the trip to Europe, the three hundred dollars she borrowed after Christmas until that magazine in L.A. paid her for her article on Latin women. I listen, not really expecting her ever to pay me, but touched that she thinks of it, glad she will begin saving, glad there is Martin to protect her. My arms around her tired and trying to absorb her tiredness, her grief. Wishing there were love in her shoulders, feeling only the solid and alienated flesh.

I have been away to Texas for a day, and landing, I remember what she will look like. Standing in so many airport lines to meet me. Two years now. Even that first time in Sacramento when I came down the escalator and saw her, a stranger in a raincoat waiting at the bottom. With a little bouquet of flowers, which surprised and embarrassed me a bit. How she used to tell everyone about that escalator, that she expected me to arrive with picket signs, fierce, formidable. And instead I was small and gentle and wore a long dress under a peacoat. The peacoat, the dress, almost objects of veneration as she named them, telling people over and over how she loved me, how from that moment . . . Remembering now, landing from Texas after a speech and away overnight, remembering everything. San Francisco below me in a glory. Remembering another landing here two years ago, back from a trip to England

and so fatuously in love with her, the first separation of any length, circling over San Francisco imagining Dante: that I would be a poet and this my home, exiled to a city fairer than Florence. And she would be waiting, the euphoria of that day. Then the breakdown that summer, an autumn away from each other and estranged, the break with Fumio in the winter, coming to her that spring to live together. Shards of the past, each so bitter because then is so much better than now. Remembering the Sita of now only as a dull ache, the new distance impossible to overcome. Remembering that she will be homely. That I will wonder all over again why I love her. Only after falling into that face again, making it beautiful, necessary, only after moments, the first almost-embarrassed greeting, the hug before the eyes of others. She will stand there looking old, that raincoat, those shieldlike alienating glasses, tense, awkward. Sita, my person to be singled out from the other persons. My person, at first strange, uninviting. I am not proud of her, can hardly remember her. And then she is upon me. And in a moment beautiful, the center of my world, and I am a satellite or a child tagging along to the luggage place. Already devoured in her face, my eyes turned up, hungry, utterly persuaded.

But not yet. Still separate in my seat. Why am I out here, the West, San Francisco coming into sight? Why the West? When I am a New York artist. Why pursuing this thing already over? Knowing that. Having just had a day and a night in Texas to think it over. That the time of love is past, the span of it that was creative, renewing. As if it were a line on a graph, a strip of fabric in a pattern, limited, mere inches long. And now what? The aftereffect, dependency, habit, the fear of endings. All endings. Time staring, my fortieth year looking toward death.

Last night I fell asleep in a motel room with the television still on. Hours then and this morning before bureaus and mirror facing my failure, my wasting life. Hours before mirrors and in showers deciding I'm getting fat, I'm not getting any work done, my life has no direction, I'm spending too much money. If only there were a job, activity, any usefulness. Motel drapes, motel bedspread, motel view of granite Dallas. The trip and the distance were no ease, only a better vantage to discover and assess, admit finally that I am lost. I have lost faith. Give up and go back to teaching? Could you even get a job? Watching the woman who has a job that afternoon, polite little luncheon at a graduate student's apartment, the professor on her sofa, describing her career, her rise, her years in service. Earlier, sitting in her grand office, watching kids troop to classes, familiar files of figures crossing lawns, the sounds of them in hallways, their faces looking up eagerly in classrooms. Electricity of people, exchange, youth. That teaching could now appear a life of action! You have to write and live alone to believe this, envy it, hunger for those student bodies on the lawn.

Sita surprises me by wearing her mink. A dress and high heels. I am always bewildered by how many women she is. Intrigued by it, captivated by this. In fact, she is all the women I never was; matron, mother, socialite, administrator, glamorous, the femininity my mere female never encompasses. Someone who can wear a mink and has lived in the suburbs and had a Mercedes and called it her ransom money after twelve years of marriage. "Pre-revolutionary," I tease her about the mink. She has come directly from a luncheon in the city, Chicana bureaucrats with reactionary opinions who needed to be impressed by the mink. "How are things at the house?" "Martin came down yesterday and we had a conference. Paul and Valerie came over from Marin and made peace with Pia." I hold my breath, watching the road, feeling her expert speed. "Are they coming back?" "Oh no, they're gone. But at least we all talked it over." How easily she accepts it, how serenely and philosophically. Her favorite project, her greatest hope. Having all her children at home. I was nothing compared to that. And now Dan exiled. Paul and Valerie defected. Emily sent to Oregon tomorrow. How suddenly it emptied.

She analyzes the combatants: Pia's stubbornness, which will not even apologize, Valerie's immaturity; the struggle between them for Paul. "Martin just said it right out loud, I was very impressed by him, Martin just told Pia right to her face that when a man takes a mate, that comes before his family." I am amused by the heroic biblical ring. How it impresses her. How she never sees the irony in our case or notices how firmly she put her family before me; not a mate in Martin's time-honored tradition, merely an awkward eunuch before the sacred straight conventions, a lover somehow invalidated, invisible. I cannot tell her this, cannot comment on Pia or Valerie or anyone. None of my business. The miles speed by, the bridge, Berkeley's lights. Just as before I left, the same problem returns—having nothing to say. Or too much to say, so much of it unsayable. The rare jewel-like moments we are alone, having no use for them.

And inside the house, the same dismal incompetent silence. I lie back on the pillows. Pillows we ordered for the apartment back on Derby Street, the first months in Berkeley when I played her decorator, her "New York faggot," we called me, loving the joke, the excitement of doing a place for her. No more of Chiquita's gypsy caravan, the countess would emerge into her own, a polar-bear rug to make love on in front of the fireplace, the works. Another time. It is painful even to drive near Derby Street now when I go through Berkeley. Now she sits in the rocking chair with the antimacassar, one of the gypsy things acquired since. Pia sprawls on the davenport watching Emily making the early-bird Valentines which are her last hold on this place and must be given out at school tomorrow since that will be her last day. Talk is desultory, fragmented by Pia's phone calls. Should she go to that party tonight? Or make arrangements for Emily's trip, calls to Martin for the plane fare, Sita's report on today's conference? I am bored. Nearly to headache. I look in my martini. Why did I come back? Sita goes to heat up some clam chowder. In a while I go in to sit by her at the dining-room table.

"Campbell's. Tastes like nothing at all." I reach over and taste it, my arm resting on the edge of the table. I look down and see my gold watch face up on my wrist. Surprised a second later to feel her fingers caressing my forearm. The strange excitement of it, the power of this little statement. The day after tomorrow we go to Mendocino for a long weekend. Driving from the airport, she said it would definitely be her last free weekend till April. Classes start on Monday and she is teaching one herself in San Francisco on Monday nights. And on every weekend till April there is a conference, a special session, something. It is still January. I listen, furious. The satisfied, almost smug manner of her announcement, almost sadistic.

Driving up to Mendocino. The rain persistent, right somehow that it should be in the rain. Certain landmarks, the packing plant with its block-letter assertion FORMULA-FED BEEF, and the big, unreasoning steer's head painted along the rooftop as you leave Berkeley. The industrial detritus of Richmond, and then the hills begin. We are silent, always and awkwardly. But in the hills and as the redwoods began, she asked me a frightening question, "Where are you now in your life?" I could not answer, hated to add it all up—the series of defeats, breakdown, separation, and now this. She went on, answering the question for herself. Now Martin was in charge of her affairs. How he would get her out of debt and begin her savings. "I've always been improvident, have it and spend it. But I begin to realize I will get old." I see her old, and worry. I see myself old, and despair. Age, death, the subjects of my continuous anxiety now; different from the suicide trip, when death was something actual, something you could choose and impose on yourself if you had the courage. Now it only stalks, taking forever to get here, but certain, finally certain. I went through forty years of life convinced I would live forever. And at forty discovered I would die, and have been waiting for it since. This is stupid, unreal, I keep reminding myself. But there is nothing else to look forward to, nothing else to expect. My art defeats me and escapes, love and the comfort of another in time and through age have eluded me twice, first with Fumio and now with her. There is no certainty, only solitude waits for me. Art is not enough in life and my art deserts me. Eating alone in a loft on the Bowery, evening on that mean street. Where will I go when I am old? She goes on talking at my side, planning her life, in charge of it, resolute. "Maybe Martin will buy that piece of land in Napa he's always talking about. And we'll all end up there, even his new lady, Laura." I cringe at climbing into the fold, imagining a pastoral forcibly shared with the kids and who knows what new lovers.

Though she has asked me to talk to her, to be full and open, it is impossible. The muteness has taken me. And the fear—if she had any notion of my desperation she would never ask. The sight of it would sicken her. The thing is obscene. Not only have I lodged unfair hopes in her, made her my reason for living—which is unforgivable—but the paucity of my other resources, my bankrupt personhood. Artists without work are naked, hungry, frantic. We do not live merely to live as she does—and how I envy her this—but for some other purpose beyond us. Merely instruments of our purpose, we are like corpses when it fails us, might as well be dead. Even feel we deserve to die. My yearning for suicide was always just the imposition of that sentence.

I do not even know how I will live in the time to come. I have money for only three years, and when it is gone there is no more to come. And then what? Teaching? Risky, I am too old for the tenure requirements, too subversive, have slipped their harness too long. There are no jobs now, and though I love teaching, I hate it too, the collar around the neck, the separation from one's own work. To grow old teaching?

When I had had such high hopes? Books, sculptures, drawings. The redwoods going by, and I would like to scream that I am barren, ended. Something is wrong when you feel such despair amid such beauty. There is an inch of snow on the road as we climb a pass. She talks of turning back, and I tease her, desperate under my banter to challenge her into going on. The road dips down again into the huge mysterious trees. We are safe, we will get there.

And our host, a gnome named Quigley, has prepared all and built a fire for us in our cabin. Large windows onto a long lawn and a strip of highway and then the terrible sea and the rocks. The rain, always the rain, but never mind, we could not do better, here is our nest, our palace, our happiness. We have champagne and cheese and nuts, a table of hors d'oeuvres. It will be wonderful, it will be magical, one of the great weekends of our lives. Mendocino—the name already tearing at me, knowing I will remember this place forever, whether happy or wretched, to remember happiness years and years into death. These two brief days she will give me, this place, the mountains and rocks and ocean, the little sea town, part artist part tourist, even this silly but superbly appointed motel. Each cashew on the table, each sip of champagne, each glance of her eyes, now finally looking and seeing me, lost in their brown and their power when she opens them to me.

We look away to the lawn and are astounded. Three deer. Sudden. Already their last movement comes to conclusion as we see them. Now motionless. Each in its place. Still with the stillness of silence. Unmoving. Looking toward us. Three. And she and I. There are the five of us in the world. And the sea. The three strange beasts on the grass, stolid and magical, their heads up, listening in the coming gloom of evening. We watch them until we can barely see them. Cars go by on the road, but the deer do not turn and flee, their heads down occasionally grazing, first one and then another lost in the coming dark, then found again. These three creatures, our omen, our supernatural occurrence, our miracle given to us. And we know them for this, both of us, aware that their appearance marks a moment, blesses it, holds it aloft and still.

Then it is dark. And then we make love. Long and slow, and quick and hot and hard, taking her gently as she takes me fiercely, the moment waited for arriving at last and perfect. We are entire and made whole, one in the unique separateness of us, each for a moment beyond self into a further place beyond reason and finally even beyond consciousness into a distant and momentary peace. Her flesh so warm and delicate, so fragile and aromatic, smooth and golden and brown, so unutterably dear to me, consumed in it, seen as vividly with my eyes closed as open, touched as unerringly with my mind as with my hands, putting all the concentration of passion into the tips of my fingers, entering her knowing she wants me and has made room, made the way smooth and liquid, hungers for my tongue as it thirsts to drink her, devour and never finish, that very blossom once blasted, damaged, the rapists, the desert—"they had to sew my clitoris back on," she told me savagely that first time, "you'll find me a little beat up," warning me gallantly—but how precious and even dearer to me for its terrible wound, moved with what particular care and compassion, the most reverential gentleness, itself the most determined passion, for I would overwhelm it with tenderness, make up for, compensate, heal and erase the scars, the hurts, all the hurts of your life, lady, dearest and loveliest and most wronged of women, mine now, this moment entirely mine, coming as she comes, with the sheer force of adoring her.

And then she sleeps. I am quiet, a guard over her rest, her protector. I read, write, fiddle. The hours go by and still she does not wake. Time for dinner. The room gets cold. The fire has gone out. I work at restarting it. It is dismal in the dark and I dare not turn on the light. The fire cannot be rekindled; the rain falls. Euphoria passes into comfort and finally into boredom. She has left me, escaping into sleep, as distant now as long before I had her. This is a dull way to spend a vacation—sitting alone in a cold dark room. I could wake her, but it seems unkind. I try again to

read and cannot concentrate, find the book tedious
after ten pages. Disappointment sets in, the briefness
of it, happiness but a moment within hours of waiting.
The rain incessant, the room prepared for a feast that
does not take place, or took place in an instant and is
now over, though the trappings remain, and I, the
solitary guest, still expect a party.

I did not want to buy a Mendocino poster.
Attractive as it was, haunting as its blurred old-time
photograph of seascape and summer clapboard, recalling Provincetown at the other side of the world. Knowing already when I saw the thing that I would hang it
in my loft, after carting it absurdly across a continent,
hang it there, near a door, or in the kitchen, somewhere where I'd see it all the time, where it would
confront me every moment the rest of a lifetime, reminding me, mercilessly, endlessly reminding me—of
this time, this slow-falling rain, this near-happiness,
this near-despair, this semblance of lovers, of secret
lovers appearing to be friends, inspecting the town, the
little art shops, the galleries, affecting an interest, desperately bored, desperately interested, cheerfully going
on in the mud to the next event, the town workshop,
the gallery up at the fork of the road, inspecting the
kilns or the painting room or the junk jewelry. I am
disguising my snobbery, my contempt for most of the
art. She is disguising whatever—her contempt, ennui,
the thousand secret places of her soul that hide from
me. And in a shop at the end of the lane I saw the
poster again, and it was harder to renounce the impulse, ignoring it only with an effort. Curing myself
with the man's collection of trivia and old phonograph
records, just as I pretended to be absorbed by the old
lady's clock collection on the main street, the china
and saucers and matching fabric, Sita holding my arm
and admiring them as if we were two old maids who
doted on complete sets. The part of her that does. The
part of her that would settle in the house in Berkeley
and continues to remind me to buy her Minton when
I go to England. A minor character. Not the adven-
turer, not even the patient and long-suffering woman
who stifles her yawn in antique shops today. Standing

now in this bearded fellow's shop, counter crowded with knickknacks, camp revivals, trying not to look at the poster, the picture haunting me from the back of my head. No, no reminders. It will be over and gone and I will not be tortured with a picture. And if it does not end I will not need the picture to remind me. And because it will end, if not now, then someday, it would be a suicidal act to buy that damn photograph. She has no idea what goes on in my mind. I appear to be interested in a poster and then grow ambivalent, indecisive, full of pauses and hesitations over something that costs only two dollars and could never be important in any case. But if I bought it, every summer of my life it would remember me, destroy me. And winters? Don't even think of winters. If I hung it in my studio on the third floor? Make it impossible to paint, fill me with regret and despair and self-loathing every time I saw it. No, damn it, not that bloody poster. So, saying nothing and showing only my quiet, futile, ineffectual self, we leave.

Meals. Meals are a problem. Last night, when she finally woke, we ate seafood at a little joint we found in the pouring rain, the car hardly able to swim on when the neon appeared miraculously by the side of the highway, authentic roadhouse, fresh fish and saw-dust floors, echoing of Provincetown and summers. But the meal made gloomy by our silence, her torpor, our pretended romance, our counterfeit holiday excitement. And at breakfast this morning, taken at the most color-ful local pub—the place full of beards and mackin-toshes and the deliberate wintry cool of the city types, flowers sewn on their jeans, all alarmingly young and hip—at breakfast we read the papers and I cringed at the display of our silence, our conspicuous pall. Warm-ing up finally, she reads me bits from the Mendocino paper: the Wilsons' boy is back from Vietnam, the Gregorys' brother and sister-in-law are visiting from Oklahoma, Mrs. Franklin ran into Mr. Franklin while backing the car out of the garage, fracturing his shoul-der and six ribs. Then come stories of her life on the little paper in Folsom when she started back to work again, emerging from her suburban era: one of a battle she won against the mayor. She is alternately tough and pathetic, whimsical and vindictive as she tells it. "I'd love to live out here and work for a little paper like this," growing lyric, sentimental, rural, pastoral, adventurous—when a moment ago she was herself in her mink of ten years ago, taking on a man rich enough to own a private plane and crash in it. She goes on considering life here, fantasizing: sneakers, jeans, and a shack, all you really need. I find myself falling into it. "Wouldn't you miss the city, San Francisco?" "You can go there any time you need, it's not far." "Four hours." "Nothing, you wouldn't even miss it." I look around the room at the creatures in their rural uniforms of commune hip, the newspapers spread on every table. No. Shacks at the end of dirt roads, broken-down cars, leaky roofs. No. Yet listening to her I'm almost hypnotized, her voice rhapsodizing about the sea. I would have her alone here. No, I'd go crazy.

Meals. Now the great meal, Saturday night, the planned and deliberate and dressed-for meal. Finding too late we've taken the wrong advice. Quigley should be strangled for recommending this vulgarity. Heavy Germanic pretension, compliments of the owner, but the rest is the most awful American falsity. Even plastic ferns, we grimace at each other. But it is already too late, the waiter has us in hand. Even then I want to protest, develop an emergency, decide we've left the car lights on, anything to get out of here. If she'd back me up. But she is philosophic, content. The meal is not the ceremony for her that it is for me, the crisis, the sacrament. Only something to get through. Dull, spiritless, each trying to rally. I waver between tears of disappointment, suppressed, and game attempts at humor, the best wine. There is even a residue of anger under the despair, resentment, hatred even for the waste of it. Meals used to be such feasts.

But then she disarms me, picking up some liniment at the store on the way home, she will rub my sore shoulder, she will massage my back. First a melancholy little drink in the hotel basement, where a nervous boy plays very difficult blues guitar almost well. "He was out of his mind on speed, couldn't you tell?" she announces as we climb the stairs. And again I am dumbfounded by her blasé, almost cynical worldliness. Then the great maternal comfort of her massage, her repeated tenderness, saying over and over how it pleases her to take care of me, nurse me, touch me, make me well. "Even this is a kind of making love," she says, her voice smooth and liquid as a caress, as the flesh of her body, as the flesh of her hands kneading my hurt muscles.

I realize as she falls asleep that it was a substitute for making love, a way of avoiding it, begging off without ever quite having to refuse, ruse and techniques I know as well as any woman, a tactic we are all familiar with, find useful with men. The startled humiliation of knowing that she has just used it on me.

I watch her sleep. Thinking of all the women she is, knowing all of them, loving them and long past judging the survivor, floozy, countess, liar and woman of honor, cornered animal and proud beauty. Speaking of her past, it is always of lovers she has left—reluctantly but necessarily—rather than further endure their wrongs. This pattern is held forth as a covert warning for the future. "My beautiful exits," she always says. "I make great exits," head held high, part parody, part melodrama. As if her whole life were a matter of walking out only because she had to, to save face, because pride was the most important thing, after all, the final thing, the only thing. Despite the occasional nearly vulgar little jokes on "class" and "classy," her rare, oblique, satiric references to her birth, this fanatic pride is the only proof that she still believes in it. And even the "we" in her "beyond everything we are proud" is indistinct: at times Latin, at times the downtrodden immigrant. Or it could be the royal "we" of the noble, Sita, drawn to her height, the head and shoulders swanlike and regal as she floats away from some mere American mortal. And I had thought each of them was a cad, knew they were unworthy, and smiled with relief that with me finally and at last she was appreciated, deserved, the connection passionate and permanent, just and immutable. Wincing at my

folly now, a naked woman in a motel room, banal, ordinary, discarded.

The past like a lost glory assailing me, bitter even to
remember. Sacramento and then Berkeley and Derby
Street, the bedroom I had made for her like a lavender
powder puff, its great white fur rug, its endless aromatic
bed like a white breast, a room perfumed with sensuality. Breakfasts she brought me in bed, her delight
in serving me, a service I tried as joyfully to repay by
washing dishes and cleaning the house while she was
at work, afternoons I'd stay there to read for classes.
Long, lovely afternoons staring at the bay between
paragraphs, afternoons too perfect even to recall. The
day she came home for lunch and a "quickie"—her
mischievous ironical recourse to smut. It amused us,
we could afford to play at it, parody it, our passion so
sure it could run the gamut of lesser emotions. And
such terms excited me, as it excited me early on, one
day when almost apropos of nothing, while driving
her car, she remarked, "I hope you'll understand, I
really like the four-letter words in bed." I turned and
saw her, this very elegant woman behind the wheel of
a Mercedes, the world's last candidate to appear a
lesbian, this woman who had so recently and tumultu-
ously become my lover, making this dashing statement
in the middle of Sacramento traffic. And on Derby
Street, as calmly as a business executive sporting with
a Fifty-seventh Street playgirl through a leisurely lunch
hour, calling it a "quickie." I imagined myself her tart
and adored it. As I adored the sight of her long, slim,
brown body in and out of the bed to the shower, to
the dressing room in the hallway, a room gone now
but piercingly remembered: its beads, its treasure of
silk and scents, seeing her here in the dark, then there
framed in that doorway, making one last witty remark, blowing one last kiss, her lovely shoulders, the
long line of her back, still seeing them duck around a
doorway.

Like a litany, the places we've been together:
Sacramento, her place there and mine, Derby Street,
Indian Rock. Derby Street and how I used to perch on
the kitchen stool while she made dinner. The low table

in the living room where we ate. Wine. Pillows. Then she lived there with Hank in the months we were estranged after my breakdown. Until finally she decided her detestation of the landlady was too great to be borne any longer. Developed the first scheme of a commune with the kids and rented a huge old house in San Francisco. The night before they were to move in, Pia and Dan withdrew from the scheme, Hank split. And I was called for. Rang me up at the farm in the East, said she was desperate and all alone. Could she come to me for Christmas? Fumio was leaving me. If I didn't kill myself, I might join her in California and start over. She rented the house on Indian Rock and kept calling me away from suicide, calling me to share the house she readied for us. And so I went. Last spring and the little idyll. Holding her now in the motel night and seeing Derby Street again and Sita rising from the bed, about to go down the hall to the dressing room. How beautifully she moves in her nakedness, sliding past the door frame, the fruits of her breasts, their brown, dark-brown nipples, most precious of all. All lost. The tears coming at last. Gone even as she lies in my arms.

In the morning a growing sense of doom. Her shower running as I lie still in bed, still in the hold of sex, wanting and not daring to ask. Her movements of preparation, the folding of clothes, the opening of bags, the rounding up of stray objects. I remember the weekend in Sausalito, but things are worse now, darker, more malign. I woke in terror, feeling the loss of the class I was to have taught as a mother mourns a child. It is something I will never have, an experience, a job, a stretch of work and action torn away from me, irreplaceable in a future otherwise so empty. I am still afraid of the class, yet now I lust for it, hunger and starve for those thirty women. They would buoy me up, give me confidence again, an excuse to be alive. People I will never know now, widowed of them without ever having met them. Since the class was canceled, calls come, letters arrive, their regret, their consternation. At first they merely scolded me, underlined the guilt for my irresponsible, irrational behavior;

contrary, ridiculous, indecisive—to schedule a class and then cancel it. And now reschedule? Absurd, a thousand times more ridiculous, impossible. But is it impossible? Lying awake, waiting impatiently for her to wake up so I can ask her, pretending it's all hypothetical and so forth, just wondered if the university would even consider, permit, and so forth. "Of course, it's very unusual, but possible. But this time you will have to mean it, otherwise I'll lose all credibility with the provost and the department." Ironical, painfully so, that the job I could once tell myself I was doing as a favor to her—the salary so trivial, the course itself so minor and negligible an effort—I have now messed up so grandly that she is doing me a favor in permitting me to regain it.

Never mind, teaching it would give me ten weeks to be with her, to be doing something definite. What are you working on now? people ask and I will finally have an answer. Accounted for, planned, the future projected, plotted. But could I stand ten weeks of this? There is no backing out, it's a state contract. They could sue me if I cut and run. Get her in trouble. But it means staying, committing myself to staying, to the women I teach. So why not, you're dying of having nothing, being uncommitted, joined to nothing, floating in the vacuum of writing that doesn't come, manuscripts that stay in the same place and do not move an inch or a paragraph. Okay, I'll give up working on the old manuscript, just teach, and work on the fool notebook I carry around with me and hardly ever write in. I'll stay with it, with what I'm doing now. I'll make it an experiment, see if I can record life as we live it, the moments ticking away in the house at Indian Rock. This love affair dying. Slowly, slowly like a diseased plant.

I will try it, crazy and useless as it probably is, a risk but also a promise. Better this, this last maybe desperate chance than going turn-tail back to New York and the emptiness, the loneliness, the dilemma of Ruth and Dobie, loving neither of them, burdened by both. Other people you call up and they're busy, the night comes on and you start drinking. I'll stay,

I'll teach the course, shaking with fear and the continuous indecision that stays on like an ague in the mind. She is content. Hardly enthusiastic, but she says she is glad I have decided to stay, there will be just the two of us in the house now and Pia, three women, we will have a good time, it will be very satisfactory. It will be Pia and the two of us, she says again, the idea pleasing her, Pia will stay on.

We sat in bed an hour, talking it over. It was tense still from the decision, frightened, in panic till it was resolved, the plans for letters to be sent out to all the students, the day of the first class established, the die cast. And then I asked her. The humiliation of asking. I think I had hardly ever done it before, hardly ever had to. There being so many other ways to ask. But I asked now because all other approaches failed. And she said no, she did not feel like making love or being made love to, but she would make love to me if that was what I wanted. And it jarred so, stung. The kindly patience, the favor of it, the gentle condescension. No. Not to lie there while she dutifully went through with it. No. With what awful sadness, saying thank you, lighting a cigarette, trying to save face, think of any trivial thing to say. Waiting till the shower runs to let my face be its naked grief. Lying there hearing the shower and seeing for the last time each piercing item. Things, the things of our time here, the objects that have been our companions these two days: the Swedish fireplace gaily painted orange, Quigley's fancy kindling wood that never worked, the big wooden table before the window covered with books, the table of our snacks and champagne, and the appearance of the deer, a few magazines on the floor near the fire, even they full of portent, melancholy. The shower stops. And the packing begins, my nervous hurry, her resolute march, her stately efficiency. The brisk transpositions into the wicker basket she travels with. Relentless. Over and over as I watch us leaving, walking through the door, like a loop of film projected again and again, I see myself turning just at the door, looking again at the bed. I would know this bed all my life, see it beyond death; this bed and this room. This bed

disappearing behind a closed door, while my body
obediently follows her to the car and gets in, but my
mind, the traitorous mind, stays behind, alone, isolated,
eyes watching this bed which remains, which remains.

Even as I stop and get out of the car and pay
Quigley his inflated price, Sita mentioning only then
that she brought no money, her new habit of expecting
me to pay, since she really can't afford it and if she
goes places with me now it will have to be at my expense. Quigley surrounded by his tiresome ledgers
and memos and scenic calendars, sprightly as ever,
I'm even propitiating the little man, begging a card
from him, "in case I should ever come back," recom-
mend it to my friends and so forth. Needing, needing
some proof of the place, even the printed evidence of
its foolish and impossible name, Oceanspray Lodge,
taking the card like a relic and preserving it in my
wallet, even its embarrassing design and color precious
now, what remains. We pass by the lawn where once
the deer stood and are gone. Stopping again just before
the road, because we'd brought a camera along and
have never used it. So she obliges me for a few moments and I pretend to learn her camera, a Rolleiflex
with a lens I am unused to and soon hate. I had
been borrowing Ruth's Nikon in New York and was
getting rather good with it and I have wanted for a
long time to photograph Sita. Close-ups, intimate
studies of her face after making love, knowing I could
capture her, reveal her, the depth of her beauty, her
sorrow, her intelligence, her humor. I have drawn her
body over and over for years and still hardly approach
it. Failure, caricature, awkward approximations, except now and then—but a photograph, I thought, if I
photographed her, seriously, making it art, the concentration and the passion of art, brought that to it,
and knowing her as I do, with what fullness and obsessive care, reverence, tenderness for her great and
so often hidden beauty. Then I would have her. Then
I would possess her in a certain and perfect way. She
would be there when she was absent, she would remain the same when she had changed, she would be
something I had discovered, unearthed, polished,

breathed upon, adored, and brought to a timeless perfection.

But she is instead only a bored and impatient woman standing by a post while I am an inept idiot complaining that I cannot focus the damn machine. "It's the simplest thing in the world," she says. All the great pictures I would make of you, lady, but instead I am revealed as someone too stupid to handle your camera. The rain drizzles on. She is a wooden object, awkward in a heavy coat. This is not the pose I wanted or the place or the mood or the image. I take one more dull snapshot and we leave.

The redwoods wind ahead. She tells me the story of her second marriage, a long long story that lasts nearly until we are home. I listen, trying to memorize each detail, learn her, commit her to heart. Ben, the navy flier, the one I know least, remembering how she told the story that first time, during dinner at an old hotel up in the gold country, remembering how I gasped as she told it, the lives she had led, the woman she was, the woman I would never be. All that she had known: poverty and money and babies and husbands, life as a clerk in jerkwater offices and as a service wife in dry back-country towns. Remembering as she tells me now, the same story, but there is more of it, more detail, complexity, ambiguity. How he appeared as a blond god alighting from a Buick convertible, resplendent in uniform, a "knock-out," as she puts it, a flicker of rueful irony shadowing ahead to the slob he became. But that is not yet, still it's drinks at the officers' club, dinner and dances set against the small Southern town, its hot nights, the cheap apartment and the roommate, a waitress from Alabama who helped pay the rent, the tawdry detested job in the credit department of the water company, Pia to raise, groceries to haul, nights too tired to go out to the movies. But the roommate went to the officers' club to see what she could find. Sita, homebound, well-bred, demure, uncertain still about the country, persuaded once to go along. And there he was: superb, shining. And bought her a drink. And had another woman, whom he dropped. But still never a wolf, al-

ways the gentleman courting with flowers and that car
and the officers' dance bands, gardenias converting the
dusty streets to something glamorous, and men, men
are the way out, the romantic strangers who descend
to the rescue. "Pia went off to camp and he stayed
over and proposed. But we still never made love. If
I'd known then—but how could I guess he was usually
impotent? The early days of that marriage I used to
ache, actually ache from wanting him. I had never
wanted Gil, my sexuality was only now coming alive,
and I wanted Ben like a fever." The redwoods thin
out, we lose them. "And the drinking. I didn't even
realize how much he drank, or that he drank more
than anyone else, I simply never noticed. He never
seemed drunk. But after I married him, I discovered
he opened a can of beer as soon as he got out of bed
in the morning. I tried with that marriage, I really
tried. I loved him that much. It was the second time
and I didn't want to fail again. And by then we'd had
a baby, Paul." Ben's slow decline, in her eyes, in the
world. "They transferred him to a flight school, which
he hated. He had to teach flying in one of those little
tandem two-seaters, terrible things, you can't even see
the student pilot. Of course it was very dangerous, and
a few of his friends cracked up. Ben got so that he
was terrified to go up. Headaches, migraine headaches.
They put him in an office job then, which he really
hated, because flying was his life. It was dull and
pointless and he drank even more." And then the
troubles began, creditors, brawls, misconduct, warnings and more warnings. They gave him one chance
after another and finally he was cashiered. "It was
like a death sentence for him. Outside that uniform he
disintegrated. It was his whole manhood, his whole
identity; the service was who he was. So he just sat
around the house all day and drank and went to
pieces. Of course he was driving me crazy too, as you
can imagine." The redwoods are gone, we are past
them now. They are gone forever. Mendocino is over.
"Finally the only solution was for him to join the
regular army, but as an enlisted man, not an officer.
And then he got a chance for officer's training if he'd

go to California. It was the last hope. We went. But things were no better here and I decided to leave him. It took months. I had two kids and no way to earn a living. Ben was being transferred to Germany. I let him go and rented a little dump for myself and the kids. It was all over." But the story goes on, on to the next man, on to Martin. After a time in the wilderness, after a still more grating and humiliating job as a "hostess" in a pretentious restaurant where the managers regarded her as some not very presentable half-breed, too dark to qualify as part of the upper staff, but not so unappealing that they could desist from whispered requests for blow jobs upstairs. Her dignity and survivorship living through this until the rape. And then she was broken.

Pregnant too, though the father might even have been Ben. "One last time, Ben asked me to go to Florida before he left the country, one last try at reconciliation. I took the bus all that long way. It was hopeless. He'd told me he had a vasectomy because I had such a hard time with Paul and was afraid ever to be pregnant again. Years later his mother told me he'd remarried and had a little girl. So he'd lied about the vasectomy." I see her with a suitcase in the heat of summer, her lameness, the bus and the exhaustion of the bus all the way back to California. And then it happened, the week after she got back, on her own now, driving in the desert one night, running out of gas, the panic, the glare of headlights, their laughter, their savagery. Her pride, how that must have undone her. "All I thought was how glad I was that someone had stopped." Because after her courtesy and her helplessness, her absurd predicament of being out of gas in the wilderness—did they ever get to the gas?— did they ever even listen to her, drunk as they were and she a lady, unmistakably giving off that sense of privilege and distinction, all that they in their drink and their brutality and demoralization, all that they despised and resented? Did she cry out or beg their mercy? I would never ask, yet I suspect not. Even when they left her torn and bleeding, she knew the futility of hope.

After the rape there was nothing. She was pregnant
and she wanted to die. It would be better for the
children; Pia's father would take over her upbringing,
he had a fortune and could easily pay for the operations on Pia's spine to correct the curvature caused by
polio. And Ben's mother could take care of Paul. They
would both be better off. She wouldn't have to bear
another child, wouldn't have to struggle to go on.
She took sleeping pills after seeing the children off for
a weekend. A neighbor who also worked at the same
restaurant came around on Saturday and found her.
When she explained her predicament at the hospital,
they didn't bother to keep her for psychiatric observation. The only problem now was time. And a method.
Then Martin entered the picture. A decent guy who
took her out to dinner once or twice. And he had a
.22 caliber pistol in his glove compartment. When he
discovered she'd stolen it, he came to visit and they
had a long talk. The upshot was that he offered to
marry her, to help, to take care of her, an abortion,
Pia's doctors and the years of surgery, Paul. Martin
was a practical solution, which is how she has always
described him to me, a protector, which is what he
still continues to be four years after separation.

We are almost home, the familiar blight of
Richmond, the doldrums of the oil tanks, the ominous
formula-fed beef marking the turn to Berkeley. Her
life is folded up like a sample of fabric, her life which
I love to gaze at, telling myself its stories over and
over, its hardships, which made me love her, even its
frivolities, which made me wonder or admire. In mid-
town Manhattan once we walked by Elizabeth Arden's
and she laughed and told me how she used to get
"done" there during her first marriage when she lived a
whole winter at the Biltmore. It is always the life I
never lived, neither its glamours and embassies nor its
banalities of housewifery and office work. Everything
about her fascinates me. Watching the lovely line of
her throat as it descends into the fabric of her blouse
as she drives, I imagine and possess that delicate flesh
in its youth, in its extremes of passion or maternity,
under the sun of summer or wet by the sea, speaking

or laughing or in tears, sleeping, swallowing, speaking. And the long fingers on the wheel, the ring with the ankh to match the one she gave me, wearing her own on her first finger almost rakishly. I have worn mine religiously, superstitiously, even in the hell of the mental hospitals, bins she had helped put me in, and yet I wore it there as an amulet, a talisman that I would ever get out, all those dark claustrophobic days that terrible summer. And if not my salvation, then a memento that at least I had lived, at least I had known her before I went down into the pit, at least I had lived that high euphoric love, the existence of the ring proved it.

Jails she had helped to put me in. But like every sufferer in these places, I continued to love and depend on those who sold me into them. And she was one of them. Together with my husband, jealous of our affair, and my older sister, scandalized by it. And my own manic hysteria before the problem of saving a political prisoner's life from the hanging he had been condemned to in Trinidad. Assigned to this case by a consortium of other civil libertarians and artists. It broke me, shattered me. The responsibility sent me over the brink. I'd never had a life to save before. Lots of political prisoners, but never a lynching to stop. Somehow it unhinged me. I talked incessantly and didn't sleep, spent days making tapes for use in speeches, half the time with the machine not running. Fumio was on a visit to California. Neither he nor Sita could cope. My older sister was called out and ordered me to the loony. Which they achieved by trickery, I was led into a trap. Went along with them credulously, a visit to a doctor's office, only to discover the place was locked. I had agreed to see a psychiatrist, who remarked sadistically that my first mistake was in believing the people who brought me there. Who else was I to believe? Each of them dear to me as life. Yet they watched while two bullies in white coats, ambulance drivers with the mentality and legal authority of cops and weighing over two hundred pounds apiece, beat me to the ground in a parking lot and tied me face down on an ambulance pallet. Even then, even after this betrayal, I played Dante to Sita's Beatrice in the elevator going to the locked sixth floor, she would be my guide to paradise after this hell. "Vergil did not get to see it, remember," I warned her, forgiving already. And each time they used her as bait when they moved me from place to place, so that the seventy-two-hour imprisonment the state permits in each of its ratholes would go on. And even then I forgave, even then I wore the ring, conjuring by it the empty days and the futile nights. I had trusted them. Gone to see their doctor, and was led into a snare, only to discover the place was locked. They had taken me by force. Only by cunning then, the cunning that pretends to agree but learns the law and waits the time, could I get out, only by patient cunning. And only through them, since the people who lock you up are also the people who can get you out, betrayers and saviors both. Not only did I need them, I loved them, learning only in my captivity the magnitude of that love. Which could forgive anything, understand even how misguided they were, and forgive that. Dependent upon their visits, the hour of coming like the last judgment each day. And that ring like the promise of salvation. That, and the amazonite in its silver band that Fumio had made for me. Sita, Fumio, my older sister—my three white horses, I used to call them, conferring symbolisms, ransacking Buddhist parable or Persian miniature or Yeats in my delirium, forgiving always after each fury at how they violated my trust and gave me into the hands of the healers, the culture police, the state and its locks and bars, loving and hating them as they must have loved and hated me.

These times lie between us always, though rarely spoken of. It was while trying to help a prisoner that I came to learn just what it is to be one. Learned what it was to have nothing, no rights and no recourse, not even a dime to call for help on the telephone. For ten cents you can start a call to anywhere in the world, and I didn't have that. Or my address book. Or the key to the door, a car to travel in, the freedom of airports or the price of a hamburger.

Even a night in solitary carelessly heaped on my
serious and lifelong claustrophobia: deliberately hal-
lucinating brush drawings on the walls, drawn with
my naked eyes as if, by sheer force of will or imagination, to cast a spell against the dangers of sensory
deprivation—for that night they had even taken my
rings from me—but I did not kill myself, did not make
my head a broken melon charging against the huge oak
door. That was California. And then the second time
I was captured that summer, St. Paul this time, compliments of my mother's gullibility before a local pun-
dit who persuaded her to commit me so he could
experiment with a wonder drug. And again with Sita's
complicity. There was a trial with the best local
civil-rights lawyers on my side, and I won. A sanity
trial, the modern counterpart of an inquisition against
a witch. Sanity is probably impossible to prove, but
they couldn't prove insanity either. We won: I would
not be committed for life. Free for a long, angry
summer upstate at the farm. Sita coming for my birthday in September, and inevitably we fought and she
left. Free again through the bleak autumn and Fumio's
desertion. The studio condemned, eviction, Fumio
despaired of. And the winter and depression and the
drift toward suicide. One attempt after another and
the thing longed for, lusted after, craved. To die, only
to die. Finally the help of medicine, the depression
lifting, the will to live coming back, the grief over
Fumio and the studio receding. Sita and I repaired our
quarrel, her own plans fell through, she came East to
the farm at Christmas; she waited while I suffered
through a lawsuit and the last hankering after death,
she took the house on Indian Rock and waited there.
And then that spring we lived together through my
last convalescence. Then a loft came up in New York
and I took it. Then the trip to Europe together last
summer, the months alone in New York last fall while
I fixed up the loft, drifting a little apart, then her visit
at Christmas putting it together again.

And now living here again with her, just as by
plan, but all strange and distant, painfully different.
Different the silence—for the silence has come on us

again—the stranger's figure next to me on the seat, different from the loving and passionate woman mistaken as she was in those hospitals, nearly breaking down herself and making the excuse always that the time in Italy was her breakdown, her delayed reaction; different from the protective woman of last spring, her kindness, her solicitude. Different now, I can already sense the difference as we park the car, as we explore the house for Pia, who doesn't seem to have been home for days, as we bring in bags and check the mail, as I hear her changing her clothes, starting the shower. A sinister difference. "I have to go out tonight, I promised some friends." My stomach clutches, she had not mentioned this before. There is something spur-of-the-moment even as she goes on explaining that it's a nuisance but she made the appointment a long time ago. Suddenly our weekend is truncated. I am unreasonably afraid. But there is a disastrous quality to her preparations, it is not only my own desperation, it is something in her manner too. And the oddness of her packing her wicker basket. As if she were bringing extra clothes. The irritation in her voice, the speech about her independence again, about having friends of her own, people she's fond of seeing. Who could they be? She doesn't bother to say or describe. I ask, trying to appear casual and am as casually told I don't know them. The inference is a couple who've invited her for dinner. Yet everything about her manner speaks more, speaks something dangerous, speaks dishonesty, the squirm of deceit. Mendocino, the weekend is violated. Relegated the moment we return. It had stood for a coming together, for a commitment, my own to stay and teach the course, and hers to live with me and Pia. We had re-formed, regrouped, made a new household. And she is already out the door. Only barely do I hear the line with which she leaves: "I'll call you tomorrow from the office."

Thunderstruck. Tomorrow. The office. For a second or two still not quite comprehending it. Then a rush, then a sudden rush of the heart to the door, to call out, to beg, to scream and wail, to denounce, to entreat,

to grab her by the very throat I love and stop her.
Waited till she was halfway out the door to say it. The
bitch, the damn incredible fucking bitch. This morning
she was too ill to make love, a touch of stomach trouble, she'd said, grinning at me, not up to it, not feeling
well. But she's well enough for him . . . Who? Neal?
Another. I'll go mad. I am seized with the greatest
fear, a physical fear even. As if the house were under
siege and terrorists or police surrounded it.

Each room is darkening, closing in like disease. Every object in the house derides me, every line and
shadow and banister depresses me—the banister, the
cheap rug in the hall, the beautiful Grecian spread on
our bed. Our bed. Of course, that was why she carried
the wicker basket. Liar. "I'll call you from the office
in the morning." Coward. The office, yet. Bureaucratic
whore. To wait until I couldn't answer back, might
not even hear her. We'd never treated each other that
way before. Even in the beginning when we were both
sleeping with other people. But not while we were together, living in the same house. Never just "took off"
this way. There were Hank and Brian, but she had
them at her house. And that one time I slept with
Sarah at Meg's place in San Francisco, Sita in another
room, she was rightfully angry; angry even when Sarah
came back to Sacramento and stayed a few days at
my own apartment. And furious when Bea slept there
during the music festival, Sita having to stay in a
motel.

But that was a long time ago. Living together last
spring, we were faithful, as if there were no other
way to live. During our separations there were other
people for both of us, but that was understood; we
were apart, after all. But to live together, to be living
with her and hear her casually announce that she'd be
sleeping with someone else, that she'd be with a lover
tonight—I had no idea how it would stun me. No idea
of the fury I would feel, the terrified insecurity, this
helpless fear. Because I am afraid, horribly afraid. To
be so at the mercy of another, to be so unprepared and
face such amorphous and uneasy danger. As if my
life were in jeopardy.

The house filling up with the evening. I can't stay
here. For nothing in the world could I stay home tonight. Bitch, I whisper, bitch. I am tricked. Said I
would teach that damn course, said I would stay. And
you do this to me the first night afterward, bitch. Bitch,
I say, but what I feel is the breaking of the heart;
anger is nothing to my sorrow. The grief of knowing.
The despair in realizing I am actually helpless. Because I love her still. Because I must suffer this, put
up with it, have not walked out. And cannot.

   The first thing I knew, even as she left, was that I
couldn't stay in, spend the evening alone in this house.
Which without her is the most foreign place in the
world. When we lived here together last spring, one
rare night when she was out, I spent an uneasy evening alone here. It was not a home at all I discovered
that night. Without her, it was an utterly meaningless
place I would never have chosen, an empty, rather
heavy bourgeois house overlooking a strange bay; the
lights outside were the lights of a foreign place, not
my town. A voice spoke inside me, What are you doing
here? As if I had wakened from a dream to find myself in some inexplicable landscape. The discovery
that only her presence brought me here, kept me here,
came like bad news long evaded. The house ominously
still, unfriendly, like a dog whose master has left it in
your care until, inexplicably, it bites you. It was her
house, not mine. And the world outside, the lights, the
landscape, and the city—all hers and suddenly unre-
lated, alien.
   If I could drive the bridge tonight, if I could feel
the speed and the air on my face, I could breathe. But
if I stay here I'll strangle. The panic mounting in my
chest. Sherman. Call Sherman. Thank God, there's
one person. One person who is not her person. Because to go now to any acquaintance who would be,
since they all are, her friends, not mine, would be betrayal. And I cannot betray her. Or us. The collective
myth of our relationship. But Sherman is an old friend,
my friend originally and still. I can tell her. Talk to her.
The ease of it, having someone to confide in. Someone

to eat with. But what if she's busy, not in, feeling un-
sociable? Then emptiness. There's only one person,
only one person in this whole damn place. I have
only one friend in California. Insane, insane I should
live in a place where there is only one friend. Get out
of here. Go home, back to New York. Knowing beforehand that is what I will say to Sherman. That I
have to go home. But what if she's not there? Hurry.

"Look, I've got to see you. Can I come over?"
"Sure." The salvation of it—my hands shaking on the
wheel, fumbling with the ignition key—that there is
this place to go in need. Sherman's talk, the understanding of old friends, dinner, the sight of their domestic bliss, even that, Marguerite making dinner, the
kitchen, the warm light, the paintings, the bowls of
flowers, the pots hanging on the walls, the old-
fashioned stove Sherman brought along from the last
studio. The ease of it. That they are a couple, that
they are together, that some are, that some last, that it
works. Even bringing this gaping wound, my humiliation, there where it will be all right, they will not
laugh, despise me, no dishonor, no loss of face.

"She planned to leave you last fall, came over and
told me you were wiped out, over." "Odd she never
told me." "Really?" Sherman looks in her wineglass, a
large glass cup, mottled, veinous, beautiful. "You mean
she never mentioned any of this to you?" "Not at all.
When we said goodbye after Europe and I stayed on
in New York while she came back out here, the plan
was for me to finish the first big work on the loft and
come out around the end of the year. Then she said
she'd come to New York for Christmas. She was on
and off with that, but finally she came. We got it together again, 'cause she'd become very distant by
November, it was hard to get her on the phone, I had
started to worry about how things were. But at Christmas we patched it up, so I came out in January. To
see how it would go. But I'd no idea she had ditched
the whole thing when she got back last fall." "Well,
she came over expressly to tell me it was all over between the two of you. That's why I was so surprised
to see you the other day. That you were out here

again. And to see the two of you together. Great, I
thought, they're back together." I laugh, a discouraged,
mortified laugh intended to be cynical.

The light falls in Sherman's living room. Marguerite
is still at work. The chicken is defrosting, only enough
for two people, but I have accepted an invitation to
dinner anyway, desperate beyond good manners. "She
loves you a great deal. She said that last September." I
am accustomed to Sita's protestations of love, protestations made to my friends, often with tears; she adores
me, I am the great love of her life, but impossible. Just
before Christmas my friend Barbara was out in California and had lunch with Sita. Barbara was the first to
bring me the news Sita was not planning to come. They
had lunch in San Francisco. Sita wept. "She's so much
in love with you, she loves you so much," Barbara reported. I smiled, pleased, self-conscious. "She's coming
for Christmas." "I don't think she will be," Barbara
said, her voice suddenly uncertain, embarrassed. "Sure
she is, we've been planning it for months." "She told
me she was planning to stay out there with her family."
But I ignored Barbara, what would she know? Then
Hatsie too, saying that Sita had told her that having
Christmas with all her children about her was the most
precious thing in the world. And indeed she had had it,
flying East to me only the day after Christmas, but
she'd said it was her job that prevented her coming
sooner, they made her work on the day of Christmas
Eve. And then it was her job that made the visit so
short, a mere four days, they had demanded she be
back right away. In coming she risked being fired. And
I believed, just as I believe the reports of her passion,
the tears, all of it. In her drama she loves me griev-
ously, weeps for herself in renouncing me, believes in
her grief as she renounces, is passionately convinced by
her passion as she recites it. Then she goes off, works,
administers, flourishes, takes on new lovers, shops for
men. But on meeting someone who knows me, on re-
flecting, she will weep and declare her love. And
whether she announces its end or gives intimations of
its survival, the listener is profoundly impressed by her
tenderness, her intoxication, her nostalgia, her grief.

"How much she loves you," they say to me, awed, admiring. As I have admired, as I have been in awe of this woman's genius at love, at the expression of love, the avowal, the declaration, the very sensuality of her voice. The soft Italian accent, the trembling vibrato of it, her beautiful eyes. Nearly three years I have been the captive of this performance, real and unreal, persuasive, compelling. My stomach melts at the sound of that voice speaking its love, I am moved past speaking or reason. Is it her love for me that I love, this melancholy and infinitely tender emotion figured forth, expressed with such perfect inflection and tone, fullness of eye? This extravagant love for me. That someone, a beautiful woman even, had loved me so plangently. This love for me now withdrawn, now bitterly withheld, hidden and eclipsed.

And of course it's been gone a long time, far longer than I knew. Sherman knew, other friends knew. But I didn't. The dusk coming into the room sad as the end of day, the paintings in their places. We are left always with things like paintings, the cold objects with which we console ourselves. It comes down to that. I walk around Sherman's studio, the little room next door: brushes, tubes of paint, pens, paper, stretchers, rolls of canvas, the messiness of a palette. I miss drawing. There is no place to do it out here; the basement, the only possible place, is still full of Paul's carving junk. And somehow that house never seems a place in which to draw. If I went home . . . suddenly wanting home, the loft, wanting to draw again, to work, to live on my own. Enough of this hanging around. Dependent sick shit. Having raved to Sherman, I already know I will stay, keep trying, hang on a little longer. I have even taken on the course. The thing we decided this morning. "It's important to you," Sherman said, assuming innocently that the course was a proper course and I a proper teacher, having no idea that the course is a pretext to stay, that I have put this love ahead of any adult considerations of work or profession, that I am simply diseased.

"Of course you can't stand it. I wouldn't put up with it for a moment," she said when I explained Sita's departure tonight. "But you see, I don't agree with you. I don't believe in monogamy, possessing people, the rightness or inevitability of jealousy. She has the right to go with anyone she likes. I'm on her side. It's just that it hurts me, it hurts terribly—I hadn't expected that; it even hurts that it hurts. It shouldn't hurt, I shouldn't feel jealous, I'm ashamed of the feeling." "Crap. Anyone do that to me, it's out the door with them." "Maybe it's the way she did it. This I'll-call-you-from-the-office business. I'm being lied to. I think I could take it if she just told me, if she were honest." "Pamela, for example, Pamela started not coming home and that was the end of it, damn it." "You see, if she explained how she felt, if she said, Look, I really want to do this; if she said, Look, here is some- one I want, though I want you too. If I had the con- fidence I used to have in her love for me, don't you see?" "Bullshit. Nobody can put up with that stuff. It's not human." "I don't agree. There were times in the past she was with someone else, and really, I was *not* jealous. I was loved, I was convinced of that." "You and your half-assed theories."

At first I don't even know where I am. Then I see Donleavy's *Ginger Man* on the pillow next to me. Reading it in my booze. Went to sleep yelling my rage into the empty house and the glass of gin and a book. With the light still on. I realize she is gone. "I'll call you from the office." How the phrase sounded as she closed the door, the words barely audible, a flicker just before the noise of the door, then the sound of her motor, the sight of her car disappearing just as I began to understand what it was she had told me. "I'll call you from the office." Her exit line. The insult of it, the sheer contempt of leaving like that, the smug bureau- cratese of the words, the dismissive arrogance of it. But more than anger, the humiliation, the crippling mortifi- cation that thwarts anger, when fury could be helpful. The result instead is despair. It is I who am worthless. The whole dizzy circle of despair, conflict, ambiva- lence. Go or stay? When you so clearly ought to go. Stay, win her back; the whisper of insanity. Remembering when she did love me, remembering how real it seemed, how utterly convincing, how beyond doubt or change.

A hangover. Breakfast. The paper. Postponing thought, the dilemma of staying or going. Because I could not tell her at lunch—since she has indeed called me from the office and invited me to have lunch—so I could tell her at lunch, just tell her, Look, I'm going home, there won't be any course. Or is it too late, has she already set the machine in motion, told the provost, sent letters to the students? Today would be the first meeting. Two o'clock this afternoon. Is there time to avert it all? Is there even time to save it? Because in the slime at the back of my mind I know already that I want to stay and search now only for means.

The method, absurd as it is. To offer a course. Then cancel. Then reinstate. A course I don't even want, am actually afraid of. Am sure to be trapped by—and yet I want it, passionately. Because it excuses my presence. The folly of staying on here. The obscene need of her. Even her cruelty. Craven without either shame or pride. Wanting to stay. To keep trying. Hope. Getting her back. Having her again, to have that love intact again, mine, warm as my arm around her back, the long, lovely muscles of her back, the delicate carvings of the bones in her spine, the perfume of her shoulders, her delectable, infinitely tender flesh.

I am distraught again, walking the rooms of the house like a madwoman. Will I go crazy again, fail, fall, live every moment in panic? The lure of suicide again, the absolute loss of direction in life. Life being over. Life being Fumio and Sita, both gone. There is no living past their love, with its death I die, living on like a zombie now, a walking dead without hope or purpose. Swallow, the heart beats as in danger, the stomach in its cramp of fear. I am no one any more. I have no work. My art is finished, failed, over. Escaped me. The sight of the newspaper folded on the table. The rug. Whether to stay or go. Wine stain on the rug. Bought it together at Macy's, split the cost. The other one, the big polar bear under the pile of cushions, that was a present to her. When she first set up an apartment in Berkeley, and I was her fancy uptown decorator. Derby Street. To go, to go home finally, give up, throw in the towel. Not to fight for her any more? Should one fight? Why should one fight? It is only fighting her; she loves me or she doesn't, one can't change that. I would want her to love me of her own accord, not through persuasion or coercion. But remember her hostility lately, the meanness of her temper. You can't change the mind of someone like that. Through patience? Playing the saint of love? Bullshit masochism. Oh, it is all masochism, don't even bother bringing that up. The word has no meaning. I would advise any friend, even an enemy, against living this way. But for me, being inside it, this is—becomes reality, the only reality. Leaving is flight, surrender, the end of hoping.

Then unexpectedly I remember the deer, the three deer at Mendocino. The burning of tears as I make, actually make a note in my notebook, put down a phrase: three deer. Sudden. Already their last movement comes to conclusion as we see them. Each in its place. Still with the stillness of silence. Unmoving. Looking toward us. These three. She and I. There are only the five of us in the world. And the sea. Three strange beasts before us. Stolid and magical. And then break off. Simply the pain of it overtaking thought or effort. Do I stay because three deer showed up on a lawn once in a resort town? Do I stay because I am a writer and this is something to write about? Because I want to have this experience, simply that? However painful, silly, demeaning. To have this experience rather than walking out on it, not having it. To have it and to record it. Even if that is in some way immoral or wrong or sick, one makes choices and I choose this suffering because at least it is feeling, at least in the vast anomie of my life now lost, vacant, at least I am driven to put down thirty or forty words in consecutive order and this is the last grasp on sanity or usefulness, hope or the notion of a future.

Or is it for the future of life? Not writing at all, but living, life itself, the conviction I have had for three years that we would be lovers all our lives, that this was a permanent relationship, a marriage even, if you will, that a bond was made and soldered, and vows and understandings given. And I am just too stupid or too stubborn to give up and go home. Even when it's so plainly all over, past, done for, blown. Even when she has filled the house with others whom she would never ask or even permit to leave and who left against her will, even when she has hemmed me out, built walls against me, taken up new lovers, given preference to some muscular young man, anonymous Neal preferred over me, preferred with such thunderous rudeness, such disciplinary force. To tell me to get lost. And I won't. No. Bitch, I'm staying. Hurry, put something on, it's time for lunch; hurry, don't lose your course, your passport.

She is on me before I know it. A puff of hair, a kiss hello. Coming up from behind at the corner of the parking lot. "I didn't see you," I say weakly. The first thing I was to say this fatal interview and it sounded so puny. "I've just come from lunch with a woman running for office. She should do very well. All the right ideas, employment programs, the works." The brisk efficiency of executive women. Where are my batteries? my protest? walking humbly alongside her. Neal. Last night. I'll wait. Say nothing till we sit down. The gravity dissipating, becoming ridiculous. Only to be with her again. Do the course, just to go on having that. To be sitting across from her like this. Her face.

And then simply her eyes. Her very long look. Her eyes. Swallowed in them, floating in them. I hold my breath. Her beauty. Has she ever been this beautiful? The eyes open and take me. The absolute tenderness of it. I used to see this making love. And have forgotten. Her eyes. So brown. Their brown power over me. Opening as if by some voluntary exercise of power, opening to their full vibrancy, the pupils expanding, taking me in like a sexual act, the terrible eroticism of that look. She can do this if she pleases, I think, she can, simply, by an act of will, by a whim, look at me this way and I am naked, open, utterly disarmed.

She smiles. Impish, naughty, flirtatious, a female

who's been out all night. An essence transported from
him, whoever he was, to me. She is intact, humorous,
roguish. The convent, Italy, serenity. I smile without
meaning to. Unable to restrain, to refuse; to refuse
would be like refusing to answer, refusing to dance, refusing to kiss. She says nothing at all. She only smiles,
saying everything. Last night is discussed and settled
in that smile. In making me smile, she makes me accept, become her accomplice. The moment takes on
light, flickers, goes out slowly. The waitress appears.
Sita exquisitely pointing out a wet spot on the tabletop. Her long finger pointing out the offending spot,
though the whole table was freshly scrubbed, proof it
had just been prepared for use, proof that this section
is open, proof that we are fortunate and in privacy.
Tea. Because she has already had lunch. And I will
have tea too. To add to the coffee, the cigarettes, the
diarrhea. Smiling again, just to be smiling at each
other, to be two women smiling over sex, a peccadillo.
Smiling as friends smile, sisters smile. The smile itself
denominating the subject, nudging it to the center of
the tabletop between us. And we sit in a tearoom,
candy factory, soda shop. Female territory. And we
smile in this debonair way, urbane, worldly. How beautifully worldly she is, this woman I love, my lady, how
humorous and knowing. How she always makes being
female a mystery, a joke, the romance of gloves and
scarves, perfume and jewelry. How she has always
made me love being a woman, and being a woman
with her, its smiles and secrets, its fascination with fabric and texture, its nuance of leather or silk or the love
of the flesh. The dressing room at Derby Street, how it
represented her with its thousands of dresses and silk
blouses, jerseys, belts, handbags, hundreds of shoes,
photographs of children and ancestors, bureaus full of
gloves and scarves, treasures of rings and bracelets.
All gone as the place is gone, as the time is gone and
who we were then, lovers tireless in bed in shower in
repairing there to dress, to perfume ourselves, skin
fresh as the lavender of her sheets, the fur rug before
the fire, the tomato juice and coffee on sunny mornings, the cherry blossoms in a china teapot, the vol-

ume of Dante by the window, the long, sweet sex of our nights, insatiable and in all positions and places, the long line of her back as I took her or she took me, the cries and whispers of our comings, our sighs and ecstasy, the light of the fire or the dawn, the roses by the bed, the moon on her flesh, the tired tenderness of her exhaustion, for I would never have enough of her, now gone entirely and forever gone. Then, gone in now.

"Lady, I don't know where I am." "Just where you were yesterday when I left you." I look at her, bleeding astonishment, the cool of it. "I love you. I will always love you. You have a very special place in my life as you must know by now." Among how many? I wonder. Children, lovers, friends. But the eyes still underlying each nuance as I hear her, caressing with old caresses, forgotten, dead, I had even thought. Afternoons in my old place in Sacramento, the wonderful rooms full of sun and plants, fuchsias piled on the balconies, camellias everywhere. The flowers she always arranged for me on my desk. Mornings waking before class, waking early to make love while the coffee perked. The evening she played truant to her own party, a farewell party for Brian, to surprise me with candles and rosé, soap and towels for the new apartment, a big black dish for flowers (I saw it only yesterday, full of junk, unanswered mail, paper clips), and Sita aglow with the wineglasses and corkscrew, my "survival kit," she called it. I was new then. Brian was a lover too, but she had slipped away from his party, come to me. It did not even occur to me to worry about him, I was new then, I was the favorite. The period of my glory, this lovely woman courting me.

"Listen, there was that time in San Francisco at Meg's apartment and you carried on with Sarah. I was there. I even stayed through it." "No, you wanted to take the bus back," I remind her, ashamed still to remember what I put her through that night and apologizing again. "It doesn't matter, I stayed finally. And when Fumio was here . . ." "But we weren't living together then, there was always somewhere else to go. Some outlet, some out." "That hardly makes a differ-

ence." "Of course it does. Look, I also remember Brian
and Hank and going back home to my apartment if I
saw Brian's car in front of your house. His last night
in town and of course I'd understand. And of course I
did. Even Hank." Dimly remembering that I'd called
her one morning when she must have been in bed with
him. Blasé we were in those days. Gay, insouciant, and
so forth. Hundreds of years ago. And the plant that
would arrive from the florist midmorning on such mornings. Almost embarrassing, the richesse, the delivery
man and the message. "Good morning, dear lady," the
voice purring at me, caressing me. The call to follow it
up. Almost embarrassing receiving the package at the
door, the grin of self-conscious pleasure, the novel and
vaguely ridiculous feeling of being courted, treasured,
swept up with gestures. No one had ever courted me.
Fumio's language of love was to sew a button on my
coat; quiet things, lovely in their considerate ingenuity,
their subtle thoughtfulness. Coming home to find that
he had invented a book rest that kept the pages from
turning when you wanted them to stay flat, that he had
remembered to buy Coke, that he had found just the
right brandy glasses. But not flowers, not Latin indulgence, not notes and telephone calls that began "Dear
lady" and went on to become graphic about delightful
sensations, sticky substances, flashes of heat.

"I want to be free. You know I have to have that.
You taught it to me yourself." I am horrified, hearing
her, my own undoing, my own stupid theories on life,
even my own actions, my insistence on New York.
"Last year I would have been your wife or made you
mine. Now I know that's not the right thing." I would
protest, but protest is futile, her tone forbids it. I wonder what it is that we are. Friends, sisters, lovers, she'd
said. "I want to share the house with you and Pia, I
want you to stay." I watch her, saying nothing, unable,
hypnotized. She is making her terms, she is in charge.
"Remember at Christmas in your loft how you said
you really enjoyed living alone. Well, I want to, too.
Or rather, not alone"—flicker of eyes, correcting herself—"but with that freedom. You know about Neal.
I told you at Christmas. And if I want to go out with

him and spend the night once in a blue moon, I've every right to. I can't go around feeling guilty or being made to feel guilty." The defensive tone again, the defiance. I smile, helpless. Avert it some way. "Next year I may not even remember his name." I blink to escape the ramifications of this. "You know I love you and how deeply I love you." "But that's just it—I don't think you do love me any more, I think you're through, exhausted." Is it my exhaustion, I wonder, my own disillusionment with this affair, do I merely project my own anomie upon her?

Her eyes smiling at me, intimate, sensual. Is it my fatigue or her mood today that brings back the high tide of love, when it was there, when every moment was charged, when just passing her a cup of coffee, or meeting each other by accident on campus, realizing fifteen feet away as she bore down on me, her coat flying around her shoulders, her hand picking a branch of camellias, how she ravished me, how she shouted our liaison to the world. How proud she was once. Around us jaws work sandwiches, women spoon ice-cream sundaes, office workers hurry hamburgers. My eyes focus on the cashier and the windows and then back to her across the table, hair swept back handsome from her face. The same beads as yesterday. The same sweater. "Free, yes of course. I can hardly argue with you. Of course it's your right. But the way you did it . . ." "How else could I?" "That ratty little line about calling me from your office." "What else?" "Efficient bitchery. Why not just tell me? Be honest. Surely the truth is better than lies or one-line exits like that. There was something cheap about it." She flinches. I've hit the mark of her honor, we are both proud here, have been rivaling each other in magnificence and probity for years. And because she is struck she takes off. And fires. "I had to shock you into understanding. I didn't want to hurt you, I don't ever want to hurt you. But I had to make you realize. So I had to do something to shock, to dramatize." "I'd rather you tell me the truth." Knowing of course she was afraid to. Had to resort to that line and then run.

Had to? No, preferred it. Just as she preferred making love with Neal.

"Look, we'd just come back from Mendocino, we'd just decided I'd stay and take the class, we'd just rearranged the house—you, Pia, and I. And suddenly you mumble something about 'seeing friends' tonight and go off announcing you'll call me in the morning. Naturally I didn't know where I was all over again, whether it was crazy to promise to teach that class, whether I could even stand it, staying that long." "Oh, that class, I wish we'd never started on the thing. Here's your letter."

She delivers the letter, my letter rescheduling the class, over to my side of the table. I had meant to use it as a lever, my bargaining point. And know far better than before that I dare not, that I couldn't possibly. She would urge me to cancel in a moment, is already repeating all her phrases about not wanting to put any pressure on me. Can I even rescue it from her? Helpless and afraid, knowing that I want to stay, must. And need the course as an excuse, a term of time, a stated interval. And the class, I think, something my own, mine. Touching the paper. Grasping at the students. Mimeographed names. The absurdity of it, to schedule the thing, cancel, reschedule. How like an indecisive fool. My face goes hot, thinking of it, the shame of all this.

And it may already be too late to recapture the students. Sita picking up the check. Back to her office, the telephone, we must hurry. Our meeting, our famous showdown took less than the full hour. And ended by her *indulging* me, *permitting* me to teach one three-credit course for peanuts. Walking up the stairs, I remember again that the first meeting is scheduled for two this very afternoon. We have twenty minutes. Sita on the phone through a labyrinth of bureaus checking to see if the sign canceling the class is up on the church door as ordered. "My God, a church?" "The First Baptist, no less. The university's very miserly with classrooms, we make do with what we can dig up. My secretary saw to the sign and then went home." Calls to the registrar to see how many students have trans-

ferred to other classes, collected their money. I pace,
fume, sweat it out. "Hadn't I better go round there
and change the sign?" Ten minutes before two. "The
registrar will call back." The thin green slips of regis-
trants in her hands. The class permits thirty-five;
seventy had applied. The fragile papers on her palm,
cradled by her long fingers. Five before two. "I'll go
over there." "There's no point, the church is locked."
More telephones, people, the green papers, tissue-thin.
A sign somewhere on a door saying canceled. "I'm going even though I don't know where this place is. I'll
find it. I can change the 'canceled' to 'postponed.' "
"There's really no point in it." "Hell, I can't help myself."

Finding it almost at once, miraculously. Great stupid
Romanesque and pompous. First Baptist. And the
little sign, yellow paper and a Magic Marker, CAN-
CELED. One lone girl turning down the stairs. Scruffy,
looks the type. Gone by the time I park. Ten after two.
Feeling foolish scribbling out the "canceled," trying to
substitute "postponed" with a ballpoint that won't
write at a vertical angle. "Do you want to borrow
this?" The girl. And her purple felt pen. I add the
telephone number for the office. Humiliated, ridiculous, while she looks on. Has no idea she's addressing
the instructor. Saving grace. "So they're going to have
it after all?" "Just call this number, they'll tell you all
about it." Magically preserving my identity. Returning
the pen. Foolishly back to my car.

A m I crazy? Buying a present. Passing a store and feeling the impulse. This morning I would have throttled her, struck, even struck her dear tender face. And now, buying a present. Just lost my last argument with her and I want to buy her a present. Sitting across from her at the teashop today, I knew for sure she would never live as I am living, in someone else's town, someone else's house, with the pretext of a silly marginal course paying only a token salary while I wheeled and dealed in my world, slept with other people while she waited up nights. Unthinkable. It is this that humbles me, this knowledge that she would not endure my circumstances one single week. And perceiving this, I worried most that she would despise me, because I gave in, took every insult. I cannot ask for gratitude, yet I so fear her contempt.

And having passed the afternoon with "other people," the other people she advises me to cultivate, having sat through coffee and a young filmmaker's epic about trains—miles of footage lavished on the Metroliner because the young woman who did it declares it's actually the "feminine spirit," the passion of her life, and so forth—I am hanging about in front of a record store hankering to go in and buy a present. The audience was so savage during the question period that I came to the filmmaker's defense, complimented the photography, the technique, the ghostlike effect in the old photographs she used. "There are always ghosts in a love affair, other people on stage," Susan Griffin whispered to me while we waited for the film to begin. "And ghosts of all the old moments of the love itself, the lovers as they were a month, a year ago, the love of then. Which is not the love of now," I said. Susan's a playwright, we were being literary. When they invited me for dinner after the film, I begged off, half regretting it later. For it had felt good being with other people, almost like New York. A life of appointments and friends and conversation. Not to be buried in that house. Morose, solitary, lugubrious place with night coming on. And yet I wanted to be alone again. To expect her again. To go home and wait. Knowing she'll be late. And passing a store, wanted to go in and buy her a present. Noticing the records, feeling the impulse.

Lovers and presents. How we used to buy them, hardly a day without them. Mostly hers. Flowers, records, a book or something to eat, trivia even. Flowers, heaps of them. Spending way beyond her means. The whole kitchen of plants she gave me when I moved in at Sacramento. Begonias, the two moccasin plants I used to literally run to water after our weekends in San Francisco. Furious they would be at me, crying out over neglect at the end of two days. Sita courting me those days. Something I hardly understood then. I had never known gifts in such profusion.

Now it's I who buy the presents. Passing the record store and then going back. Not knowing what to buy till I remember the Alice Stuart that Sherman has. Alice Stuart, recalling the name just when I need it, tossing it to the clerk. "Central aisle." Steward, no, Stuart, no, next to it, finding it just when I'd given up. The one with the motorcycle on the cover. And another one too that I haven't heard yet. Clerk wrinkles her nose at the other. Maybe she does me a favor. "It's early and not very good." "All right, just this one then."

Waiting for her downstairs, the record on the couch where I will not forget it. The rain in torrents. Will she stay at school? Put up with a friend? Go to Neal's? The time passes. Nine-thirty, when I expected her. Then ten. And past ten. And still the rain. Huge impersonal flood. How will she ever survive it? Then a taillight reflected through the glass of the front door. Seeing it like some sort of miracle, unforeseen, beyond desert. I call to her from the open door. Her voice answering me, her brown coat around my arms.

Settled on the sofa, we sit where she sat that night with Pia, comforting her after the quarrel with Valerie, and I hovered in the kitchen, cooking a chicken to comfort them. But tonight I sat where Pia sat, tonight it is I, the center of her attention, her delight. She crows over the record and plays it, listening in my arms. For the first time in weeks I feel she is actually present when she is with me. Her body speaks to me. "Makes you want to dance," she whispers. I remember dancing as from some former life. "Friday let's go dancing at Peg's," she says, bouncing nearly, having thought of it. Excited by her nearness, her kisses, the pressure returned against my body. But afraid to press further.

In bed she seems ready for me. Permitting me brief access, one bittersweet opportunity to enter and be her lover. Does she remember him and compare, measure me against him, Neal of only last night. If I went down on her, would I find him there, his odor still about her after a shower? Forget it, take what you have, what is given in her new sweetness, her willingness. The aftereffect of the other perhaps, the rebate, but still mine. Yet so short this turn of mine before she finishes, expels me, ceases to respond. My own inability or her lack of interest?

Then leaning over me, taking me, always what she prefers. Her face looking down on the joy given, registered unashamedly, uncontrollably. Her satisfaction. Her godlike powers. In and out of me each time stronger more certain more inevitable until she has found a new touch, slowly ever so slowly, touching the whole outer flesh, each stroke separate resonant astounding. I dare not speak, even encourage her with words as I love to do, sly lechery of language to excite us both, forgone now, I can only cry out softly with each stroke as she guides, controls, masters, nurtures, and completes. I the creature given over, straining, accepting, accepting all I am given. Stroke after stroke, curious the high of it, the cool of it, and the plateau of it surprising and a little frightening. Wave after wave of heat. Stillness and motion, then the sudden shuddering. Have you ever done this to me before, I ask, bewildered, ever quite like this? That miracle, the finding, the discovery of new sensation where all was familiar, all had been known.

I am lifted, I am hidden, I am in danger and suspended in air and fall and rise again and dizzy, then battered, then exalted. I am her cunt and against my will I tell her so, slavish, owned, devoted, open, a thing to be used. At the mercy of her force and her strength and her fingers, her caprice or her tenderness or her majesty over me. Her eyes open to me, giving pleasure, knowing her certainty to make me rich or afraid or victorious with each caress. Giving because it pleases her to give now, this moment. As it pleased her to give another last night. And I can only admire, prisoner of the touch of her hand on the quick of me, the slow mysterious move of her fingertips around the lips of my mouth gaping to be filled with her, pleading for her fullness and her force in me, the blow of her arrival at the cervix, itself another mouth, another door opening to her touch. Have me, have me, I'm yours, altogether yours, my mind saying what I refuse to say aloud or say only to repent it, the complete abnegation submission surrender, the long fingers of her assaulting me breathless or sly shoved high and now and now this instant. Crying out in the little cries she gives me, crooning to me as I come to her, my creator, comforter. A coming strange and strangely disappointing.

Pia's home. It's been days now. The last note, the one found on Sunday when we came down from Mendocino, specified "a few days to think and get it together." Yet she never tells me where she's been. She stands at my doorway and I invite her in for a cigarette. She sprawls on the bed: long beautiful limbs, perfect and delicate girl's beauty, the face almost of a child. Like Emily's, but finer. "Emily's just great, loves it up there. The only thing she misses is her big Donald Duck." "Well, if that's the only thing on her mind, she must be taking to the change very well." "Sure, she's

getting along just swell. That part's all okay . . ." We
lapse into a silence. "Staying here while you guys were
gone last weekend really got to me. Over in my room
it's full of Dan's clothes and stuff. And when I
go downstairs I see Emily's bed. Like the whole place
was too full of echoes. So I just had to take off for a
while, don't you know?"

I do, and then of course I don't. Have no idea where
she's been. And the "being alone just to get into my
own head" seems fairly unlikely. In San Francisco or
even Berkeley she would have had to stay with someone. Michael is out of the question; his wife has come
back to him. I cannot ask her where she's been. And
she clearly doesn't mean to tell me. Further silence.
The phone rings. "If that's my mom, I don't want her
to know I'm back yet." It isn't. We try a few topics:
the income tax, the used car Martin has given her, the
band. "Jack was supposed to call me back but he
never did. Guess old Jack was just stringing me along,
wanted to show me the sights, that number." I am disappointed. "They didn't play the right kind of music,
anyway. Stevie Wonder. I can't get off on that stuff.
It's all atonal and that big band honking away behind
me. I need a melodic line, don't you see?" She fiddles
with a bracelet. Wonders where she's left a glove. The
cigarette is nearly finished. Is she back with Dan? Is
she still clean? Wanting to ask. Unable. Awkwardness
filling the room. "Gotta get these big old shoes fixed,"
displaying the outrageous pair of wedgies that made
her fall down the steps into the front hall the last time
she wore them. It worries me to see her wear them
when she drives. "These are my only job interview
trotters. Had 'em tacked together with a Band-Aid
here but that didn't hold up so good." Smiles. Adjusts
a bracelet. Leaves.

Back in a moment with "a few things." Nightgown,
dresses. "I'm off again." My affection falters, wishing
she would talk to me, stay. "I left this note for Mom."
My eyes, scanning the thing pinned to the frame of the
door, usual stuff about "needing time and space to
think everything out." Sad little exchange about the
note. "Do you think this is the best place for her to

find it?"—the note tacked rather foolishly to the naked frame of the door. "I'll tell her it's here." "Well . . . off I go . . . oh no, did I forget those gloves again?" Long, elaborate search for the gloves.

It hardly seems an hour later when she calls. "The most terrible thing has happened. I hit somebody. Not in my own car, but I hit this guy." "Tell me what happened. Take your time." Her voice pinched, terrified, she keeps going over it until it's clear. "I was driving Dan's car, see . . ." I don't see, when she has one of her own, when Martin has just bothered to buy her a car of her own, part of the plan for her independence and rehabilitation. "And this guy on Van Ness, wouldn't you know he has to jump out and yell whiplash." "Start over." "Well, I was getting along fine in San Francisco and the hills and all, pumping the brakes. You know, Dan's car doesn't have any brakes." I close my eyes, knowing, remembering he was "going to get them fixed" at least two weeks ago. No use asking why anyone drives a car without brakes in San Francisco. "Well, I got to the stop sign at Van Ness and suddenly all the cars bunched up at once and I couldn't stop fast enough, couldn't pump 'em up quick enough and I rammed into this guy in front of me. Wouldn't you know, he disappears under the seat. And then comes roaring out with this whiplash thing." "Did you hit him very hard?" "Just my luck in this whole city to get the biggest creep!" I would laugh if I had the energy. Were not afraid for her. "So he starts yelling that it's a hit-and-run and the scene of the crime and all that stuff, just 'cause I can't stand there forever, 'cause I had to bring Dan's car back to him and get my own." Why? I wonder. "This guy has a Datsun or something and I haven't hurt his car too much, but Dan's front end is a mess. You know how those little Volkswagens just fold up." Bewildered, I am left with the knowledge of how Volkswagens crumple, this general truth, this commonplace. She bounds on. "So I took Dan's car back and picked up mine and I'm going back there now, scene of the crime, he calls it, just to show him I keep my word. But he's got this phone number and my address, so I just wanted

you to know, in case he calls up." "Sure." "I'm terrified, I'm just terrified. He could go after me for every
cent he could get." "Try not to worry right now, try
to calm down. Relax a little." "What can he do to me?
Attach my welfare check? I'm broke, man." "If he
calls I'll talk to him." "I just wanted you to know
ahead of time. Tell Mom not to worry."

Thinking that I have now, my stated interval, my
term of time. Thinking it as I watch her at breakfast.
My stretch of days, my allotment of proximity, days,
weeks, months. Then nothing. Go back to New York
and it will be over. But for now there is this, guaranteed. Thinking it as I watch her over breakfast. Warm,
secure in her presence, momentarily secure, watching
her eat. Her poise, her assurance, her movement
taking a piece of toast and buttering it, both dainty
and bold somehow, and curiously admirable to me,
smooth and fluid like the smoothness of her skin. Admiring the shape of her breasts in their green sweater,
her long legs as she stands and goes into the kitchen.
Her movements as she cleaned the ice box last night,
the stride, the efficiency. Even her confidence before
a mess of spoiled vegetables, some recalcitrant stain.
I would have made a project of this, dreaded it all
day, stretched it to hours if I'd gotten to it at all. She
does it in four whirling minutes. Even the arcane fit-
tings of the plastic shelves, those troublesome boxes
at the bottom, all deceitfully easy under her command, trays sliding neatly back into place.
    Then her committee arrived for a meeting she'd
assured me would last only three minutes. I went
upstairs to read and be out of the way. Discovered I
had left the glass of wine I was drinking downstairs.
Too late. The book I'm reading inescapably dull, the
print too fine, my neck begins to ache from reading
prone on the bed. Try again, sitting up. Worse still.
They have been down there an hour already. I begin
to hate and resent them. It's dinnertime, why don't
they go home? Percy, his boasting noise coming up
through the floor. Then a white man's voice, nasal,

irritating, going on about his asinine "five-point scale" for making decisions. "We must ask ourselves, will this experience benefit my intellectual and emotional growth?" I close my eyes, this sort of language always gives me the creeps. California hokum, therapeutic weekends, how can she bear these people? But this project, this "dialogue between male and female: toward a new communion and understanding," is at the moment the darling of her heart. It has already consumed two of our evenings and will devour a three-day weekend in February. It is about to overcook tonight's own chicken as well. The male voice goes on: "Does it take me to restful places likely to nourish and stimulate that growth?" Charming, well-modulated moron. Go home, the chicken will be overdone. This is my dinner you are drying out. I have a headache from hunger, from being cooped in a room like a domestic animal.

And when they finally left two hours later, she rescued me. Hearing her step on the stairs, I had already forgiven everything. The dear soft voice of her apology. How charming the Italian in its accent, which fluctuates according to the occasion but is always stronger when she is confused or sorry or ill at ease. Or perhaps it is the Portuguese, for it is the Indian in her that apologizes or waits, once waited two whole days for me when I missed a plane. Light-years ago. Never mind, she is laughing, hugging me, laughing at them, laughing with delight that they are finally gone, laughing at the chicken. And I am laughing too, warm in her embrace, the scent of her lovely sweater, the silk around her neck, the fine gold of the bracelet at her wrist. I forget everything in her presence: the absurdity of my position here, the unfairness. They are dismissed in an instant by her complicity, her romantic transformation of all life into an assignation. She'd once spoken, smiling, of "the proper conduct of a love affair." I had never realized that love affairs were conducted, I thought they merely happened. I had much to learn.

Now at breakfast she is planning Paul's birthday

party. This or that couple from the office. One pair
can't come because it's their fifth wedding anniversary
and they have other plans. I do not look forward to it.
It sounds very dull and heterosexual. "What usually
happens is that Pia and Paul's friends end up upstairs
playing music and smoking dope—I'll get beer and
crackers for them—and the rest of us have a good
time downstairs. George McFarland is coming. You
remember George. And Neal. And I think I'll invite . . ." But I hear only Neal. I would have thought
she could do without this, without making me meet
him. Perhaps it's better. Perhaps if she has her own
way in everything, is unopposed. Completely free. Is
that freedom?

Last night when she woke in the middle of the
night, because the back door was open and had been
banging, I was positively surly. She laughs, repeating
my growl. " 'Sita, what the hell are you doing?' is what
you said, as a matter of fact." "I'm so sorry, darling."
Wishing now I had held, had kissed her, enjoyed her,
the soft of her flesh. "I've known worse. People who
wake up in the middle of the night and talk. Talk,
mind you. Hank used to walk around in his sleep." I
see Hank, ghostlike, another past, his great naked
body dwarfing his cock. When you are secure, they
never bother you, never challenge, these pictures. You
can flick them away. In the old days I triumphed so
over Hank, over all of them, Sita so outrageously in
love with me then that they simply never mattered.

Last night I did not offer lovemaking. Afraid now
as always lately. Afraid of her rejection, even more
afraid of her having to reject, finding a way to say it
kindly. Or annoyed and forced to show annoyance.
No, not forced, merely unable to hide it or disguise
her antipathy. But this too puts a burden on her. And
I am loath to put her to that trouble, that ill nature,
that guilt. And I am afraid, too, to know how bad it
is, how small my chances are. And so it is always her
decision now, a decision rather than what it used to
be, a coming together and igniting and who knows
which ignored, for it was that close, the spark in the

loins that mutual, the fever coming into the forehead and finding relief in the mouth. Wishing as I held her in my arms before sleep, wishing as I have wished a thousand times to descend her body and eat, feast in the damp between her legs, drink as at a fountain. Suckle there and play and sate myself, hours of it, the greed of it, the concentration as I hear her cries, breathing in the scent of her, the dear lovely taste of her always so fresh. Time to do this, the afternoons we used to have, evenings devoted to lust. And joy. The joy of those times. Now there is neither time nor inclination.

But there is this stretch of weeks. There is this, there is still this. Over inevitably, as inevitably she will put down her coffee and go to her office. And leave me here to wait her return nine long hours later. But I will have this time, savor it, experience it as completely as I can, drain it. It is the end of love, the dregs. The last crumbling and embarrassed moments of its collapse. All that I am given.

Knowing it is limited. Not like before, when riches poured down, occasions came unsought, surprising me as she descended on me in a morning I did not expect her, casually, beautifully undressing, an act she always did with the most consummate grace and ease. Or Sita met by chance on campus, flattering me when she would burst into my office at the end of a day. A bunch of daffodils in her hand. Or found at the door of my classroom, Sita claiming she had just discovered a new place we should drive to for dinner. Once even with Hank, we drove up to the gold country, the three of us riding in the front seat of my convertible with the top down in the fine serene evening. If she likes, I could even take on Hank. Remembering a wistful comment she'd made that a woman lover she'd had once hadn't liked him, was unreasonably jealous, and that she had always wanted to have a weekend in the country, up at the ranch where Hank lived, the three of them, just to be in nature, to swim naked there and lie in the sun. Wondering if I could do that. Liking Hank. When we got to Sutter Creek and began to explore the ruins, he teased me, the three of us standing together, both of them so much taller than I, "shrimp," he called me, and I suddenly found I resented him, discovering I was not a woman to him but a boy, or he would try to convert me to a boy, someone smaller, and I was not the desirable stranger but a rival. At dinner he drank badly and was morose, jealous, irritating. But he insisted he drive my car down the mountain because I drove the pitch-black road so slowly. He had just wrecked Sita's car. But she did not back me up, said she was too tipsy to drive herself, and seemed to think it a fine idea he should. I refused to let him drive and he called me a cunt—"Just like any cunt in a bar, all cunts, whoever the fuck they think they are"—a remark she has always professed she never heard, even though he shouted it. I drove, but for the first time my confidence as a driver was broken. Her confidence in me too. When we go anywhere now, she drives. Even in my car. It is part of my subjection to her.

Mad, the whole thing is mad. Mad to be here, mad to linger in a relationship where you don't even drive your own car, where you are hanging on in somebody else's house and town and life without a purpose and your own sense of adequacy, ability, competence utterly shattered, so that you no longer really work or believe in your work. Thinking of suicide again. And congratulate yourself on having ten weeks of this guaranteed to you? Glad of it.

There is this space ahead, this time. Last night after dinner, merely watching the television. She sat beside me on the floor, then stretched out on the couch while I sat below her, an arm around her knees, giggling together at the pretensions of Bronowski or Alistair Cooke's narrations, the gravity of televised "culture," groaning at the superb generalities of their capsulized history but admiring their footage on Greece. Then lying back on the pillows in the bay window, no longer even watching the set and its dull pop-singer hero, only inhaling the fragrance of her flesh, the security, the eternal because so momentary safety of her arms. This time.

The sound of Hare Krishna people along Telegraph Avenue. Dark of a coffeehouse. Loneliness of the afternoon. A rainy day in Berkeley. Why am I wasting myself here, far from home, pursuing what has already fled? Why, when death is so soon? Around me beards and coffee cups, madras bedspreads on the wall, other people's conversations. The impenetrable lives of strangers. On the street a young woman carrying an infant covered with a blanket against the light rain. She looks utterly lost but has more purpose in life than I do. Young men in their ponchos and hats and padded jackets, their big boots and watch caps. All the paraphernalia of youth. I become old, watching. A youngster crowing over his professor: "This guy used to teach at Harvard." Waiters on their listless feet. "So I went into his office this morning and he told me two or three things that are gonna be on the midterm. With the answers, man. Be no problem there." The busboy picks up a dirty cup. "This guy writes so smooth, you know, it just flows." Pull of the espresso machine. A girl in the corner behind huge dark glasses drinks coffee soulfully. The espresso machine pulls again, suction and whistle.

She will be home late again tonight. Only an hour, an hour and a half together before she sleeps. A couple come in and discuss God. Are they madder than I? "They can still be saved," the woman's voice labors on, didactic, anxious. Ineffably tedious. He rattles her with questions, objections. "No, no, when you are praying, ask the Lord to help you with the things you can't accept. Having been a Christian for twenty years, I can understand a lot more than someone who's been in the movement for just a few months." He quibbles over her age, closer to nineteen really. Idiot reactionary fanaticism and this child calls it a "movement." How self-important they all are, what a collection of phonies, of mediocre minds. Berkeley. The waiter finally brings my coffee.

I must not dig in too hard, hold on, anchor myself in her, I thought to myself last night at the Riviera, watching her arm, enjoying the rose flesh of it, my eyes touching it like fingers. Watching her during an

Italian film; the woman director was present, answering questions afterward. And Sita, her mouth half open in delight, following the play of dialogue in both languages. The look of joy on her face as she heard her own Italian spoken. And later, outside the café, coming upon an Italian professor: *"E Mario." "Come va." "Va bene."* How her voice dances over the words, rises and falls and sings them. Her English so much more restrained, restraining. But seeing her again speaking Italian, how she lights up, how she relishes each word in her mouth. Her laughter, her gaiety. I go on a few steps to wait for her apart, enjoying her from afar, happy for her happiness. She calls me back to introduce me. "You do not speak Italian?" the professor asks. I admit my ignorance, feeling irredeemably stupid before his surprise. It would take too long to explain my lust for the language last summer, my eagerness to learn it, and then the wall she lowered between me and her country. "I could have picked up a lot, just didn't seem to have the knack"—but no one hears me; they are reminiscing about friends in Sacramento. After he leaves she tells a long and naughty story about the professor's wife, the mood of the evening still with her as she drinks cappuccino, her voice still floating into laughter, into that particular lilt and vivacity it takes from contact with the Italian. As if English were a kind of prison and America too a duller place, heavy and plodding like its language, somewhere you might go to escape a war or a depression, but tepid and ugly finally, a cold exile from the Tuscan hills she loves so deeply. That summer, especially the last time she saw them, en route back to Germany and the charter flight, tears in her eyes so that she could barely drive, she hated so to leave them. And I, looking at them that last time, had actually come to hate them. And Italy. All that I had loved so in my Oxford days, the great trip to Italy alone after my examinations. Years ago, and had loved the place, the people, the profusion of art and excitement and good nature. And by the end of a summer there with her had come to hate it, the heat and the tiled roofs, even her good and always impeccably polite family. A hate that was love utterly disappointed. How easy it would have been to learn the language, how easy to love her family—how easy if she had not been there. Preventing. In some mysterious way preventing me from speaking or from becoming friends.

Her brother was invariably, even punctiliously kind. So it is hard to explain, but perhaps it was that little incident even before we got down to the villa and the shore and the countryside, the second day actually, just a few hours after we left Milan. I needed cigarettes. Paolo was not very eager to stop the car. And it was hot that day, not yet lunchtime, but the traffic was heavy already. I had to plead a little to get him to stop. Then I jumped right out and into the store, thinking to hurry. Hardly noticing his command that I wait until he was at my back in the shop, shouting at me. I had already used my new and experimental Italian on the shopkeeper, and made my request, was rather pleased with myself, when I turned to see Paolo furious. "Who do you think you are?" I'm astonished, merely stare at him. He countermands my order for cigarettes. I stand there discredited, ridiculous. He buys another package, pays, and orders me to leave. "What on earth is the matter, Paolo?" "Who do you think you are, going around like you know everyone?" He slams the door on his side of the car. I look back to Sita for guidance. She hasn't any. Like Paolo, she merely assumes that I stay in the car while a male deals with the world, keep silent in a country where I do not know the language. And be served. But paid for too? How many times has it been made clear to me that Paolo finds it hard to pay for the life he leads. I had meant only to save my host the trouble. And I had also taken it for granted that one helps oneself, is independent, and the American woman in me had no desire to be served, still less to put up with the bullying that comes out if you show any signs of independence. I found Paolo harder to like after that, though I did like him anyway. Or rather I admired his character in maintaining an exemplary courtesy to me through a whole summer in his house, when I knew he neither liked nor approved of me. I'm not certain what he imagined my relationship with his sister to be.

On several occasions he referred to Hank as Sita's lover of the moment, a fiction I did not know whether to contradict or not. During the first week of our stay he read a book I'd written, *Flying,* that was expressly lesbian in certain passages. Bravo, I thought, he has taken this extremely well. The next day our beds were changed from a double to two singles. The reason given was that Sita had a cold. She may well have asked for the change herself, though of course she denied it. On the rare occasions when we spoke. For she was consumed now, reabsorbed into the bosom of the family, the language, the ways, the countryside, the long afternoons at the beach, the conversation of her sister-in-law, her walks with Paolo, her hours of badinage with the children. She was lost to me, lost in the crowds of friends and relations, a couple from Milan, the grandmother, the maid, the thirteen who sat at dinner. And I was a shadow reading books in our room, grinning foolishly when addressed in English, puzzled and idiotic when addressed in Italian. In as much as she could arrange it, I was simply not there. I had been the means of transport, a convenience in bringing her to Italy, but now dispensable. In as much as I could arrange it, I would rather neither of us were there, but she would not leave, and our two-week visit slowly and hideously became two months. I begged and was occasionally conceded a weekend in San Gimignano, a night in Siena, and finally, by myself, fleeing really, a week in Florence.

That an entire summer in Europe could be so wasted, so boring, so friendless, seems hard to believe now. All the expectations I had had, the adventure of it, being with her in Italy, so loved, so long talked about, imagined, planned, anticipated. And of course there was much in what we had that could have been enchanting, even glamorous. The great stone-floored villa in the fields, a farmer's house from the eighteenth century, huge, full of rooms and guests and long lunches, banquets at night, the party they gave for me the night I left alone for Florence, the champagne and cakes, the table spread outside in the mists of the evening, romantic it was, magnificent. Somehow only a mockery. Even our crazy dancing that night, the one occasion of hilarity, license, the whole lot of us, children and all in a frenzy of cha-chas and twists, tarantellas and rock 'n' roll. There will always be something lonely about remembering this, I'd thought at the time, thinking it was because I was leaving them all, leaving her here with them. But it was more than that, there was a strange betrayal even in the feast. An empty ceremony.

Remembering it now in a Berkeley coffeehouse on a rainy afternoon, I find it unspeakably bitter. To remember Italy at all is unpleasant, remembering it as I am losing her is unbearable. But why didn't I see it then? Not really believing her odd little explanations for her behavior—that she was suffering depression, that she was having a little nervous breakdown in return for my bigger one, and that I, if anyone would, should understand and sympathize. On other days she would say it was her health—glandular deficiencies, hormones, nerves, her doctor would look into all of it further when she got home. Poor lady, she was simply bored to death with me and had not yet found the way to relieve herself of the affliction. Coming home in September, she could serenely tell Sherman the affair was over and rearrange her house and life and associates accordingly. She had simply neglected to tell me. Till being here becomes finding out. And letting me come was a weakness she permitted herself after the visit at Christmas. There was still a spark. She wouldn't quite give it a chance, but perhaps she could not quite bring herself to extinguish it completely. She'd wait and see. So do I. I wait and see.

And I drink bad coffee in cafés on rainy days in Berkeley, and prowl bookstores, and have nothing to do for whole afternoons. Because I am waiting. Knowing already that if ever I were to win, I would be just as confused. I have done her the disservice of making her my need. I have used her to find purpose in my life. You can't do that to someone. My own terror lies like a mat under a rug; makes me tremble browsing through a bit of Henry Miller, his *Insomnia,* the obsession of an old man with a young and indifferent girl, but my story too. Yet whatever fool he was in the middle of the night, he was still a writer. And I have lost who I am. A follower following nothing, my hands empty along the way. Do I cling and pursue this love because I have really nothing else to do—or am I unable to write because my slavery to this infatuation makes work impossible? The former. No, the latter. The former because you have not finished a book in three years. The latter, because that is the period of time you have known her. Never blame problems with your work on other people; you have simply had no book to write for three years. Probably never again. Done for. And done for with her too. Both at the same moment. Nice timing. That curly-haired boy waiting on table knows who he is. The religious fanatic knows who she is. Even the wavering and uncertain figures passing the windows in the rain, even they understand who they are, each in his lazy California manner, "mellowed out," "laid back," whatever occult fizz passes for wisdom in their confused minds, they all know what they are doing. But I am only waiting for nightfall.

I spread her out on the couch. Laughing at me. "Kate! Why are you getting me to take off my clothes now? We're going out soon. You were going to call your sister before we left." "Later, later. This now." "But she'll be out here in ten days, we should confirm with her . . ." "I'll write her a note." "People can see us. If someone came up to the front door . . ." still laughing, unsure perhaps as I am unsure. How she would have adored this once, the madness, the risk, the spontaneity. Now I am very far from sure if she will even give in, permit me. But sitting near her on the floor as she sat on the sofa, it came to me, like a wildness, like a hope—the notion of spreading her legs and taking suck. Suddenly how I wanted that—how charming and offhand, how silly and willful and easy it seemed. I had only to coax off her trousers, spread her legs, and

the warm dark loveliness would be there at my mouth.
If I can persuade her, cajole, tease. Appearing to be
utterly sure of myself, without qualm or question. If I
can make it be then, that time and its willingness, its
lust and hurry and ease. We never refused each other
anything those days, could often hardly wait until we
got home. When I landed from Seattle once, we took
a room in Sausalito simply because it was a closer bed
than Berkeley. Rented a room because we could not
wait or drive any farther. Deciding the thing in the
airport parking lot, amused, feeling wicked and a little
silly but very pleased with ourselves, with our savoir
faire and nonchalance, our imagination and ingenuity
—or rather hers, for it was her idea, I was far too
provincial and stingy to think of renting a hotel room
to satisfy an urge. But how charming the idea was
when she suggested it, how worldly and blasé. Scarcely
able to wait till we got there, falling upon each other,
each as if by some mute intuition taking each other in
the anus as well. We laughed—can this be the reward
of a Catholic girlhood? Just as I'd laughed when she
came to me finally at my farm that September after the
breakdown and the loony bins, the moment arrived at
last when in touching her flesh again I would know all
those nights in hell were over and had been worth it,
had been lived through only that I might feel her in
my arms again, her embrace, her skin under the fingers
of my hand, and when she took me and entered me,
I wept and said, the joke only a pretense for its utter
earnestness—Ave Innocenza, do you realize you're my
religion? But she had no idea what I meant. Maybe
that was the beginning of the end, for we quarreled
the whole time and she left three days later.

The anger of the bin was in me, my fury at what
they had done in order to lock me up, to dope me and
hold me and make me despair of freedom. I tried but
I could not forgive her. And she would permit me no
anger, imagined I was still mad. And I suppose I was,
a little. And she drove me madder. The last awful
business upriver at some college where she was to
speak and was traveling as a big shot to confer with
other big shots. I was supposed to perform as well, but

hadn't accepted the invitation in time and had been
replaced. So I traveled along as companion, baggage
handler, nonentity, and then shamed her horribly by
heckling from the audience. Stuffed-shirt chapel atmosphere and I put a bit of the old bomb-throwing
radical into it, discomforting the little Wasp children
in the audience and mortifying Sita. After that it was
over. No amount of begging or pleading could get her
to stay. A long tearful delirious night and she left on
the 6 a.m. plane. It was over, all over again. Then, in
the late fall, her plans for a commune with the kids
fell through and Hank left because the rent was too
high for him. She began calling me. Answered my first
tentative gift. It seemed she couldn't forget me. Or perhaps I was handy, other options failing her. And mine
were failing too. Fumio announced his desertion. I
began the long spiral downward into suicide. Six tries,
two of them in earnest. When the depression had run
its course, she was there for me, she had taken the
house in Indian Rock. We would live together, it
would be our home. Refuge and asylum and all settled. Until I failed her, or it seems I did, by taking a
new loft in New York for a few months of the year.
Having no idea it meant so much to her, having no
idea it would bring about the disaffection that came out
in Italy, the slow, but perhaps not slow, perhaps sudden erosion of trust or even interest that must have
taken place in her while I was in New York these past
months fixing the loft. And so we come to here, what
I find when I return, the house on Indian Rock alienated, Sita absent, hostile. The process I stay here fighting, the death of love, its breakup, its wilting, its
decay.

Hoping by an act of fantasy now to revive it, hoping
by such reckless gestures as spreading her upon a
couch to reach some spring of Eros never touched and
still new, still fresh. I know, even as I perform the
miracle of undressing her, I know the futility of what
I do. And do anyway, doggedly, stubbornly, with the
faith of desperation. Because it is desperate: to imagine it would matter at all if she gave into my whim,
submitted to my obsession—this once. What is once?

What would it possibly matter in the sure and relentless loss of yardage, the inevitable sliding down the bank grabbing at saplings and weeds, what would it matter if once, a mere once, she indulged me? But that is what I want. As if this once were all time in one moment. Without consequence. As time is for lovers.

Further laughing and persuasion, yes, darling, just a little whim, it occurred to me we had a good ten minutes, just right for something instant, how pretty you are, your long brown legs, your soft brown hair here. She protests again about the door, about her shower, about her long day at the office and no shower, it cannot be pleasant, she would prefer to shower, she would prefer to go upstairs. And out of my clutches. And the shower too is a canard, she is as fragrant as she always is, tasting her as she laughs in resignation and places her hand on my head, crooning as I wish now I could croon and speak, speak the words of my love and lust, the words that would excite her further, stoke her, fire her to cries and madness. For she is interested, she is finally intrigued and then warmed and then willing. But not as I would have her willing. The very act of getting my way, of succeeding, is my failure, the realization of how alone I am. I had wanted her to love me back, to love me as I love her, as much, as compulsively, as passionately as we once both loved each other. But this is then and then is not now. Now is merely my diseased persistence, seeing again the beloved skin of her thighs, the soft brown hairs over her cunt. Her cunt that is almost a being to me, so long have I loved it, known it, kissed it, wept for its wounds, its small twisted clitoris. After the rape in the desert, the six drunks who stopped when her car broke down —the joy that help had arrived—the nightmare that followed the surgery. Why, after such outrage, why, when penetration must be so physically as well as psychologically painful to her, why would she permit, even seek Neal's probably large and certainly painful prick? Why, when she is loath even to let me go down on her with infinite gentleness and relish? Surely he cannot know and love her as I do. The old rancor, that she would fuck a man, permit him to enter, gross and rude and large after the crime of the six drunken rapists has left her so, why of her own free will accept another one? And why in preference? There is no knowing, only the moment with the sweet salt taste of her in my mouth, trying, trying to give her joy or bliss or something to come back for, accept me again because of some particular pleasure, some satisfaction for love or skill or even adulation. Because this is surely the act of homage. Saying to her once as we walked by the sea, saying what had been so hard to say, and saying it with a bitterness that surprised me—"Why is it always I who goes down, never you? Is that some of your damn European aristocrat business?" And she of course protested. But it was true, even in the early days, when all I saw was her great and enormous desire to make love to me, to give me such pleasures as I had never known; even then, she did not often perform that act. Yet now, it is still she who is the lover, her endless and wonderful ability to make love to me, all that is left of our sensual relationship. Whereas once she assured me no one had ever really given her pleasure before—and how easy I found it to believe that tribute, why not, there had been the rape, a succession of clumsy or inattentive husbands—now there is really nothing left but her making love to me. An exercise of power perhaps, a favor, charity, guilt. But to satisfy herself she has found men again, the one last time, others. Labor, even as I labor, listening for her cries and her hands stroking my cheeks, lighting around my head, I have no real hope. At bottom my heart already accepts defeat, expects the little sounds of her pleasure and then the sigh of her satisfaction— and knows it for fraud, if not the fraud of faked orgasm, the fraud of shallow and mere physical pleasure. I have lost my hold on her; even as I take her in my mouth, I understand how I have lost my hold. Were she to have refused me, I would not know with this same disappointed certainty. Having wanted and having gotten, now I know. Really know I have gotten nothing. Hardly even the heart to look at her as she speeds past me to her shower.

This is not love. This is sickness. Only some utterly negative aspect of what once was love. Like meat gone rotten. The failure of the illusion, the winding down, the acknowledgment of death. Debility, weakness, loss. All the hateful, the despicable traits. Dependence most of all, a paralyzing, humiliating dependence. The aftermath of love. Like its corpse. Long after the body ceases to live, the blood to run. But the vitality it gave off once, how it made me feel young, alive, intelligent, capable. Now this blue-gray thing of evening. Remembering her professions of love, an experience so deep it will go on to the day she dies, never leave her. She had never loved anyone this way before. Now I experience it ending. What she must have meant is that she will always remember having wanted me, not that she will always go on wanting me. But I had hoped we were exceptional, long-lived lovers. Not an affair of a year or two and then erased. And do I mourn her love's death or my own? Because I too cease to love as I knew it. What's left is not love, only despondency, fear, the little hopes, the great clinging.

But to think of a time without her. New York without her. Of course. But for how long? The day I can no longer be with her, the day I cannot come back. Finally it is her absence in the future that I fear. The line to the theater shifts, moves forward three feet. I am "entertaining myself" because she is gone tonight, won't be home for dinner, is staying at the office late because of registration. It is the third night in a row. It is possible that she is simply having dinner with someone else. Neal? Who? If you begin that route, you are sure to go crazy. Forget it. The line crawls on with film-archives tedium. She pins up the notices of the "cultural events" on campus in the kitchen. I pick almost at random, desperate for a way to fill an afternoon or an evening or the hours from five to seven.

I leave the line for a moment to make a note in my notebook. It has become my friend, solace, obsession. I will live in it, in the ability to record experience which makes me more than its victim. Putting feeling into words, and the words onto paper. Magical transformation of pain into substance, meaning, something of my own. The notebook then, like a shield against all that happens, each turn of events, the suffering of each evening. I am recording a process, keeping track of an event, noting with almost clinical observation and accuracy the death of something organic. But back in the line I am merely a nondescript waiting patiently to see a movie that fails to interest me at all. And even as I finish my scribbling, I am seized with the cold knowledge of New York, the loft alone. A future without her. Gray years stretching to death. The notebook assumes its real aspect, an untidy scribble without meaning or body or direction. The cheapest illusion. What will happen is what I have written and the cold understanding in it: finally, it is her absence in the future I fear.

I am home a little later than she is, her car is already parked in front of the house. As I mount the stairs I see her coming toward me in the hall, the familiar purple wool caftan (over her brown skin how many times) and that absurd flannel nightgown underneath. Watching television by herself. I sit down at a little distance, drinking a glass of wine. "Shall I bring a glass for you?" "No." Then I drink it alone, sitting alone, giving her space, sensing that she would like that just now. Or she may even move over toward me. A Japanese film tonight, long miserable business of hara-kiri. Just when I am settled into it, absorbed, I am startled to see her rise and leave the room. Probably just to the bathroom. Surprised to see her return with the ubiquitous curlers. "I'm exhausted, I'm going to bed. You stay up and watch it."

I am afraid, afraid of a middle-aged woman in hair curlers abandoning me to the little screen of shadows. Go with her? She doesn't want me. Nothing could be clearer. And I would now like to watch the film. Then be sensible, stay here. Letting a few moments pass before I must rise, go up the stairs, the room already pitch dark. "I wanted to say good night." Her kiss perfunctory, meant to repel, send me back downstairs. Well, I have tried. Watching the film again, the slow terrible agonies of the feudal code, its courtesies, rituals, obligations. Then the light is on upstairs. Without even saying it to myself, I know. She is choosing another bed. Pia's in one room or Valerie and Paul's in the other. Knowing already that the move is a command not to follow. I go to the bottom of the stairs. She is before me on the landing, taller, so much taller, the length of her nightgown.

"I am in one of my wanting-to-be-alone moods right now." I feel the tension in my shoulders, discovering they are raised three inches higher around my neck, my arms rigid. I look at her. "Have I done anything wrong?" "No, of course not." I feel the tension in my shoulders ease a bit, aware I am lowering them. Does she see me? "Are you angry?" "It has nothing to do with you. I've told you before, I need space sometimes, you'll just have to try to understand." The voice querulous, annoyed. She turns to mount the stairs.

The fear is greater now, a certain thing. I watch the film in a trance of dread, deadening myself with it, drugging my mounting terror with its patterns and images, faces and figures. The frame, the shot, the rhythm of architectural line, of black and white. You do not call back love. If one lover takes it away, withdraws bearing the missing half, then the unfortunate, the loser, the fool still willing, cannot furnish it alone. Her refusal is absolute, without appeal. And I do not appeal it, only wait for grace: a change of mood, the swing of the pendulum, the inevitable (no, perhaps not inevitable) rebate. After her night with Neal she was a greater sweetness to me. But this diminishes. May diminish to a smaller and smaller mite each time. Whether to play the lover as saint—"love must never beg or entreat or demand"—or whether to be modern, practical—insist on the rights of a peer? Vacillating between the two, successful at neither. Insufficiently committed to either course. Meanwhile, the shadows of an old world before me, the figures in the drama go about their predestined ways to death. Slow, graceful. The samurai condemned to seppuku with a bamboo dagger. Terrible their poverty and honor and courage. Extreme, remote, and perfect.

Alone in this living room thousands of miles from my home. And she, obdurate in her room upstairs, whichever room, whichever bed. She goes from me by steps, each expected but then surprising, each fore-known and then a shock as it occurs, something I could never have predicted. There is no way to fore-stall, as there is no way to recall, to bid back, to re-store. That she does not want, that she does not wish —is everything, an enormous power. And wanting, I am powerless. Her serenity, her solid ego and identity —is it that she knows herself so sublimely, commands her time and place and destiny so thoroughly? How do you become so strong? Through denial only? I see her marriages anew, not as the inflictions she has de-scribed, but as the exercise of her will over Martin, over Ben, even over Gil. She could have made their lives hell. No, not your place to judge these things, you know nothing really anyway, watch the screen, the samurai preparing to die, the square tatami of his suf-fering. She is a presence above me in a room.

My eyes uncovering the empty bed. No need for the light. Or the stealth I had promised, were she here, stealth to undress without waking her. Banging the closet door against a hanging plant irritatingly hung at just the wrong juncture. Taking my nightgown from its hanger. Just yesterday she had praised its color. Out the windows, the desired view where I can never move my desk, the lights of San Francisco gleam-ing across the bay, magical, alluring, the old dream of living there. Teaching the course again next year, hav-ing a future for us here. Now in the dark seeing her pillow gone.

Of course I can't stay here. This will be recurrent. And Neal on Sunday at the party, and wondering all day if she will go home with him afterward. Monday my first class. Still time to cancel again. Before the students kick in their money. Go and explain gra-ciously, urgent research, publishers' deadlines, family illness all require I return posthaste to New York. And merely stay through February. I can't stand much beyond February. My eyes traversing the rug as I get into bed on my side. The mere sight of the rug telling me in an instant of my boredom here, my dislike of the place. But what if she were to do as she did last year, make it a fortress, a castle of her protective adoration? I would strangle. What if she wanted me to stay, stay on through the year? Never leave California. No, I would die without New York, suffocate. So why not leave now? Why be here at all? No, these months, these few months, this last experience.

Lying in bed. Knowing she is lying in bed in another room. Pia's room behind the closed door. This night harder even than the other when she didn't come home, since then I could go out to Sherman's. The rain falls. Sounds of the house, this house of old sounds. Rain on the roof sounding as if it were falling directly through the ceiling and into the hall. Just a few feet away, the steady tap like a leaky faucet. The other night I could drink and rave, read *The Ginger Man* till I passed out in fantasy. But tonight her hostile presence just yards away.

I light a cigarette, unable to sleep. The lights of San Francisco if you raise your head from the pillow. Such a beautiful room for a bedroom, we thought when we got it, the great yellow painting on the wall, the black-and-white-flowered sheets, the Greek bedspread. Simple, perfect. And now this disorder of objects persists even after she has eliminated some, weeded the place out after we came home from Mendocino. And I had hoped so that I would be given Paul's room to write in. From the beginning, when we talked of shifting things around, using Paul's room, I was afraid, afraid it would be a matter of her moving herself out, away from me, rather than making a place for me to write as I hoped. My forlorn manuscript still all over the desk right at my elbow. I didn't get the room.

And now sleeping apart. It will go on. The damn class keeping me here, months of this torture, this bullshit. Monday is the first class. Over the weekend I must talk to her, ask her gently if she's sure she wants me to stay, or can foresee that it might be too great a strain, that much time. And then if we cancel it? Further looking foolish in public, but at least not bound by the law to stick it out. There's a contract. And state law. Have they got me already? Fear like a net over the bed. In what strange place have I fallen captive all by my own undoing? I had a life, New York pulling at me all day—get out of here. Losing myself in staying, losing her if I go.

In the morning I saw that she had slept in Paul's room. A peach-colored blanket, and under it a yellow one over the spread. There were no sheets. I had noticed before that when Paul and Valerie left, they took their sheets with them. I smiled and thought of them as children, indigent children in love. And she chose this. Chose to sleep without sheets under two light blankets. Preferred it. It was what she preferred.

Sitting on the couch Friday afternoon, the week over. A glass of wine. She is gay, relaxed, out of time, full of reminiscences. I enjoy her, simply and openly delight in her. "And what sort of people did you know in Japan?" She lies along the sofa, her body young, elastic, glamorous. "The Brazilian ambassador, who had grown up with my mother, and the French chargé d'affaires. His wife was a great friend of mine, she had a little girl the same age as Pia. Only a few Americans. But one couple, the O'Neils. Both over six feet tall, and she had black hair and blue eyes. Everywhere they went they were smashing. Then one night Tim O'Neil was coming home drunk and ran over a Japanese civilian. An old man with a white oxen and honey buckets and the oxen loomed up around a corner, but Tim just never saw the old man. It was a terrible thing: inquest, court-martial, the whole works. He deserved it." "Were the Americans bullies?" "For sure. Luckily I was not an American, so there were all sorts of places I could go that Gil couldn't. And this way I got to know a lot of Japanese, visited their houses, became friends." I see her in those days, young under great wide hats. Spoiled, beautiful. "Gil loved to buy me hats." The Sita of then, another Sita, the

young Italian dragged out to Japan to join her American husband, forced to leave Italy because of an affair
with a student there, her parents insisting she was
causing scandal, her place was with her husband. And
rejoining him, loath but obedient, for the distractions
of diplomatic life, parties, cocktail dresses, the liquor
ration that had to be consumed by the end of the
month. Gloves and shoes and jewelry. A chauffeur.
On the chauffeur's day off a mad ride in a jeep with
Ginny O'Neil, the two ladies on their way to a garden
party, the naval sentries unable to stop them and
bound to salute the commander's vehicle. Gaiety, a
swirl of people, dances, uniforms, gifts, invitations,
clothes. A summer house in Karasawa. And Sita married to a man thirty-five years her senior, a man her
mother had forced her to marry when they fled Italy
for Brazil and poverty, the rich American who was to
be everyone's means of escape. A good man and he
must have loved her, but she grew to hate him. "When
we were sent back to San Francisco, he wanted to
buy me everything in Magnin's and the City of Paris
and Gump's. He wanted to buy me San Francisco. It
was the first time I'd ever seen California and I loved
it. Then he was ordered to Detroit. I didn't want to go
to Detroit, and my father had just died. That closed
the door. I didn't have to be married any more. It was
over."

It is almost time to go, to relinquish our cushions
and comforts, to proceed with our evening. We have
scotched a reception in the city and will just go straight
to Matthew's for drinks, have dinner, and then dance
at Peg's. Paul calls. Plans for his birthday. I move aside
in a special euphoria, from the wine, the talk, hearing
her relive an earlier life, learning her again in greater
detail, further nuance. Then startled, as if a great
hook has torn the flesh of my stomach, by what she is
saying into the phone: "I've moved into the front bedroom, so you'll find all my stuff in your room when
you come over." A laugh. "Yes, and I've been warming your bed." More bright laughter, then the expected closing, "See you Sunday." I sit stunned while
she goes to change her clothes. Has she really moved

into that room? Was last night the beginning of a permanent arrangement? I had heard her talk only about some posters, moving in her desk and the file cabinets, and her clothes, because the room has a big empty closet. And is this where she will sleep now? The whole structure falling again, the fragile little edifice of my peace, my sanity. Do I have to stay here ten weeks in separate bedrooms? Never. Cancel the class, I must cancel the class, get out of here. Now finally I must leave.

Thinking as we drive along, It's the last night. As we cross the long arm of land toward the bridge and the city. The dilemma burning inside me like a stomach ulcer. I will have to tell her this weekend. Tell her the course is off and I'm going back to New York. But tonight, bury it, bury all the agitation and grievance, live only in the moment, the moment of our last night on the town. Each segment still untouched, drinks at Matthew's place, dinner by ourselves, the dancing at Peg's. FORMULA-FED BEEF speeds by and the debris sculpture on the beach, those strange concoctions of old boards and driftwood continually made and destroyed and remade by invisible strangers—how they remind me of my own ephemeral life—and the great bridge spiring off into the distance, beyond it the enchantment of the lights and towers. Making our approach, we agree, surprising and lovely concurrence, that it is better to live in sight of the city, at a distance, where you can see and savor and have the thrill of entering this way, than merely to live in it, where you see little at all and never the skyline. I help her search for a parking place, I find the spot, I succeed for us in the little challenge. And her umbrella protects me like her arm. We are one, warm, musical our rapport. I do not ask her about Paul's room. I will not spoil it.

The last night, each moment resonant and separate as a Christmas-tree ornament. Past the chic polyurethane panel Matthew has hung across his glass door, some ultra packaging device converted ingeniously to decor. And the red carpeted stairs. I remember them. And the plants, hundreds of plants. Most of all the brown rooms, that he had painted all the rooms a deep and elegant brown. A showplace, the kind of place that's good to visit because after you've admired it, it reminds you how much you like your own house —as she has said. But I compliment Matthew, am impressed, in awe of his house, one part of me just as delighted to be free of it as she is, but enjoying the creation of it, the peculiar achievement of it, that it exists with a greater authority than we do.

I meet Richard, Matthew's new lover, younger, very handsome. Richard talks all the time. From the moment we sit down we are his prisoners. He insists we drink a new concoction (contents unspecified—we must taste it first) that he calls a "Gold Dick." Sita laughs. "Haven't had one of those in a long time." A bit too cool, I think, growing uneasy. A not-so-veiled reference to her old flame Brian Oyama, a Nisei. But surely it was meant only to amuse. Richard goes on, insisting we hear all about each and every apartment he ever had in New York. Crowding us, suffocating us with his talk, his endless one-man avalanche. I am a New Yorker and he pulls New York away from me as a greedy child pulls away a map. An apartment he shared with his sister and three black stewardesses. We obligingly ask the right questions about privacy. "Oh, we got to know each other intimately, intimately. But what I couldn't stand was coming home to find Harlem in my living room. All those spooky dudes they went out with! So I moved over to the East Side, Upper East Side, East Seventies. I did much better there. Just couldn't handle that West Side funk, just couldn't handle it at all." "You were right not to persevere," I say, catching a wry, ironic grin on Matthew's face. Knowing his boy. Infatuated, but still knowing.

Richard goes on, indefatigable. I tune him out and save what is left to me, the sight of Sita kneeling to fix me a piece of farmer's cheese on a cracker, the comfort of our two leather chairs side by side, facing the men, the mere knowledge of her presence, Matthew's friendly being across from her, the beauty of the room. The drink draws to its close. This portion of the evening, this fresh and precious ration. Like seeing a fortune diminish.

And we still have not accomplished our mission. "What are we going to do about Sherman?" Sita asks. "Get her a show," Matthew says. "I can't do anything for her in the freelance way now, market's too tough. But let's see what we can do to get her a show." Richard's just full of ideas: rent a gallery on Saturday night and invite the dealers. Hire a band too, I groan to myself. Richard elaborates, flies off into public-relations fantasy, hoopla. I concentrate on Matthew, addressing him seriously, talking for the first time this evening, trying to fight through the silliness of Richard's hard sell to insist on Sherman's undiscovered greatness. She belongs squarely to the New York School, a peer of Gorky or Kline's, but always overlooked because a woman, not only that but a lesbian, not only that but a dyke who has worn it on jeans and men's shirts for years like a cross. Though her work is beautiful and original, she is a recluse painting in obscurity, suffering years of poverty and neglect, but always painting, painting in whatever neglect or despair or on booze or broke, painting still the great strong pictures of her own style structure and line. "She is yet to be discovered, but I don't want it to happen after she is dead," I tell him. A bit self-conscious after my speech. They murmur agreement, I've had my effect. They promise to see Sherman on Sunday. Matthew is an art director with many contacts in the city. We all have hopes.

On the last night even the smallest moments have an urgency: the lifting of a piece of French bread at dinner, the passing of the butter, the choosing of the wine, even the choice of the place itself, a small fashionable restaurant on Castro Street, the awkward, overpublic wait for a table, the two of us poised right before a swinging door. My heart cries out to be settled down, at ease and in comfort over the meal, the ceremonial meal. And when it is begun, I already fear and anticipate its conclusion, the moment when it ends, the segment of the evening ending with it. This, the last night.

And at Peg's in the roar of music, the wonderful near-sinister rhythm of butch and disco and hard bartender, the great tall black beauties of women, the rabid finesse of the dancers, the whirling colored lights reaching from the ceiling toward every fantasy smalltown prom and big band and nightclub and acid, but effective only if you will plunge yourself entirely, spinning until you stagger in your dizziness. And this is hard for us. Removed so far from this world, tourists once or twice a year, the first moments uneasy in the place. Because it is tough and gay and at the edge. Everything we admire in it, but still another world. Being here at all is some sort of commitment or declaration. I watch her to see its effect. Will her retreat from me show in this place, will the absurdity of the whirling lights, the jejune music, the frantic gyrations of the dance, the public act of dancing with another woman, will it all merely throw our futility into high relief? But with that smoothness of manner, that charming democracy, that tact and poise in any situation which I both love and hate in her, she smiles and is agreeable, exchanging a word or two with some woman whose drink sits next to ours on a railing (there are no tables, it's big Friday night), even accepts an offer to dance with a huge peroxided blonde I am forced to envy though thankful for the opportunity to watch, merely watch her dance. This is different from dancing with her, a thing I never do very well, Sita unable to match my American rhythms or I that odd little South American beat she never relinquishes. And yet tonight we are closer to being in tune than in all the years I've known her, closer to having that euphoric sensation of being perfectly in step, communicating with the body, the face, the mind—all one integrated little pageant that has the special cachet of being performed in public, before spectators. Whether they watch or not, one is stating and proclaiming a relationship before the world, showing off an emotional attachment never otherwise permitted such display.

Perhaps it was for this reason I so resented the man. A nondescript creep, the sort who frequents this kind of bar, with hang-ups of his own, yet unlike the voyeur

leaning up against the wall, or the two sailors who
have come for kicks and to dare each other into getting one of these broads to dance. This one is different.
Determined. Fearless. He asks woman after woman to
dance with him. And succeeds. He has even split up a
couple, engaging one of the women in something like
a necking match, only to drop her the moment of his
conquest, the moment she stops her embarrassed protestations, the moment she seems to have adjusted herself to his step and his insolent gnawing upon her neck.
I watch, feeling a special humiliation. I am no bigot
and would probably argue that such places were best
open to the public, loathing rules and exclusiveness
and bouncers at the door, but I hate this man. A sudden irrational anger, as if he were the center of all
malice, as if his predatory way, his hunt and his stealth
were the very image of all that threatens me, every
danger in my life now. It is almost over, my mind
keeps reminding me, this last night, this last occasion.
I mention the man to her, pointing him out. She has
noticed him too, agrees with me—yes, it's terrible how
they come here, yes, it is annoying. Someone asks her
to dance. She is gone from me again. The night is almost over. Bar calls for the last drink. Still watching
the alien male closing in on a new partner. She is back
with me now, holding me, taller than I am as we
dance. Feeling at one with her and then separate as the
lights explode, the final drink is bought, the voice
booms at us over the microphone. They are having a
ball game, a picnic, are a community with Sunday sup-
pers and birthdays and anniversaries. We do not really
belong, there is her university across the bay, her neat
administrative post, her necklaces and Italian leather
boots, her children and grandchild, her party of straight
couples tomorrow. The little tawdry world collapses as
they turn on the lights, waitresses begin clearing the
tables. It is over. Even the malign specter of the man
has disappeared. Ahead of us only the bare late-night
street, finding the car, the drive home.

All I remember of the party is Neal. But of course it took hours before that happened. The early afternoon and Paul's gang to be entertained, their tedious jokes about Allen's red car, about Paul's haircut, about Tom's skiing trips, about his girlfriends, about their busboy ambitions, the new restaurant in Sausalito. I watched the afternoon sun and tried to help entertain them but found it difficult. Pia relieved us a bit, Pia the prodigal returning home after the mysterious absence of a week, Pia seeing Valerie for the first time since their fight. Her entrance was remarkably dramatic, with effusive whoops, lots of jewelry sweeping into the room, trailing jokes and kisses. High. Very up. Seeing the unnatural energy, I wondered if she was on drugs again. But perhaps this is only strategy to cover an awkward situation. She kisses Paul and notices his haircut—the general subject of conversation for the last two hours. She does not kiss Valerie. I am shocked by her stubbornness, impressed by her bravura and defiance. It would have been so easy to be gracious—yet she wouldn't stoop. And yet she triumphs, gives us all a sense of life as we sit languishing in boredom. After Pia, the family party lapses into the general, hordes of people crowd the rooms. But for me nothing changed.

I think I have never hated a party so much. I have always loved parties, can even summon the nerve to speak to strangers at them. But I spoke to no one. Not even the few people I knew, like Marsha Crabtree, who once shot an unfinished film with me and now sits next to me, loyally and kindly urging me to go ahead and edit it. "We've got some really good footage

145

there," I dimly hear her say at my elbow. I nod, smile
wanly. How can I explain I'm going back to New
York, maybe tomorrow? The city yelling all day in my
head, urgent as a suitcase to be packed. All day while
cleaning the rugs and arranging potato chips I have
packed and repacked my hopes—it remains only to
tell Sita. Sita a figure in the distance, greeting her
guests, performing hostess at her party; charming,
beautiful, witty, and full of laughter and serenity. In
charge, completely in charge. And I a tongue-tied
figure in a corner, unable to say a word, peculiar,
downright embarrassing, certainly noticeable. Nothing
unfreezes my silent idiocy except the one anxiety. Neal.
Imagining him in every man who enters the room.
When a very handsome, gray-haired man walks across
the dining room with her, tall as she is tall, it must be
Neal. I am undone by how well they look together, how
superb each of them separately, how they match and
complement each other as a pair. One cannot argue
with this perfection, I must of course defer. But she in-
troduces him to someone as Walter. Of course, Neal is
thirty-five, he could not have Walter's beautiful gray
hair even over such a youthful face. Wait, watch again
for Neal. He is coming. You have only to wait in a gut
of nerves, moving often to cover the fact that you never
speak, occasionally useful with chips and sandwiches,
but essentially mute, useless. Only to wait until he
comes, like a sentence to be executed.

And then I see him. A florid young man with huge
mutton-chop whiskers. A bit plump despite her stories
of his athleticism. Through some mysterious, baleful
intuition I recognized his hunting jacket on a kitchen
chair even before I saw his face over the dining-room
table. He follows her into the living room, general in-
troductions. He smiles a special smile at me. I cringe.
He sits at her feet as she sits across the room from me
by the fireplace, a little above him on the chair, and
Neal, like the others sitting on the floor, a face in a sea
of faces as she presides, queenly, regal, the prow of a
ship around which they constitute the waves. Her manner of introduction somehow proclaimed him, his man-

ner of sitting at her feet as well. I feel a subtle, nervous twinge go through the guests—they have sensed it, sensed Neal and myself and some displacement, some way in which his arrival has displaced me. There is the little extra burden of bearing up under ridicule. Or at least trying not to appear ridiculous.

But perhaps my inertness, my silence, is protection, the way I blend into the cushions or the wall. But of course that too is ridiculous. And ridiculous too when I find myself seated next to Neal, who has lumbered over and now squats on his haunches to talk to me. I can think of absolutely nothing to say. A crisis of inarticulateness. "I hear you're going to be doing some teaching for us." His voice is paternal, grand, as if his post entitles him to speak in avuncular fashion for the entire university. I look at him, this puffy, slightly shy young man, embarrassed perhaps as I am, but being decent for God's sake, trying, you've got to admit that. Almost liking him. My answer, which could have been witty—given the number of times I've made a botch of that course, there are ample opportunities for making my answer a joke on my own scandalous vacillation—my answer just a weak little smile and some drivel about looking forward to it. Neal then treats me to a gunner's report on courses that fail for lack of students, courses that must be canceled, courses where the instructor is sent home empty-handed "because the whole thing has to be run like a business, you know." That settles it—squatting back on his heels, he is a football player or a Vietnam veteran or a hunter beside his kill, but he is not the shy and likable young man I had conjured up a moment ago. He speaks *de haut en bas,* an administrator to a mere faculty member, a male to a female, and out of a wealth of masculine assurance and assumption that takes my breath away. How can she endure this pompous young man, how can she endure his heavy limbs and his quietly overbearing manner!

I look up to see her smiling at the two of us. Pleased to see us together. For her sake then, continuing to listen to Neal administer the university, pay its debts, arrange its priorities, and watching him later as he sits across the room, a bit spoiled-looking, a bit put out that he should have to come to this party at all, see her with other people. I understand him, even sympathize. I am also on his side as he looks with annoyance at the proper young couple on the sofa, boring everyone with academic shop talk and subservient reference to the provost. I stay apart with Crabtree and her man and their hashish, hoping a bit of it will carry me out of myself, make it possible to talk, to enjoy the party. No luck. Neal prepares to leave. Will she go with him? Or will she simply install him in Paul's bedroom and subject me to having him in the house all night? She has a cold, she says. Is that a clue, a signal for her departure? Neal disappears. And soon she tells her guests her cold is driving her off to bed, but they must stay and enjoy themselves as long as they like.

It's an impressive performance, walking out on your own party. I cannot help but admire the sangfroid with which she manages it. But now I am left to conduct this foul event—it's not my party, these are not my friends; indeed the experience has convinced me that Sita and I don't live in the same world, could never really live together at all. I do not find these people interesting, even dislike them and consider their presence intrusive. And yet on another day she could invite fifty entirely different people. So various she is, so capricious. And tonight she quietly withdrew the moment she felt like it.

The guests linger. Pia and I see to the stragglers and sit up late with a neighbor who arrived at the last moment, one of the few interesting and likable people. But it is now past one, and even this real personality, with her talk of actual life, palls and flags. We see her out and I go upstairs to find "our" bedroom empty. She has gone out with Neal. Knew it, suspected it, feared it. If I knock on the door to Paul's room, will she be there at all? Will she be there alone? Will he be there as well? Her voice calls to me, feeble, devastatingly ill, "Come in." She is by herself, very sick with a cold. I am overcome with tenderness for her, remorse.

The class files in. I have done it, have gotten this far. After a whole morning of intending to tell her I would cancel. But she was so ill it seemed impossible to proceed, and my one oblique little attempt—"What would happen if I didn't do the class after all?"—elicited a very straightforward "Then I'd lose all credibility with the provost and my department." I could go no further, though the impulse to run was on me all morning, a morning spent in hectic trips to the bank and then to the co-op for her medicines, lies to the druggist that I am she, even the lie of signing her name to some fool slip exempting them from responsibility when I innocently asked to take the medicine in ordinary containers rather than those with the elaborate and apparently standard "child-proof" tops. There is a further hassle about whether she has a co-op number. Pretending to be Sita, since I am afraid the co-op will not fill the prescription otherwise, I feel particularly silly having to telephone her for the membership number. Turns out you don't need one, but I now realize I do not have enough money for all the medicine, which costs more than the twenty-five dollars I just took out of the bank. I cannot write them a check using my own name, so must go again to the bank. All the while my inner voice is screaming, Get out of here, for God's sake, go home, leave their lousy sunshine and vegetation and prissy regulations and get back to reality Downtown.

Back from the bank, the precious medicines in hand at last, I leave her for my class, Mark having arrived to sit with her. The class files in. We have been waiting a long time in the corridor for the room to empty. I look around at their faces. Grown women—how on earth am I to be their guru? If they only knew. And the awkwardness of standing about, packed together, waiting for a room in a stuffy YMCA building. Tacky, and off-campus, the Y scarcely seems an improvement over the First Baptist. We are packed into its depressing little foyer, staring in embarrassment at each other.

Maybe this will be only another error. I start out, trying to give off energy, to swell my voice, which sounds small and ineffective, my lecture notes squirreling around on the page before me. I make some distinctions for them, playing with the notion of a feminist sensibility versus a feminine sensibility in writing, the effect of history upon artists and then of artists themselves in turn upon their society and culture and those who come after. Their attention hangs on me, they expect too much. I go on, finding there is more to say than I had imagined. A few are bored. Afraid, seeing their faces withdraw, realizing they are too far away, crowded into the back of the room. No, still alive, very much alive, all of them, by this time speaking up, challenging. I am astonished at their information, how widely they have read, how many of them write. Will I be good enough for them? And an odd little hope that they can help me, that I can learn from them, benefit from the mutual support that one of them has just mentioned.

The period draws to a close, and I am almost sorry. I have been better than this with other classes, more vital, humorous, subtle, erudite—but that I could do it at all, pull it off at this time, there's a relief in that. Even a little triumph. Afterward I go for coffee with two of the students, Janice, a young college instructor, and Virginia, a poet. We sit in a little café near the parking lot while Janice describes Anaïs Nin to us. She has met her, says she is dying now in Los Angeles. "How does one come to know such a woman?" I ask, curious about the great and the extent of their accessibility. She tells me that Nin spends her evenings answering letters from her readers. I admire, I more than admire, yet the idea appalls me. The poet has with her some leaflets advertising readings in the city, a world beyond these confines, the claustrophobic world of Indian Rock. I have now met two people who know me rather than Sita. I am lighthearted when we part, eager to buy another notebook, to write, to work, to study.

Crossing the street on this errand and suddenly believing I could teach again, make that a life. But where to find a job, the market being what it is now? Imagining myself teaching in New York, a life busy, active. No more of the loneliness of the loft and the struggle to write. A life full of people, students, colleagues, old friends fitted into a circle. Feeling confident and competent. No more of this dependency, uncertainty, homelessness. I find a few more errands, extending the time. Knowing I will miss her since she goes over to San Francisco for her own class tonight. I will get home after she's left. I even look forward to having the house to myself.

I am still floating when I drive up and see her car in front of the house, realize she is too sick to go to the city, has of course stayed home. And Mark is still in attendance. Upstairs to her room, seeing her enthroned on pillows and Mark like a son waiting on her, I wonder if I, too, return to her as to a mother. But also an enchantress, our goddess whom we serve with wine and toast and chicken soup.

Mark sits on the big corduroy couch with his shaggy hair, jeans, stocking feet. I sit on a little stool near the phonograph. A record of ballads, the mood for a drink. I bring us all wine. Mark borrows a pack of cigarettes. We smoke together. Our lady upon her pillows. Mark is silent, even more silent than I. As Sita and I chat over the day, Mark says nothing. He is a heavy presence in the room. Such a presence as I have been lately. How strange the dynamic of persons, their emanations, the effects of their mere movements or expressions. How more powerful and definitive finally than words. Mark interrupting something I am saying by slowly, awkwardly standing, going over to the bed, looking at something. He has destroyed what I said, smashed her attention, even my own concentration. Does he do this knowingly or instinctively, and what is the difference?

They have spent the day going over old papers of her—speeches, manuscripts, stories. She has made use of him to move the file cabinet out of Pia's closet and over here into "her room." The room that had been Paul's. The room she has been referring to so much lately. "The front room is mine," she tells people. I remember hearing her say it at the party, sensing Neal hear her say it. And her kids know of course, everyone around her does. Mark too now can observe the separate-bedroom principle.

I go down to warm her soup. Mark follows to heat up macaroni for himself. The food begins to burn in the pan as he forgets it. Almost unwillingly, I take it off the burner, stir it to save it for him. I am relieved to see him leaving, after one last attempt of several to borrow her car. He is pulling on his boots, ready to hitchhike. At last to be rid of him, to have him out of the way. Then I am inconsistent and regretful almost as he kisses me goodbye. How stupid of me to be so possessive. Yet his going leaves us a warm and lighted room, cozy, the intimacy of the sickroom. I have already appropriated the corduroy sofa, having envied Mark as my back ached sitting on the stool. Merely to sit with her, to read, to be together in the quiet evening.

I begin reading one of her manuscripts. It is not all that good, but that is not my interest. An introduction about a journalist "in search of a new angle," a series on the love affairs of older women with much younger men—a transparent device to tell her own story over and over again. It is Sita and Hank, Sita after she left Martin. And each of the three women is a side of herself: the plastic, high-powered, Los Angeles woman executive; the aristocratic woman moving in foreign diplomatic circles; and the one most like her in externals, a suburban housewife who follows her daughter to a commune where she meets a painter. Leaves her husband, a businessman, for the bearded artist and the countryside. The young man in each case an idealized, beautiful, erotic object, highly charged but utterly devoted. And the husband, a nonentity, a jailer. They'd had separate bedrooms for years.

Reading, I see her fantasy self, the drift of her emotions, her attitudes, her hopes and patterns, real or imagined. The pattern of husband as ogre, then rescue by a young man. She has imposed it again on this house and even on me. Separate bedrooms. Making me the husband, Neal the young savior. I tell her this and she laughs. "Neal couldn't rescue anyone from anything. He's young, he's very young. Impossibly young." "But don't you see?" "Not at all, don't be silly." I go on reading. What had hurt me so savagely when I first realized it, this parallel with a jailer husband—this blast against my womanhood, my love for her, this slander—now also seems tedious, simpleminded.

Very well, teach the course and leave. Till then live on your own, I tell myself. Picking up another manuscript, this one rather better, one she is working on now, a grim little parable of the war in Italy. She had protested, "No, don't read it now, some other time." "Would you rather talk," I asked, "or are you only being polite and would really like me to read it?" "I'm being polite." She is couched on her pillow, watching me. But when I leave off reading for a moment, I discover my eyes examine other parts of the room now, they do not run for hers like little fishes seeking food. I feel contained.

I feel free of her. The class and reading her story, with its naked and simple illusions, have freed me, left me a space for indifference, for neutrality, disengagement, even for self. I go willingly to my bedroom, suggesting my own withdrawal. "You must be tired now." She is standing, on her way back from the bathroom, and she hugs me. Inside her hug and feeling it merely as pleasant, as warmth without necessity. Lovely new indifference. "Perhaps if I'm better tomorrow I can come sleep with you. Get out of this hospital." She calls this after me as I close the door. "If I let you," I wanted to say. Wanting so much to say it even minutes after the time has passed.

But if I withdraw, it may be only another blind alley, another defeat. Remembering what she used to say of Martin, that he left her alone all the time, was married to his job, to mere money. By answering her departure of spirit with one of his own, he only contracted another fault, something else to be reported as a reason that he was impossible to live with, sterile, without feeling. "If I let you," I had wanted to say, even by teasing to imply that I too had choice, assumed it. But would I? Would I merely heat and want her,

helpless in wanting, crippled by the fact of loving,
handicapped by that, certain to lose. And how I
loathe making a game of it, oneupmanship, maneuver-
ing, outsmarting. How that cheapens it all.

Going away is better, cleaner, it does not profane
the love. But I cannot go away now, am staying,
committed to staying. By the class. Yet the class makes
a turning point. Reading a bit before I sleep, I realize
that tonight, strangely, for the first time, I am at peace.
Remembering how just last night I read a few pages
on Magritte without registering a word and was utterly
miserable, a misery hard now even to recall.

The feeling holds. When I wake and cross the hall
to the bathroom, past her bedroom, opening its door
first to wake her gently, I can still feel it. That the class
has made me alive and almost indifferent to her. I
look at her sleeping face as at a friend's, but not as
a creature looks upon its god. Its slave master. Very
well, that's the point. We are all moderns and slavery
is not progressive. I look at her face again. No, it is
something new, if not indifference, then it's the cool
thrill of liberty I feel.

And I feel well. As after an illness. I am someone
again, if only the someone that conducts that class—
at least a mind, some personality, a certain modicum
of effective intelligence, purpose. I was swallowed by
her and now I am coughed up; swallowed by her
world, her friends, her family, her job. Not their
fault, of course, but they simply drowned me. Brushing
my teeth, I remember someone in New York, my friend
Alita. I imagine conversations with Alita when I return, long afternoons in her studio, the cats on the rug,
teacups, talking as equals. Delighted by that feeling,
able to remember it again. Friendship, one's peers. The
class has done this for me, restored me to the world
I'd forgotten.

As I wash my face, the cold water restores to me my
dreams of last night. Hectic, wonderful things. Alita
telling me she had balled with Ken and another lady,
Ken balling them both, and she loved it. I said I would
never do that with Fumio, I would surely be too jeal-

ous. But then in the next sequence of the dream joyously balling with Rip and another woman. And then woke to realize that all this has never happened and that Rip is a rich SoHo art dealer now, not the gamboling blond athlete I used to know. But the dream had its sap, its pagan ease, its out-of-time, out-of-space pleasures, like a carnival and the people spread out in caves beyond the city, lecherous but languid, flesh shining in the misty evening light.

On waking I wondered vaguely if a man would want me or am I too old? Forty. Sita nearly fifty and has her men, all too many of them. Realizing that I think her the better woman: body, dress, manner. Beginning to take account of my subjection, this vast and monstrous sea of inferiority in which I have washed about for three weeks now. Emerging, I sit on my bed in the room that is mine now, rather liking that. Sherman's oil again, my own drawings, my desk, my big red Mexican sweater hung on the door, the beautiful blue and white bedspread from Greece. Even the carpet no longer haunts me. Perhaps what I had been so in terror of was living here alone with her, having nothing else but that enslavement to her. Now it is not that alone. There is the class. There is even some of myself returned again, coming back.

The piggy-back plant hangs high over my desk. The early-morning sky, gray clouds with the sun lighting them underneath. It is the first time I have been up before her in the morning, had the house and the day to myself.

Today is like yesterday. She was still sick then, too, the two of us home all day together, yet curiously apart, estranged, remote. She in her room and I in mine, the hours going by. I work, she sleeps or lies awake by herself, not needing me, not wanting me. She does not call out to me for things. I must suggest the soup, the tea, the apples. She looks tired and very old. She does not call me, she calls others, thinking aloud to herself that her friend Edith might be good at massage, or that Mary Jane could bring her papers from the office. When I go near her room, I feel a need to knock, to stand in the doorway and seek permission. We are in a curious place, we who used to be lovers, so headlong in it once, rapt, intoxicated. Earlier selves I can hardly recall or believe in now, and remember with wonder and astonishment.

Now neither of us speaks. The effort of repressing so much leaves us nothing to say. All talk is dangerous. I rebel against this continuously, go near her room, meaning to say something, anything—meaning to connect. And seeing her I cannot, something is forbidding in her tired face. Of course she is ill. The tedium of illness. Stopping off at the market yesterday, buying two steaks in the hope that she would be well enough to relish them. She wasn't. Only more soup. I ate yoghurt and waited for another night. But even entering the market I could feel that special foreboding you feel with illness in the house, foreknowledge that meals will not be celebrations, that the evening will go by unmarked by that coming together. When you can't even look forward to dinner, life loses most of its color, we used to say on the Bowery, an adage out of our bohemian days, our art world, bon vivant life. How far away it all seems now. It took so long for me to understand that her hedonism was not the same as ours. Not until I had learned much from her, a new way of life dedicated to pleasure, to the sun and California weather and the life apart from the job. But I don't have a job, my work is my life. There is always this difference between us, growing larger over time.

How gloomy the day is through the windows. I've finally gotten my table before the windows. Not the old ones of course, the ones in what is now Pia's room, though she hasn't slept there in weeks, but here in "my room"—what had once been our bedroom. Here with the same rains coming every day, the same lowering clouds, trees and bushes blowing, the city across the bay only a morose and steely blue. The rainy season. Last night when I came home from the market she seemed inaccessible. No wine, no music as when Mark was here, no recognition of the evening and its customary warmth, leisure. I took myself away, couldn't stand sitting on the little stool at her side, holding her prisoner with a presence she didn't want. "If you need anything, or even if you just want to talk, call." Almost calm, indifferent. An independence I achieved by watching the evening news downstairs. And then she astonished me, coming into the living room in flannel jacket and bathrobe, establishing herself on the couch, joining me of her own volition.

Pia and Paul are to play for an art opening in Berkeley tonight. Pia seems to have blown it already by not showing up for rehearsal, failing to get the guitar she was to borrow since she had never fixed the broken string on her own, and finally by leaving Paul stuck out in Marin County without a ride. I am happy with Sita, warm, at home, snuggled into a domestic moment watching a documentary on the Second World War, but I must go out, attend the opening, hear them play, be their audience—if they have even gotten there.

And the opening is a sorry sight. Six people when I arrive, soon reduced to four. Pitifully, there are no less than three homemade cakes for the guests who never arrive. I feel sorry for the artist and spend a long time looking at her pictures. Even sorry for the kids, who did come after all, and are even playing, though carelessly and without much effort. How their music fails to interest me at all now and yet how bewitched I was by it once. In the beginning. Disenchantment. How it all "went" with her when I first knew her, these beautiful children making music, the fragile and haunted daughter who sang, the funny and talented son who played guitar. And this lovely woman who was their mother, my lover. Sat at their feet and begged them to play, and she beamed, proud of them. Loving her was loving them, inheriting them as a gift. In all of her life there was but one thing I envied then, telling her once, If I envy you at all, feel poorer in any way, it is that I envy you your children. "You will share them," she had said.

But they were not to be shared, their allegiance was to her and her only, tough as the rind of a fruit. And I lost my sheen after the breakdown and grew discredited in their eyes as she passed through the stages of abandoning me. Last fall when she came home from

Europe and told Sherman it was over, she must have
told the kids as well; I was never expected to show up
again. And they must know this is merely an aftereffect, like the last ripple in a pond long after the stone
has fallen. Paul knows his bed is warmed, she's taken
care to let him know that, and it must have registered.
Yet Pia must still have some feeling for me, greeting
me with a full performance of Brenda Starr: the neat
new job she may get, the super bosses she may have,
the big commissions, the hot salary—"Unless this
chick who knows Dictaphone beats me to it. They were
all so taken with my magnetic personality they just
clean forgot to ask if I knew Dictaphone." I smile and
try to be encouraging. She is so lovable, so vulnerable,
doing her "routine" for us, acting it out, the bosses and
the dewy-eyed new secretary, and a moment later,
dancing the Charleston while singing a raunchy song.
Lovable and yet so tragic, with such predestined sorrow. The job won't happen, the heroin may come
again in this life she's now taken up with Dan at the
Mission Hotel. Pia, her lovely face, the long, elegantly
slender body, her ridiculous fashionable shoes. That
face, so perfect in its Saxon beauty—how proud of that
Sita is, that miracle of blond and blue to have come
from her own darkness, her Indio blood.

When I first knew them all, having lunch in the city
with Pia, high up in the sun at Ghirardelli Square,
looking out over the water, Pia telling me her mother
had pushed the Anglo look in her, worshipped it as
all she could never be here, the fair ideal of this foreign place. And Pia had the singing lessons, dancing
lessons, acting lessons, was a cheerleader, went the
route, even modeled in New York. Then rebelled with
Leary's band of outlaws, Janis's crowd. Pia blaming
her mother, then not blaming her, understanding the
needs she was meant to satisfy vicariously. The sun
shone on us. We were full of compassion and the most
profound understanding that day. We were frivolous.

Which is the greater truth, that day of golden possibility or this evening of preordained failure? I know
the first time was joy in living, Sita's love converting
every moment, sight, incident into radiance. And now

this life extended after death, the sight of the empty living room as I open the door. Back to her bed.

She thanks me profusely for having gone, knowing I didn't want to. I am touched, feeling sad little afterlights of love as she puts an arm around my shoulder, apologizing for being sick. Reassuring her, comforting, offering to rub her back with lotion.

And the sight of her back, naked and beautiful, surprises me with love. I thought I had stifled it, but there was the ache of it, the pull of it again. A flowering of lovely freckles, the firm delicious flesh, feeling it under my fingers, my eyes loving the wonderful lines of it, especially as it disappears under the covers into her white buttocks, the slenderness of waist and then their hidden fullness. I would lift the covers and see their round white flesh, the supreme moment when they part and come together, that so sensual ridge, declivity of flesh. The strange little mound of flesh she has just at the base of her spine—I would know her body in the dark by that sign. Stroking the small of her back, lusting to go below it, catching a glimpse of my desire by pulling off the covers for a moment. Satisfied and unsatisfied. Wanting her past speaking and into tears and then refraining.

Then back to her shoulders, the back of her neck, doing the work of a friend as well as a lover. I feel the tension in the shoulders ease, hear her sighs of gratification. Strange way to make love.

Bidding her good night. She promised again to be well enough to sleep with me tomorrow. "If I invite you," I said, softly smiling at her. Very likely she did not hear me. And I wonder if my daring has paid off at all. Today she is more distant than ever. So where have we got to now? Stasis. The rains. The city in mist. Rain against the window glass, its strange irregular patterns, the suburban roofs of Berkeley. I have lost my opportunity to leave of my own will, lost it permanently. When April closes I will leave anyway, of course. But the chance to flee, to walk out on a bad job—that's over. The class keeps me here until something like the original expected period of time is over.

When I parked my car in the driveway, I sat behind the wheel a long time, dazed, wondering what I should do with it when I leave. Because I will not be coming back. Nervous a little, even saying that, speaking the words. Teaching here every winter into spring, the old original plan, that's over. Over with the emotion that might have made it possible.

Rain striking the tin roof. The tulips she bought for me upright on my desk. And in the great shallow black dish, a group of camellias that she picked and arranged for me last Sunday morning. Like the tulips, rare deviations into the past, its old ceremonies. They rebuke me now. Ingrate. I hear her in the bathroom, the splash of her shower behind me, the rain before, this afternoon too has passed without speaking. A few words over the errands I have run—the bank, shopping. Giving her a telephone message just as she steps out of the shower, I come upon her nakedness, her legs below her sex and its poignant little patch of hair, how slender her thighs, almost piteous the way they part below the hair, how they hollow out a space, seem so fragile outlining the small void below the pubis. Has she gotten thinner through her illness, I wonder, or was there always this defenseless little space between her legs? Loving it just as I am surprised by it, almost a voyeur, catching sight of the forbidden, something never revealed before in all this time. She stands with the towel in her hands, drying her face, the absurd puff of a shower cap on her head, overtaken in her nakedness, her vulnerability. Bothered in her illness, with business, with telephone messages. I feel a great protective tenderness, then I feel nothing.

Her face by candlelight. Sita peeling an orange and making fun of Henry Kissinger. "You missed the news. The fat little man's off again for Egypt and his big wife's bought herself a pith helmet. A huge inexplicable veil all over it like mosquito netting. Like a giraffe in disguise." After her shower she put on a long skirt and went downstairs. Instant action in the kitchen, beef stew begun and the whole house put in order in minutes. She is well again, or almost well. She comes back to me, talks, laughs, gives off energy. The silence, the despair evaporate. We have a full-fledged, comfortable dinner, with all her graces. Wine and candles and steak and good talk. It was probably how she talked at dinner that first made me love her; a love affair is all those evenings and the light of candles and the talk and the wine and her eyes suddenly at the end of a sentence. I can think of things to say again. By candlelight I can adore her, the classic loveliness of her face in profile, and her wicked, humorous talk.

Afterward she rests her head on my knees while I read, this delightful arrangement her own idea. But first she invites me to sit next to her on the couch. For days I have sat at a distance, the distance of her cold and her coldness. So close to her body now and our hands in each other's.

"Hang on to me, lady." I look at her, pleased by her saying that, but still not sure. "What do you mean?" "Probably that I want to hang on to you." "So?" "So." And then the subject changes, interrupted by a movement or some household banality impulsively remembered. Earlier she had spread herself along the sofa and, looking up at me, said suddenly, "I love you," transfixing me where I stood. "Thank you" was all I could say, not knowing, as I am forever not knowing now, how to respond, how much. Even whether I should at all. Or whether to go on withdrawing as a tactic. Absurd, hateful pretenses of love —you love or you don't—so why the game and the chess moves and the sleights? Or whether to withdraw in earnest, to go on extricating myself from love, attachment, dependence—seeing this becoming possible perhaps now. My indifference, friendly, even serene, as I go to bed alone this night just as the last. And the nights before it.

The lights of San Francisco across the bay, and above them a strange supernatural light, an aureole in the mist. The rain has cleared for a moment, and above the city and its million jeweled buildings, this peculiar halo of mysterious light, not a reflection of the diamonds in the windows of skyline, the sumptuous buildings crackling across the water, not that. Something other, some other prescient force lighting up the sky above them like a halo in an old picture.

But then I wake, caught, as by something unpleasant suddenly remembered, to realize that she may come back, may sleep with me tomorrow night. Would I have the courage to refuse her? Never. Could I, however sweetly, ask her not to come? Thwart her? No, I know already that would be beyond me. And if she offered lovemaking, then what? Looking back, I realize that I never have refused her. A few times in the past, yes, from being tired, but this was not seen as refusal by either of us, merely lack of response. Until this stay here, we had neither of us ever put it on the line, come to an open difference over it, a flat denial. "Learn to say no," she taunted me last week, the phrase still like a slap. And if I did, would she cease to ask? That is what I fear, just that. So little faith in my own powers to be coy, to attract, even to distract. I who have been on hand (grimacing to myself at the pun) or on tap anyway, every moment. There for her when Neal isn't, or the children, or committees, or Mark, or the job or the countless friends and well-wishers. I who have stood by, hangdog or carefully neutral, her shadow, her nuisance.

I sympathize with her impatience. Placed as she is, cooped up with a lovelorn soul she does not exactly love. Yes, of course, I can understand. Taken all around, she has been kind, remarkably forbearing. For someone who does not love, to be immured with one who does is torture. But do I love? Or love enough for it to be so described? Though this is far too simple. Not only in that perhaps she does *indeed* love—to some extent, surely—but also in that *I* do not—or not entirely. I cannot leave my own ambivalence out of account, my longing for New York and my own life, my utter horror of staying here permanently or for any length of time. "Married" to her or to this house. For someone who does not love, to be immured with one who does is torture—was that last spring? Would it be this one too if she were still infatuated with me? Isn't it simply that she is the first to know the end of love, or maybe only the first to be honest and admit it? Don't

I know it's over too, over within me—and am merely unwilling to let it end? Not wanting it to die, I proclaim its continued life by prolonging it as mere misery.

Mere vaporizing. This was supposed to be a life together. Maybe what drives me to frenzy is my failure before my own absolutes. Should I have loved her entirely and forsaken New York and, cutting all ties, come here to live—as she once wanted? But does no longer. Good enough then. She would never consider making such sacrifices for me—there had been one reckless offer to come East to live with me when I was so depressed and near suicide at the farm one Christmas, safe I'd never take her up on it, make her lose her job—no, it was obviously I who had to leave everything behind and come to her. Good thing I didn't. Or did she cease to want that only when I failed to give it, the turning point last spring when I took the loft? Did she just despair, give up, and not care any more? And will I do likewise, tiring finally, worn down finally, acceding finally to the separate bedrooms, the careful partition of lives like the cellophane and cardboard in the packaging of especially perishable goods?

I'm not going to Los Angeles. She flies there tomorrow for a conference, had asked me along, and almost without thinking or knowing what the exact date was, I had said yes. Because it would be a chance to be with her, share one of those many weekends away. But a few nights ago, when she reminded me it was this weekend, I did a remarkable thing. Said I'd rather not. Would prefer to spend the Saturday preparing for my class. The trip is expensive, she would be busy all day, and faculty clubs are not good love nests. No, I'd prefer to spend Saturday working. Astonishing myself. The forbearance. Astonishing myself still further by acting to please myself—I really would prefer to stay home, work, see a film in the evening. Or maybe see Sherman. Suddenly there are so many things to do. A week ago it was hard to get through the day. Now I have resources, am beginning to stand alone. Still I have doubts, a moment looking around the kitchen, how desolate it always seems when she's gone. I wonder if I should have said yes.

When she returns from San Francisco after a long meeting, she asks about my day. Splendid, I tell her. "I finished that article on Sherman and had dinner with Susan Griffin." In fact, it was a wonderful day, sunny at last after the maddening stretch of rain, the joy of writing again, finishing something, typing it up, getting it ready to send off. The cure of work, its health. And the delight of another writer's company, a drink at the Marina in the full glory of the sea, sashimi at a little Japanese restaurant. Home to do a bit more work, even write some letters. Feeling cured, myself again.

When she came home she sat on my bed, reading my new piece and scratching her flea bites, Limbo's fleas, which eat us now that the dog has followed Paul out of the house. Next she stands in the door, talking to me. Then sits on a little wooden stool in the hallway, just beyond the door, as if there were an invisible line she is forbidden to cross. I laugh at her, the sight of her scratching away at the flea bites, laughing with delight, laughing a long time. "What in hell are you doing, are you forbidden to cross the threshold?" "Well, it's your room and I respect your privacy." Have we come to this with her separate-bedroom nonsense? Requests to knock and enter, etiquette. Suddenly the whole thing seems so viciously silly, tiresome. Too tedious to hurt any more.

Because I have mentioned a crick in my neck from typing, she offers to rub my back. I smile at the transparency of it all, pleased as well as amused. All evening I have thought she might deign to sleep with me. But she has to get up at six, still has a bit of a cold. When she recedes into her own room I am content. I did not have to face the decision, should she have asked, and did not ask her myself. Content then when she is off in her bed, her room and my room, content in my room to read late, to look out the windows at San Francisco's lights and water, to get up and write a note reminding myself to buy raw fish for Saturday, the night she will be away.

I had brought her daffodils, poking about the little wooden cart in front of the flower shop on Solano, wondering what I could get for the cash I had with me, realizing only gradually that it was Valentine's Day. Sentimental crap of course. Feeling a bit silly as I carried them up to the front door, then completely disarmed by the delight in her face. "How yellow they are, Kate, how much like spring!" The spirit of the day takes over, asserts itself against all better judgment, all hanging back. "I have something for you too, dear lady," she sings at me, brandishing a champagne bottle. Silver paper, great pink ribbon, she has been to Barber and Stewart, had it gift-wrapped. All for me. She has remembered. What if I hadn't absentmindedly bought those daffodils? She would have beaten me at what I had thought was my game.

But it is hers tonight as well. She has become the benevolent dictator, the fairy godmother. We'll have dinner at the Marina, she says, celebrate. The lilt of her at times like this, the call in her eyes, in the movement of her head. First we'll have a drink, wait till the sunset is just ripe before we watch it across the water. "The champagne now?" "No, let's save it for later; when we come back we'll build a fire, drink it before we go to bed." Something's up. Suddenly she is all romance, witchery, good fortune. Mellow the talk, the mood, the fine evening; like the past come back. She is restored to me in stages, in a glance, in a smile, in the full warm brown of her eyes. I do not want to believe but I feel myself sliding, persuaded. At dinner she is flirtatious, saying again that she does not want to lose me, her eyes full on me, the power of them open and compelling. I am being called, beckoned, even pleaded with. She is courting me from across the table, with a look or a smile or a joke, with teasing and reminiscing, with the flattering recall of a detail, an occasion, a friend.

The lilt of her at times like this, the call in her eyes, in the movement of her head. The pleading nearly in those fine brown eyes, the pathos of this aging and beautiful woman asking me not to leave her. "It's that I never felt or, rather, never felt before that you had any respect for me." "Sita, don't be absurd." "It's true. You never gave me the feeling that I was worth anything in your eyes." Maneuvers, I think, of course she must know how I admire her in everything, I have told her so a thousand times. And she has even used it against me. "I had to make you respect me." "You have only made me miserable." "Until this time, until you came out here this time, I've never been anything more than a shadow in your life, tagging along, someone in the background." "That's ridiculous." "It's how I feel. It's how I've always felt." I look at the great beauty in her eyes, the utter sincerity, the unimpeachable conviction. All completely of the moment, all true, all false. She has persuaded herself of this during the past five minutes and believes it completely. Five minutes ago or hence, she will be imperious again, mouthing speeches about her freedom, or full of sentiment, persuading me that what we suffer now is merely a moment in our long relationship, a mere segment in the band of time that unites us, will unite us always, each passage like a pattern in a bolt of cloth, now one color, now another, now a leaf, now an arabesque, now a flower or a hill. "We have come to a very wonderful place in our relationship," she goes on. "We have come to a point of struggle where all the initial conflicts had to explode, be resolved. We will be more equal now, we've reached a point of separateness, independence. We've grown up in a sense." "I have no more expectations," I tell her, afraid even to say this, controlling the bitterness and the soreness of what I say. But she does not hear me, telling me again how deeply she loves me, the one great passionate love of her life.

There is no resisting her eyes, the softness of her voice, its little thrill of an accent speaking a word, softening it, making it intimate, nearly as intimate as the Italian words she used to say making love to me— "*tesoro bello,*" "*ti voglio bene,*" the most intimate sounds I had ever heard. I even forget that she no longer says them. Listening to her now, the gesture of her throat courting me, the liquid of her eyes pleading or snapping into the flirtation of wit, the coaxing of her humor, her mischievousness. Even her infidelities are proofs of her love; ploys, sleights, gestures to strengthen the fiber of this wonderful creation that lies between us.

We are at our old place on the Marina, Solomon Grundy's, with the sea and the city spread out beyond the glass walls, the gulls sweeping, the last sailboats hurrying home, their great wings brushing by our windows. Beauty of sky, sea, the lights of the bridges, and the city. This is our place, we are at home, each great moment of our affair played out somehow, echoed against this scene which is as much Sita as it is itself. She who is always California for me. If I should lose it . . . a tear stinging the thought. But before me now her whole self dedicated to the idea of retrieving me. Yes, I have expectations. "There's a Persian proverb I'll tell you when we're comfortably installed in front of the fire," she says.

Just as I light the fire, New York interrupts us with a quarrel and a petition, long, convoluted prose recited over three thousand miles of telephone wire and demanding immediate attention: prisoners and denunciations, informers and accusations, arrests, positions of principle. I want very much to say, "Look, I just happen to be busy making love now and cannot quite enter your mood." But I don't say it; no one ever does.

After this, the peace of the fire and the room and our quietude. We have hours to make love. Leisure. I will wait and let her seduce me, sitting back from the flames on a low stool next to the red Chinese table, watching the fire, sipping champagne as, gradually, by the slowest and most insidious of motions, her hand winds its way up the full sleeve of my gown. It is so deliberate, so agreed upon, so assured. The entire evening is prelude only to this moment, pledged to it, all preparation and diplomacy toward this consummation. Our talk is only a summons to this actualization.

Remembering how she took me sitting down, sitting on a low stool, her hand reaching under my long skirt, entering me as I sit. Legs apart, perched forward but still sitting. The little straw stool, drumlike, made of string and bamboo, curiously and elaborately fashioned

over a straw frame. Pakistani, fruit of one of our enchanted shopping sprees at the import houses of San
Francisco, on fine mornings two years ago when I first
furnished my apartment in Sacramento, the great luxurious weekend visits of our first love, rapt hours of
lovemaking at the Sausalito Hotel. Now the fire and
her figure crouched on the floor next to me, her hand
searching, reaming, digging within me. Somehow it is
particularly exciting that I sit, that I am sitting just
above her as she reclines on the rug, her arm extending up inside me. Sitting. The frisson of perversity in
it. Forcing myself almost to go on sitting, which is difficult. So excited I am, so much I long to sprawl on the
floor under her so she may hover above me, nearly
mount me, and my legs flung wide and open. But sitting still, or if not still, yet maintaining myself on the
little stool through the pure ecstasy of her explorations,
her little touches, her experiments, her caresses, her
attacks. Those long, strong fingers plunging into me,
then withdrawn to hang about the lips of love, the
small bud of clitoris erect, swollen, full almost to crying out. And still upon this little stool, this curious
sedate little chair, gasping into her mouth, take me,
take me, our tongues crowding into each other, divine
intercourse each its penis and protrusion, or turn about,
womb and cave-like the mouth arches and waits the
other's tongue, pleading and prodding to fill, overwhelm.

Still perched upon the little stool. And finally can
bear no more confinement but must have the floor, the
great red Persian under me and the fire before me as I
groan under her full thrusts, having quietly slid the
stool away, slowly surrendering the strange gratification it gave, its limits and discipline. Now for the full
open force of her, the full stretch of my legs, buttocks
tense and taut as they raise me against her terrible
entry, its power and fire. Hot you have made me, so
hot, I whisper. Her tongue in my ear for answer,
coquetry. Knowing so well her mastery, her authority.
I would give her everything, blood, self, life. Open for
her, whispering into her ear as she takes the higher
inner ridge of flesh in me, wrings it and makes it come

like rain, juices weep upon her hand, telling her as she brings one cloudburst after another from this strange hidden height, telling her I am hers, her creature her thing her woman her cunt her own to have, do unto, surrendering with each gush of that pink and hidden place she has only to press and it flows, surrendering self as well as body.

And now I will have her. Wanting to open her upon the floor, take her on the rug. There, then. Thirsting for her, already imagining how she will taste and feel, how it will be entering her, the joy of it, the great tenderness I bring to her body, subtle against her nipples, moved beyond myself, kissing her throat, wanting her now. "Wait till we get upstairs, I'm the staid type, I like beds." But when we got there she stops to open Emily's note. The child's block letters on the page. She hands it to me, turning away: "Dear Grandma I just wanted to say thank you very very much for the Little Lulu valentine card. Well I'm running out of things to say. Love Emily." Impossible not to smile. But she is weeping. Lost to me now. The sight of little Emily being loaded onto the plane, the sordid hamburger joint near the BART station where we tried to cheer her up, the odor of the coffee urns, aura of small-town bus stations and proletarian sorrow. Emily in her winter coat waving goodbye as Pia hurried her along and away. Grief has removed Sita miles from the woman of a moment ago. Grief and other people, dear, close, and with better claims. They have all left her now. A month ago she was a matriarch presiding over a home bursting with family, now there is only me against her loneliness. I share her sadness; loving her, I feel a strange little pain over all partings and separations, like the knowledge of death, but I want her back, my lover again. Not possible. She is gone.

Waking, I fight the sadness of every waking here, the moments before I beat down panic, assure myself I am safe, that the sun is shining and I am recovering myself, learning to survive. But she is gone, the bed is already empty. "Phony," the word coming up out of my subconscious, I hardly recognize it for a moment.

"Phony, she's phony." Come on, have you no gratitude for last night, for all she gave? But that is the point. I was seduced, won over again, coaxed back into the cage only to be abandoned there again. Nonsense, she's just gone for one day, she'll be back from L.A. tomorrow. A pleasant day by myself, study, some first-rate Hawaiian tuna, if I can find it, eat it raw for dinner, a film. And she's restored to me tomorrow morning. We are going to the museum in the afternoon and to see Susan's play in the evening. Sita has already seen it but is going again for my sake.

The note is waiting for me on the ice-box door. I don't even read it right away, imagining at first it's the usual "Beautiful Lady, etc.," the charming and inevitable little message admonishing me to enjoy the day and meet her plane at such and such an hour. And then incredulously reading: "After consulting my schedule I find that I will have to stay over an extra day in Los Angeles and so won't be back until Monday morning." "Consulting her schedule," "discovering" she'll have to stay another day. Lies. So Neal will join her there? So there will be no Sunday together at all. "Due to flight schedules" she cannot be home until Monday. The whole weekend without her, the whole weekend alone. How can she do this after last night? Didn't it exist for her, was she only adventuring? Neal will be just as interesting an adventure on Sunday.

I remember when I suggested the Beat Show at the museum and wanting to see the play, I remember saying then—in my own room, out of sight, even with a grin—"We could go somewhere else, or maybe you might want to see Neal that night since you've already been to the play?" Hearing her miraculously drawl back that no, she'd be pleased to go with me. Lies. And when did she change her mind? When did she call him? Had she arranged it with him before last night and our feast, our lovemaking? Neal. Or someone else? Someone there in Los Angeles. Why not tell me, why not give me the truth, at least that? Because this is "kindness"? Then this hateful little note blasting the weekend and all its hopes, hopes built since yesterday. Built on lovemaking, built on new tendernesses, dependencies, the ties of the flesh, the feel of her in my hands, the quick of me hot under her fingertips. Only a new trap, a new deficiency. God, why did I whisper those bits of folly, that I was hers, her woman, in friction and heat vowing that it was hers, this place in me, entered and held, her "house," she'd laughed in my ear, taking me. What a fool to give myself. She'd made no such commitments, simply enjoyed it.

And what can I do? Passing the Mixmaster on the way to the bathroom, its aluminum bowl registering irrelevantly out of the corner of my eye. Prisoner all weekend of this empty kitchen, these meaningless objects. Why didn't I go with her down there? What a mistake that was, that little notion of independence. Nothing, I can do nothing. Am helpless, impotent, the initiative is always taken from me. She acts and I react. This is subjection. And how clever of her to have been the one to bring up the idea of "respect" last night, insisting that I did not respect her. Even mentioned the word "subjection," that we had never been equals before, that she used to feel everything revolved too much around me. She has certainly changed all that if it were ever so in the first place. But how clever to steal a march, appropriate these very complaints to herself, put me in the position of assuring her of the depth of my respect. Monstrous and feudal respect. Virtual despotism. I am her inferior in everything now.

And then the note stymies me again, staggers me with its duplicity, its smug hit-and-run language. Like the routine of telling me she'll call me from the office. How do I get through this weekend, rebuild enough self-sufficiency to last through it, enough films, enough reasons to visit the city? And all the usual bland talk last night that we will be lovers always, for years and years, permanently, whether together or apart, this long and splendid relationship. No, we will not be lovers after I leave, nine weeks from now it is over. And yet she can't give me her free time even now. Next weekend is her committee's workshop in the mountains. Friday, Saturday, and Sunday, all three

days. And who will it be then? Neal, Walter, who is
going to attend? "Such good friends for so many years
—probably because we've never slept together." She
may elect to change that. There's also Percy. You'll
go nuts thinking these thoughts. Stop.

Remembering how she took me sitting on the little
straw stool. How good it was, knowing she would
make love to me, knowing I would get that, have that
again, that it was certain, the luxury of time. Folderol.
Bullshit.

Look out the window, it's magnificent weather. The
city glistens across the water, beckoning. You're in
California, even if it's empty and without purpose. The
sun of spring. There's good work to do, places to go,
a glorious weekend. Absurd to mope around and be
tied to her. How much better to be free, to be myself,
whole, new. Very possible, this new independence,
very possible, this new self every day closer within my
reach. An end to being haunted, to neuroticism. Love
is ridiculous, Sherman and I agree over the phone. She
is leaving Marguerite. Soon I will be leaving Sita,
though it is hardly the same thing.

Chewing it over in my mind. And on paper. The
blue notebook, the one out of sequence, the one I
can ramble through, the one for problem solving and
obsessions. And the things most difficult to say. Sex,
for example, my continuous sense of exasperation and
defeat there. Is this what we fight over? Over sex?
How undignified. She resists me, will not let me make
love to her. Will not let my passion inspire her, holds
out against my love and defeats me. Even these terms,
how demeaning, how distant from love itself, how
redolent of war and struggle and hostility. That it can
come to this, this plague and vexation and under-
current of animosity. When what I began with, the
emotion, the reaching out, the desire and the urge to
touch, was so different, so flushed with tenderness.
And then it is turned back, snubbed, thwarted, mortified, and defeated. I will never get her back. I will
never have her completely, entirely open to me, laid
bare and open, a road panting and waiting and want-

ing me as I am, completely hers. Instead, I am the one saying it, even against my will and principles, theories and scruples, all the rest mere nonsense when she enters me, saying aloud or crying it in my mind—I'm yours. Your cunt your clitoris your heaving thigh and belly, your cheek of ass, your anus, your vulva, its soft thick flesh turned to clinging velvet turned to soft butter, waiting like a survivor alone on an island waving at a ship, waiting for the rescue of the stroke of your hand.

But she does not want me the same way. Only the brief permission of entry, the few moments of my skill, artless and without direction, the soft sigh of her finishing. I want to spread her limbs and eat her, devour her for hours, savor the sweetness of her odor and her taste. But she has no such ambitions. Always in my unsatisfied mind, always in my thirsty hurt unconscious, only there shall I open her legs and the little dark mouth and sup and dine and drink, the brown legs open only in my mind, the terrible sweetness of her soft mouse-colored mound, the tender hair. Only the mind can have her heave and struggle with passion, cry out for more and more and all: entry, tongue and fingers burrowing, opening further, taking her anus as well as the cleft below the thatch of hair, tongue laving all. Even the forbidden, turning her over, caressing the beautiful globes of her buttocks, smooth perfect shapes, stroking them over and over again and taking her, entering slow and moist and gentle.

But it is just this I cannot do. Just this abandonment I cannot bring about. Her ardor is for me, or for her own magnificent powers as a lover, her mastery, her control, the perfection of force and intimacy in her fingers, their speaking power over me. But not as the beloved, not as the one given to passion, surrendered to emotion and desire, helpless for it, lusting and craving and needing. No, she does not need. She gives. And when it pleases her. Otherwise not. So I do not initiate, I wait. And the waiting is my resentment, my continuous frustration, my grief. I rage and grumble: this is unequal, this is unilateral, this is without reciprocity.

In sex one wants or one does not want. And the grief, the sorrow of life is that one cannot make or coerce or persuade the wanting, cannot command it, cannot request it by mail order or finagle it through bureaucratic channels. And I live with her knowing she does not finally want me. And have the humility or cowardice or weakness or despair to go on living with her in the hope that it will change.

I examine the past, searching for clues. Was it different during the days in Sacramento, the first wild wonderful days? Those first two nights probably I never noticed, so overcome by the way she made love to me, the power in her fingers. Their articulate voice came later. At first it was merely their force. No one had ever used such force within me, surely no woman. I was stunned, almost afraid. It would destroy me, cripple me. And yet I could bear it. Just bear it. And then it became easier and easier. For I learned to listen to her hands, apprehend what the fingers said, talking to me, each thrust, each minute or subtle move a whole essay of love, a sentence of passion, fierce, naïve, romantic, manly or womanly, intimate, sister-like, the lust of a stranger or a mate. Sometimes I would still the heave of lust and lie very quietly with her inside me barely moving, charting my interior, which I had never so understood before, discovering new crevices, hearing her fingers' blood beating against the cervix, her fingertips discovering a shield near the rear of the lower portion of the canal which when touched caused automatic spasm. This is the place of the orgasm, we thought, marking it in our minds. And I marked it too in her body. But how open was she then? Wasn't the emphasis then too upon her making love to me? And upon her scars and bruises, the disfigured clitoris that I loved with a fiercer love because it had suffered every crime and indignity and I would avenge them all, heal with the fine euphoria of my adoration. What arrogance. I could not heal it. Now I can scarcely rouse it. She who will let Neal's great penis, or some other's, enter here, an object of a size and force that must surely hurt, will not or will only rarely let my mere finger enter, my soft and adoring tongue genuflect and worship. Having to live with that.

Every morning when I wake I search for the sign. Waking is terrible. Out of dreams so dark, so irrational, waiting for the clue of today. Imagining it will come in a word, in a thing recalled or formulated, in some line or direction taken. And then there is only the good clear sky, and the bewildered fear subsides; it is a fine day, it is Sunday. I am still alive, well, sane, have little to fear, much to look forward to. The city, the museum, a visit with Sherman in the afternoon, the theater in the evening. It's all planned, programmed.

Making breakfast alone, I grow philosophic. I've simply been a victim of jealousy; ignoble, the most ignoble of emotions, the most reactionary. Why shouldn't she have other lovers, enjoy her freedom? Love is not to be constrained. We have one of your modern relationships, self-conscious, slightly hypocritical, built on a good large dose of ideology. It's supposed to be an "open" relationship with room for other lovers during the months we're apart. All you have to do is extend that to the months when we're together, which is what she's pressing for now, and provided there's a good foundation of trust and affection, the rivals aren't rivals and they don't threaten what lies between us. The trouble is that they do. If I felt her love, if I had the sureness of its presence, I really would be able to bear the existence of other lovers and bear it very well, much as I used to. But her love simply isn't there any more now, is not persuasive.

So give up. I leave in a few weeks. It is only a matter of time. What was it that I wanted, anyway? Simulated domesticity strangled me. The sight of her graying hair, nightie, slippers, hair curlers, all in some permanent state of guard over me would make me cut and run faster than this, this strange prolonged waiting for the end. The fact is, she interests me now. Hardly her purpose probably in pursuing her own way, but surely its effect. Sita in her long, green-trousered legs, her slender waist, her green sweater over the lovely shoulders and breasts, her gold necklaces, her hair swept back from her face, pursuing her way. Lively and radiant somewhere. Somewhere in L.A. or Berkeley or San Francisco. Gladdening Neal's day or someone else's. Maybe even attending her conference, flirting with the world, scattering her vivacious Italian charm, or the darker, nearly Indian tranquillity of her Brazilian side. Beaming at the people around her, many of them younger, duller Sitas, beaming them her humor, her grace in age, the miracle of her subtle erotic self.

Wherever she is I bless her, admire her, salute her. What if I were to renounce the last remnants of vanity, gradually burned away by my humiliations here, and embrace a really selfless love? Not merely the foxy taking what I can get, what bones of affection and attention are thrown to me, but to lay off my hands altogether, bring them away palm upward and back to my sides, clean, asking nothing at all? Bid her to be, simply to be, since her being is such a triumph over life, her own past, her age, her own disappointed hopes, the lives she wept for never having had last Saturday when I came upon her listening to *Bohème* —it was knowing, she said, knowing she would not, would never be the writer or the conqueror she'd dreamed of being once in some earlier self, the adolescent ballerina with her huge haunted eyes. Now a woman facing fifty.

"Really feeling her oats, isn't she?" Sherman had rumbled over the phone when I mentioned Sita was gone this weekend. And why not, why shouldn't she have that, that last glorious burst of energy, not merely erotic but total, giving her whole body zest, her walk, her voice, her face. Why shouldn't she have it? Maybe I have never loved her enough, or well enough. To love is simply to allow another to be, live, grow, expand, become. An appreciation that demands and expects nothing in return. The end of love—or its beginning.

She surprised me by coming back as early as ten on Monday morning. It's a school holiday, Neal has the day off too. I'm taken aback, had never expected her so soon. The dishes from my long bachelor weekend aren't even washed. I am ashamed, a little confused. Suddenly she is with me again after the long absence. Yet I feel nothing at first, only a neutral nothing when she hugs me hello, this stranger in her pink wool blouse and sweater, her face a little aged in the morning light. Strange, neutral feeling, my main concern the unwashed dishes. "I didn't fly all the way from L.A. to worry you about the dishes." She laughs, sitting herself down at the table where I'm reading for my class, nervous because I'm not yet through the assignment, while she describes her conference. "I saw your old friend Ivy yesterday." I wonder, did she really spend the whole time in Los Angeles? Was I wrong, was she really telling me the truth? She goes on describing a comic band that entertained them Sunday afternoon. "One hilarious lady with a pompon and a headband —like this. And these, what do you call them, gloves without fingers and big wide open sleeves. And there was one like you, delicious, voluptuous little thing shaped like a turtle dove and poured into this brown dress with a pelisse, and a bustle, you know, that she'd bump and grind in time to the music." A turtle dove? I wonder. Was she really there, did it really happen, or did it just happen on Saturday instead?

"Some damn-fool guru and his disciples were on campus too and held us up for hours Sunday, we couldn't get into our meeting room, so we convened very late Sunday evening, but we got a lot done, made a real start for women in California. Maude Tracy was elected our part-time advocate for the whole state. We have almost enough in the treasury to cover a salary." I listen, confused, my mind partly on the dishes, partly on the book I must finish reading in the next few hours. She goes on, spinning, weaving, embroidering, creating a whole weekend, event after event, meetings and people and the college where they stayed, the faculty club, the participants. Even the band and the musicians, their outrageous clothes, their spirit. I no longer know what to think, am numb with trying not to care.

Then as I wash the dishes, she reads the paper, sitting on the couch. When I have finished, counting the hours and minutes left before class, I decide to risk joining her for a little while to test this bewildered indifference. I sit down next to her, discovering there is not enough room, awkwardly obliging her to move over, feeling silly. She puts her arm around me, says she is glad to be back. I see her and feel her, not really seeing or feeling. Why do I feel so little? What does she feel? The same neutral emptiness probably. But she is kind. It is a sort of happiness just to feel her warmth, the rose-colored wool of her shirt sleeve around my shoulder. I no longer know any more. Except that it hurts less. Even that is a loss; to arrive at mere indifference after such a love. Refusing even to remember the reunions of the past, their ecstasies, their gifts and surprises, their surges and throbs of voluptuous pleasure. We would surely never have restrained ourselves, would surely have made love. Couch, floor, kitchen, dining room, nothing would have stopped us. And now I go dutifully upstairs to read my book.

Wondering, as I sit sequestered here, off in "my own room" with the door shut, hearing her busy showering, the sound of her rearranging the room Paul and Valerie have stripped over the weekend, even their bed gone, leaving only a little sponge-rubber pallet on the floor ("her bed" in "her room"?), wondering if she will miss me, feel any want or emptiness now that I am out of reach for the whole morning and early afternoon until the class. Then a knock, polite, discreet. Would I like anything to eat? Some tea, an apple? Bringing a whole tray replete with teapot and a small camellia blossom, the lovely flower smiling at me against the brown wood of my desk; elegant, precious, framed upon its snapping dark-green leaves, having ridden serenely upstairs upon a pretty blue napkin. Such touches as I fell in love with.

After my class, after her meeting, we are to have drinks on the water at Solomon Grundy's. I arrive home first, having turned down coffee with my students. No, I tell them, I'm going to have a drink at the Marina, want to hurry not to miss the sundown, sure of myself, young, excited, the evening ahead of me, the happiness of a Friday night or a holiday, the night glamorous and full of promise, the bay misty before me down through the hills as I drive. She is not home yet. I debate what to do—leave a note asking her to meet me there? or wait for her here? The sun is setting, the special moment hurrying on. She'll probably go straight to the Marina from the city. Go. Hurry. Leave her a note. Hasty thing composed by two faltering ballpoints, the first giving out halfway. But plain enough. And with a foolish little flower scrawled on the bottom.

And then I begin down the hill, going a new way, faster, one of her methods. But missing the exit, imagining there's a special one for the Marina just beyond the University Avenue exit. No such thing. On my way to Oakland or some such fate. Off again at the nearest ramp. I will miss her. Long, desperate search for an entrance back, going the other way, returning to Berkeley. A sign tells me I'm headed for Sacramento, seventy-eight miles. I curse a New Yorker's curse on California, freeways, the modern world. And look up to see the University Avenue exit. Saved. Now a little sign pointing to the Marina. I follow. A long frontage road going nowhere. She will have come home, seen my note, gone to the Marina, seen I wasn't there, gone home again. Turn around, go back to University Avenue. Give it another try. Through long streets of warehouses and railroad tracks back to the main thoroughfare, the only one I understand. I will miss her, I will be late. She will have left. The signs, the correct turns. Wondering if I should turn back, go home. Surely it was a mistake to leave the note calling her down here. But it was agreed we'd go. No, she will think it peremptory. She may get home and decide she doesn't want to go out again. Just what I was hoping to prevent with the note, to assure that she'd come. And now the sun has gone while I have been lost on freeways, the moment over and past that we had come to see. That note, the whole device was an error. I had thought it independence, fire, temperament. An act on my part, going ahead, taking the initiative.

The conduct of a love affair, I say to myself, seeing the parking lot finally through the car window—arrived, safe—the conduct of a love affair requires the right moves, adroitness. And this is misconduct, error, mismanagement, bungling. Walking up to the place, loving just the sight of it. Solomon Grundy's is built like a Japanese castle on the sea, with great wooden beams, a bridgeway across a chasm of water, the waves rolling under it echoing to the towering beams and the delicate wooden fishbone of the canopy overhead. All the sides that face the sea are nothing but pure glass, section on section of sky and water sealed in view as from a gigantic observation platform. I look along the side of the building to the windows of the bar, way back near the sea where they begin. All the hundred occasions of our love have met here.

Surprised and glad to find a table, lucky really, even though the sunset has long passed. Of course she is not here. Or not yet. Beginning to grow afraid. Will she make me wait here for nothing? It's inconceivable. But she may come home and just decide not to bother. Telling me later that she was tired, that she didn't want to drive so far. How long should I wait? Till eight? Past eight? Call her? That gives her a chance to refuse, and by now I need her here. The waitress comes by for my order. I say I am waiting for a friend.

Sitting before the pitch-black sea beyond the cold windows, I feel utterly helpless. Nothing I can do to change anything, affect her in any way, draw her back. No tactic, no device. When it becomes a question of wills, the one who has made it so holds all the cards and the one who goes on loving is powerless. When it becomes a game, there is already no winning. To hurt back, to take revenge is both impossible and unwanted. It is she who makes every decision, every demand, every stipulation, who conditions every peripheral aspect of our lives. We are eating at home tonight rather than here because she is tired of restaurant food after a weekend in hotels. Just as we get up in the morning at the hour we do because of her job, just as I wait for five for it to release her to me.

But it is not in these material, inevitable things that she controls me. It is in her silences or bursts of affection, her willed absences, her hundred methods of withdrawing, evading, leaving me nothing but sisterly good nights, a friendly good morning. "Have a nice class," she said as I left, as she got into her own car and headed for the city. Yet I was hungering for her; for luck almost, I climbed out of my car again to see her face as she drove down the hill, feeling blessed that she had thrown me a kiss.

Her greetings, now so measured, objective. And her "I love you"s, her "It's nice to see you again"s, how perfunctory, polite, without meaning. The black water through the windows; she did not bother to come. The terrible sadness of the end of love, its loneliness. The illusion no longer shared. I look out at the waves and at the lights of San Francisco, the wharf and the bridges. The two small stars, the planets Venus and Jupiter that my students had mentioned—how airy and delightful it was with them today—hang isolated and poignant in the sky. Just as promised. Hum of the people around me, reflection of the bright fireplace in the windows, this intimate and cozy place impossibly lonely. She hasn't come, isn't going to. I realize finally that it is perfectly possible for her to yawn at my note on the door, find her keys in her bag, and simply decide not to bother—"She'll come back when she gets tired of waiting."

I turn around and see her, coming almost shyly toward me in her tired camel's-hair coat.

To be two women living in this house. I look off to the sea and away to the city. To be two women living in this house, to what profit, to what purpose? How narrow the margins grow, the limitations close in. She made love to me last night. After permitting me the same, or rather, not really the same, a short, almost futile attempt. Men interest her more now, at this period of her life—that was how she put it to me as we lay in bed afterward. And I am no Neal, no great stretch of flesh within her. I watched her face, both as I struggled to give her pleasure and as she turned to me next, looming over me. It was the face of someone I loved, a wealth of tenderness for its wide cheeks and beautiful dark eyes, loving its line of chin and lips and nose, its brows and lashes, the mole just above her lip. I looked straight into her eyes as she entered me. Looking straight into her eyes and seeing nothing. Her Indian eyes. Under her beautiful mask of the loving and sensual woman, under and beyond that, the inscrutable Indian self buried and obdurate.

I had never thought she would come to me last night. Had seen her sitting naked on Pia's bed. Is this to be "her bed" in "her room," now that Paul's bedstead is gone? I wondered, despairing at how she outwits me, eludes me at every turn. Now that Paul's bed is gone, the sponge-rubber pallet may not be to her taste, I had thought. She'll come back now to "my bed," which was our bed. But then the sight of her in Pia's room, calmly sitting naked on the bed, waiting for me to finish with the bathroom, that was too much. I would have wept if I had the energy, if I did not feel such despair. Sitting in bed, waiting for the good nights to be over, waiting to read myself to sleep. And then she appeared in the door. "Are you open to receiving guests and other wayfarers?"

How she disposes, how all is at her disposition, how I am acted upon, passive, hedged about. And how willing, having her in my arms, how willing to be hedged and warmed and heated and alive to her leg between mine and my hand to find her. "I have wanted to make love to you all day," she says, "all evening." And how was I to guess, how even to believe? Believing.

We'd gone out to the movies, a little rustle of festivity since we so rarely go out at night, coming home late. And the day had been good, going swimming with Susan at her club, seeing the trees and the hills rise like a bowl all around the water, looking up at the apartments perched steep above us. And the concentration of twenty laps, the sting of chlorine, the hot shower after, and the sauna. Gratitude of the flesh for motion and water and warmth, the comfort of its exertion. Never mind, I had thought, I will live here, in my body; perfect it, isolate it; I will become essentially solitary, an independent existence, send down a root from my backbone into the place where I stand.

And she slept with me that night. Usual folderol of wonderment, her arbitrary preparations in Pia's room, the expectation she would come, the certainty she wouldn't, renewed expectation. The drama of her nightly arrangements. How I tire of it, am humiliated and sated, able to bear no further misery. Yet go on bearing. Pompous she is, absurd, but all-powerful. How many people go through this business of separate rooms, visits, beds declared vacant or closed or independent, nightly hopes, fears, disappointments. Everywhere in the world it must go on and I never thought much about it, believed everyone slept in double beds without a qualm or a flurry. Never suspected the possible stratagems, moves, advances and retreats of pieces and pawns, the thousand possibilities of inflicting torture, withering little shoots of hope annihilated in the soft closure of a door. I'll read, I decide,

smoke, enjoy my solitude, keep later hours—still listening to the sounds in the hall, the precise stage
directions of the bathroom, the toothbrush, the fau-
cets.

And then her figure in the door. A woman in a
wrinkled flannel nightgown. I have set my heart and
life upon this apparition. Though tonight, unlike last
night, it turns to sleep in a moment, tonight she is
separate, off on her side of the bed, the warmth of her
body my only reward.

And yet the very next day there is a new deprivation. She will be very late tonight. Her friend Maud,
her great conspicuous friendship with Maud—"Maud,
my best friend," she always says, the statement never
failing to hurt and irritate me. Or Neal, I wonder, is
this just a cover for having dinner with him? And
then an overnight I will only discover when the time
comes. Yet when I come home from hanging out with
my students in a coffeehouse, she is already in bed.
Pia's room. Asleep already, but she has left me a note,
says she tried to call me in the afternoon, has to get
up very early tomorrow morning. Doesn't want to "disturb" me. "You are loved," the note says. Just like the
other one, the night of the party. And for a crazy moment I wonder if the note is a ruse, if she's even in the
house.

I undress quietly without waking her, but around
eleven-thirty the telephone rings. A man's voice.
Neal's? But there are others: Mark, Walter, how many
others? She wakes as I am answering it and I hand
her the receiver. "I'm sound asleep," she keeps telling
him. "Yes, yes, I'm glad your speech went well." Neal,
precipitate fool, at this hour waking her with news of
his vain little speech. Hairy-armed Rotarian. She disappears swiftly back into her room, an irritated specter.
I lie in bed alone, having come three thousand miles
to the cold comfort of separate bedrooms, knowing
everything, knowing it all to its dregs, all the folly of
it. And still here. There are eight weeks left.

Unexpectedly, I remembered what it was like. Realizing only through the contrast. In the coffeehouse last

night, one of my students reading a poem describing some lovers. It was all there again, the frankness, the joy, the ease and intimacy of bed. Sitting up and chatting, laughing, getting up for coffee, diving back into the flesh again. As the poet read I could feel the sliding fabric of sheets, mornings of lovemaking, coffee cups, whole afternoons of sex, sunlight that is luxury and time without hurry, without goals, only the goal of living in that high moment which is forever, both past and future, that second which expands to fill the world, blotting out childhood and old age, transforming each segment of life into the refracted light of now, the moment to which all others led and can only follow.

And I thought of our taut and nervous bodies now, like two long, gray metal bars laid parallel in bed. Suddenly it seemed curious that we can sleep at all, our flesh now so without ease or spontaneity. So out of touch and harmony. But it did happen once. And that's what I remember now, having almost forgotten it. How we sat up in bed and chattered, drank wine, smoked. Sacramento those first dawns, making love before classes or as soon as the world released us into evening. The speed and grace with which she removed her clothes, how it always astonished me. Quite wonderfully, without shame or hesitation. Her arms removing a blouse on entering the room. And suddenly she would be there in her brown skin and flanks, the great brown circles of her nipples. And we had all that, that ease, the freedom of feeling, quick and alive, young in our joy, our frank knowing of each other in flesh and spirit and talk. Such a feast of talk, endless talk. Our naked bodies moving between bed and bath and kitchen, downstairs to the coffee or the plants, the talk continuous, witty and relaxed, intimate but objective, or gossiping or partisan, lofty or flippant, talking of a book or a meeting or a personality. How it all flowed.

The little bedroom there, its shadowy light of candles the nights she visited, its pearl-gray mornings after I had stayed up all night reading for a class, having to cram because we had spent the evening in lovemaking. And then she would sleep while I kept vigil, doing the two hundred necessary pages before a nine o'clock. I cross the hall from my study, sensing the strange pale light, knowing that now I must wake her. Hesitating, hating to do it. But after a moment, there is no sorrow at all—we were never tired. Sita waking to love again and a shower and coffee. Mornings when her presence, her great happiness was like a song through the house, through the coffee, through the clean early sunlight. How different we are these mornings. Strained little moments at the dining-room table, each reading the paper. Or if she does not read, I also forbear in courtesy. And the hope of a moment's attention. But I lust for the paper, the opiate of it, the cover to our emptiness, our so obvious emptiness.

It is the distance of our bodies. That more than anything, that is the index, that our bodies no longer know each other in the same way as once, are no longer friends. It is the distance in our bodies. And our minds and our souls. But you see it in the bodies. If you can even remember, of course. But I remembered it in the poet's phrase, a certain piquant image of lovers and their bodies, the good friendliness of their bodies in bed, their good will, their excited, almost childlike escape from all self-consciousness, their special camaraderie. Only then did I feel the loss, the difference, and understand the terrible change. As lovers how our movements now are curtailed. It is difficult for us to be ample, attend to the whole body, be generous with care and attention; I cannot throw back the covers and find her thighs with my mouth. Our lovemaking is cut-rate now, short of fabric, skimpy. Like girls in boarding school fearful of waking a house mistress, campers sly not to arouse the counselors—no, they all enjoy themselves—like prisoners then. Like prisoners, stealthy and adroit, minimal. Sly we are, secretive. As if we were ashamed.

Once how far otherwise, free with our flesh, our bodies nude from room to room, unconcerned about our cries through the thin little apartment walls. And now, merely this hasty little act below the covers, this mockery. Hidden, out of sight. Is it always so, the end of love? Always that abbreviation of the former drama, its play and invention and embroidery, its long, serene caresses snipped, eliminated, pruned, divested of their ritual, leaving only a quick push for orgasm—the goal, the finish, the having it over?

It was not a remarkable poem, only that it conveyed the magnetism between bodies; together with their innocence, their friendliness even. And that made me understand, with one blow, measure the distance and be appalled. What do you do then, when you realize you have fallen so far, when you can calculate and must admit it, like an account finally investigated by a bank auditor, the evidence confounding you? What do you do? Admit it's gone? Leave? Or relapse into vacancy, into not knowing, into hope, into expecting change? Do you confer? But conferences are already admissions of failure, and our failure is too ominous to withstand a conference. If I take a hard line, if I say it is over, she will agree. If I do not, she will go on about the years ahead, how I "will always be a part of her life," how we are in a "stage," a particular "moment of growth." And say that she loves me, with that diluted, almost sisterly affection she now considers love. But we are not lovers, our flesh has lost its knowledge of each other. Not only that glorious electrical affinity that kept us up all night, but even its relaxation, its contentment, its friendship. And you cannot define something so nebulous as the trust between bodies. Or restore it merely by taking note of its absence.

If I had not listened to this poem. If I had not remembered. If I had not realized. If I did not know.

A life of waiting. Waiting till she gets home at night, till her day is finished, till she gets back from Sacramento, where she has a meeting today. Days consumed in waiting, days empty except for the prospect of her return. Existence relative, dependent, vacant. I might be a wife, a child, or some marginal and parasitic creature. My own work is little comfort and does not sustain. Hardly her fault; my failure is my own. But her absences, her withdrawals, psychic as well as physical, leave me drained, impotent, unable to concentrate. Yet once when she left each day I was filled,

replete, eager to work, believing. Why should my belief be contingent upon her love, hers or anyone else's?
If you are an artist, you work, simply that; the belief
has to come from within.

Now I no longer believe, only wait. Waiting, finally
and eventually, for the time when I leave. Eight weeks.
So little time. And then it's over? Finally and eventually over. Harder than waiting for evening, this prospect. When a thing saps you, corrodes, dissipates your
energy . . . I say to myself, being sensible. Rational.
Thinking of self-preservations, smelling disease.

But life beyond and without her? Not freedom, only
greater poverty. Life closing down. Fewer and fewer
remain. Ruth and a few friends in New York, the man
I used to be married to—lately a strange, nervous
friendship, new in places but underneath the same
tragic fiber and fabric. And Sherman. So few people,
so little left. Age closes in. She and I were to share it
together somehow, an idea she still professes to believe
in, talking about Martin's retreat in Napa. I see myself
there in age and solitude, coming there afraid of the
cold, reduced, glad even to share the sun with Neal
or whatever other Neals show up.

When you can live neither with nor without her . . .
Absurd, but it comes to that. Is it only need, loneliness
that ties me to her? Memory? Memory of the past,
the love then, its food and health and quality. Or some
strange mixture of the two, the second, failing, becomes transformed into the first. And dignity disappears. For the defeated lover such things are luxuries
hardly remembered. But how one gets to hate this
creature inside oneself, this rag without selfhood or
pride, unable, quite unable to afford such things. The
other, older self, the self who was loved and cherished,
seeing love disappear, bridles, pulls up sharply. Pam-
pered, it cannot imagine itself despised, makes as to
leave, simply to exit from such an untenable circumstance. And falls just before the door, its leg tied in
some explicable way to memory. Inconceivable that
this could be taking place, this thing of being no longer
loved, when memory knows such a different world.
There, in memory, in the past, staring right at you

from the same face that now rejects you, a face hardly changed, slight changes compared to years and the distance of a continent, only this faint shift of expression between boredom and infatuation. And then you are addicted to that inch. If you could move it, erase it, slide—imperceptibly at first but by subtle degrees—slide it away and restore the past. Or wake up to have it suddenly intact again one morning.

I wait for her now to come home from Sacramento. Lately she has taken up a yoga class on Tuesday evenings, one more little escape from me, one further evasion. I heard her describe it as you might listen to someone explaining how they'd wrecked one side of your car. Such a theft it seemed of the little time I am given. The hour grown later and later. We will miss Susan Sontag's talk at the university. Dishes washed, salad made. I am of two minds whether to season the meat yet. Going to the door or the window, looking out. Pulled, yearning, like a wife in an old fable. The table set, the candles ready for lighting. A car pulls up. I hurry to finish my preparation, sure it is she, not needing to run and look out. But I do, only to see the car pull away. Maybe she just changed her mind, decided it would be more amusing to look up Neal, got home and just didn't feel like coming in. Or maybe she wanted to turn the car around, drive up to the top of the hill and come down and park on the other side. Waiting for the headlights again. They don't come back.

Later and later. We will almost surely miss the lecture. To keep from going mad, to prevent hysteria, I will read. Half a page before the phone rings. She is at the bottom of the hill. Will be home in a minute. Like grace.

Curious the operations of jealousy. And jealousy too simple a word. At dinner she mentioned, quietly and in passing, that she would not be home Friday night. I never blinked. Neal. Neal's night. And in bed she wanted me, her hand finding my breast surprised and willing. My mind measures and resists—tomorrow is Neal and so tonight, the night before him, and per-

Sita

haps Saturday too, the night after him, there will be this rebate. The payoff. Is it her guilt or actual desire? No way to judge. My body doesn't judge at all, the loins wanting her, writhing for the touch of her hand, the bud of flame between the legs lit by her touch, her fingers sauntering, dallying, expert. Hot and cold as she circles, opening, preparing. "Talk to me," I whisper. "I have wanted you all day. You were everywhere around me in Sacramento, I remembered you in every street and building. I've waited for this." "You never say so, you never say these things." She chuckles, raising herself on her elbow as I lie under her, cloaked and covered and tremulous and waiting the moment when she plunges inside me, when one sensation gives way to another. I tell her we do not take time as we used to, time to enjoy our bodies fully, to explore and savor. Telling her in my lust the things I would do, my hands covering her buttocks, stroking and caressing the line of parting before the cleft I do not enter but only touch, each fingertip exciting me as her hand on my cunt faster and faster excites me now to frenzy. I do not even think any more, only thrash, her creature as she enters me.

Afterward I wept in her arms. "It will be all right," she says, holding me. But she would not give herself, let me make love to her. Immediately I think of Neal. I have lost, been outclassed by the competition. Wanting to make a joke of it, and not daring. I feel tricked now, cheated. What if I had resisted? But I wanted her. So often these days, during so many occasional moments, I ask myself—brushing my teeth or working or parking the car—what if you refused, went without? How would she react? Further withdrawal? Or perhaps she wouldn't care at all.

Surely this is wrong, foolish, reactionary. Surely she has a right to her pleasure and I none to my pain and misery. A love without possessiveness, restraint— surely we both believe in that. Or rather I believed and proclaimed it and she was jealous, violently and painfully jealous, when on two occasions I took a lover. I will never forget the sight of her standing up naked on my bed one night in Sacramento, a diva in full tantrum because she had just been bitten by one of Bea's hairpins lurking treacherously in the sheets. I very nearly laughed. But whenever she felt jealousy it was sorrow, and her every sorrow grieved me. Sita never struggled with jealousy—it came upon her and it happened. She was a Latin, she was entitled to it. It was I who had notions, terms, theories, and Sita who was fiercely possessive, protective as a lioness, forbidding. There were times when it became unreasonable, even grotesque; she punished me for weeks over an affectionate indiscretion she came across in a letter, a letter to a prisoner, where it was merely academic if he would ever spend Christmas with me one day in the country, a thing I proposed to cheer him up. Having read the letter by accident, she wrote me a dramatic note to the effect that we were doomed. She used to date my defection from then, regarding the loft I took merely as confirmation of an essential infidelity. But now she has come round to my views, practicing them with a vengeance. And I am not proof against them.

This morbid curiosity, the sense of betrayal, the world upset by a word, by a segment of time missing, stolen away, by a night away. The emptiness stretching between now and tomorrow. Her voice on the phone this morning calling from her office: "So I'll see you tomorrow afternoon then." She will be away all night with someone. The thing accepted, taken for granted between us at breakfast and when we drive to the garage to pick up her car—see you tomorrow, hear from you tomorrow. Tomorrow, when she is taking me to the Chinese New Year parade and dinner in Chinatown—my reward for patience. As if I were some particularly well-behaved child. Or perhaps simply a child, a dependent being one buys with treats and favors. Why should it be such a humiliation, this bright sensible new way to live?

Just as I had perfected my gloom and self-pity, she called and asked me to lunch—she is thinking of firing her secretary. I am the secretary living in fear throughout lunch.

After a night with Sherman, drinking and complaining
—Marguerite's illnesses, Sita's infidelities—like two
old boozing pirates, boring ourselves and each other.
In the restaurant at one point I thought I would scream
with tedium, as Sherman expounded to her old friend
Selma why New York is so exciting and San Francisco
is so dull, a performance I have heard a thousand
times. My left shoe hurts, my foot is going to sleep.
Even with the shoe off the foot hurts terribly, the bones
seem squeezed. Selma describes the filth of New
York, the rudeness. "I was there just one weekend and
it was two days too long for me—never again." I put
my foot across my knee and massage it under the table. Selma and her child lover, a college girl, finally
rising to leave.

Sherman's voice when they are gone, droning over
my pain: "I needed to see you tonight. I've really had
it. I can't paint in this mess, I can't even live. She's
totally dependent on me, has no family in this country, no money, no place. Now the damn hospital, the
hospital bills. Just what wiped me out last time. I can't
even think any more." We are back at our first conversation, while drinking a few hours ago in a tough
gay bar on San Francisco's Broadway. Sherman had
called early this evening, looking for me, got Sita, just
dressing to go out. "Sita was on her way to a seminar." "Bullshit. She's on her way to Neal." "Who's
that?" "The guy she's fucking tonight." Appalled at
my own voice, the crudeness and violence of the term.
Almost an assault. An assault I would never have
made but for the lie. And my fears that she may have
persuaded Sherman, seduced her to her own views.
"I'm really disappointed," Sherman says softly.

But I must find out more, what else was said. In
fear now that I have lost my only ally. Sherman reverts
to Marguerite, staying with a friend tonight, right near
the hospital. Her illness is very serious and may last
months. The doctors are finding it hard even to diag-
nose. "I can't stand it, I can't stand living like this."
"I feel the same way, endless distraction, up and down
in her moods, her decisions, her nights in and out. It's
a completely totalitarian relationship." "I can't go on

this way, just fucking can't." "Neither can I, but I do. Loving her, not loving her." "She says you have lovely times in between." "Sure, great romantic fires, fireworks. Then she's off again." "She told me on the phone that she wanted an adult, independent relationship." "That means she fucks Neal when the mood strikes her. And I put up with it." "Never, I'd never be able to stand that." "For some reason, I can. Just barely. Look, I believe in her freedom." "Sure, she's seeing age and she wants to live—zoom." Sherman gestures in a line with her finger.

"I can appreciate that," I say, the feel of the bar stool under me, the clink of glasses, the faces along the bar facing the evening, drinking their Friday evening, the jukebox, a band setting up in the back of the room. "Look, Sherman, I can appreciate it all, even admire it aesthetically, if you like, Sita's a beautiful woman. And if she wants to grab life and wring it dry —why not, we all do. And I don't really even know what I want from her finally." "She keeps you interested, that's more than I can say. This being-sick trip is driving me up the wall." "Well, Marguerite doesn't want to be sick—you're acting like it's her fault." "Yes . . ." But Sherman turns to Moxie on the right, quips with Selma behind the bar, acknowledges a gaggle of young lesbians eyeing her from the end of the counter. How can I keep her to my subject, attacked again and again till I understand it, as if talking aloud might solve it, bring insight, undo the riddle? Selma finishes behind the bar and joins us. We will have one more, then go for dinner. Dinner alone, the two of us, with our two obsessions.

But it's Peter's birthday today. Wonderful, who's Peter? Bartender at the restaurant we're going to, a new one. Sherman says the Air Freight, our favorite haunt, has taken a nose dive. Or rather, since she prefers gestures to words, a habit particularly emphatic when she drinks, she does the nose dive with a gesture of her thumb descending like a crashing plane. So we must go to this new place, and Selma and her lover (young, silent, pretty) will go along with us just for one more drink and to wish Peter a happy birth-

day. I'm fond of Selma, an old crony of Sherman's, a
retired union official, tough and gentle, but tonight I
wish her away as I suffer through the monologues
Sherman directs at her, waiting for my time, for my
obsessions to reassert themselves. When the other two
leave, the dialogue goes on, even repeated: Sherman's
frustration before Marguerite's invalidism, psychic and
physical—"Cortisone the rest of her life, can you
imagine? Poor damn kid, but how can I go on with
this, sick, all the time sick, day after day, it never
stops." And my own complaints, each indication from
Sita, what it portends, even as I talk feeling the bones
of my foot aching in this odd inexplicable way, wanting
to leave, to walk, to exercise, to stamp out the pain.
And wanting to stay, to keep gouging the wound, exploring it.

"I don't know where it goes. I want both things,
here and New York. But it can't work." "Beautiful if
it did, to be able to have all that. But your cake and
eat it too? Now really." "Overambitious"—feeling
guilty before Sherman's monogamous judgment, her
settled life in one town. "But otherwise it just means
going home at the end of a few more weeks, giving
up." "She won't let you go." "Sure she will, she'd drive
me to the airport tomorrow." "You're wrong. She loves
you." "I love her too. But I don't know what it means."
More wine, more repetition, more spinning of the
wheels, less understanding, further despair. More state-
ments of impatience, more punching and kicking at
circumstances, less hope for change. Sherman's bearish
voice: "Let's quit, I'm sleepy."

Back home I see the living room transformed subtly
as for company. Neal. He came here to pick her up.
Since I was in the city at the doctor's, he was able to
call for her here. Be entertained. Glasses in the kitchen?
Don't bother looking. But a silent butler on the Chinese table, the cushions hunched up under the windows, the shape of his back implanted. And flowers,
the chrysanthemum plant I bought her when she was
sick, wilted in its pot lately. But she has clipped the
flowers, put them in water, where they shine in a little
majolica pitcher. What a genius she has for making a

room special, festive with merely a touch, the slightest
rearrangement. But something else is new, Sherman's
other painting is on the wall above the console, re-
placing Pia's hideous Maxfield Parrish poster. For a
second I am furious. Even before I can admire, re-
joice that the painting is hung again, brought out from
under the sheet where it had been banished when the
kids moved in—even before I am glad, I am furious.
My friend Sherman's picture was hung for Neal, Sherman's painting hung to impress him, to make the room
"gracious" for his reception. No, forget it, mount the
stairs. Read a little. Sleep. She is not coming home
tonight.

The first note is on a little rocker before my bedroom door. Yes, of course, there'll be notes, the usual
nervous little assertions that I am "loved." And the
expected instructions on how to get to the hotel in San
Francisco where we meet tomorrow—the exits, times,
locations. She has even changed the time. Not four
now, but five. Merest wince of disappointment. Well,
I will read myself to sleep. Turning on the bedside
lamp to find another note posted beside a huge pink-
white hydrangea filling a Chinese bowl. *"Tesoro bello,*
this exuberant blossom—with its delicate pale-pink
petals and its simply luscious fullness—reminded me
of your breasts. File this under H for horny thoughts.
My love, Innocenza." More than a genius—this flower,
what we used to call a "snowball" when we were
children—was, until she touched it, merely a large
ugly thing on a stalk in the front yard. Now it is a
miracle in a blue bowl, now it is a message. I am
touched, persuaded, conquered. Somehow between
dressing and transforming the house and doing the
dishes, somehow in all her preparations, preparations
for another lover, somehow she found time and
thought to do this. In her strange, excited eroticism,
which borrows from one to give to the other (and I
have known that feeling too, loved one lover more for
loving the other, another), she has stretched the perfume of her sensuality across us both. I see the little
note pinned to the lampshade and believe, am flattered
with the old, almost shy embarrassment of riches her

courting used to give me. Such courtesy, such charm.
I am treasured and cherished and wrapped in the furs
of her attention. Reading alone in bed on a night she
has left me for another lover, I am loved, adored,
protected, watched over as if by spirits.

And in the morning I notice another note set for me
at the dining-room table, more chrysanthemums, the
piece of paper leaning against them. "Good morning,
my love"—though she wrote it last night—"Another
outrageously beautiful sunset . . . and they will go on
—longer than we will, and then we won't even miss
them. But I missed sharing this with you now. Death
is forever—and life is so short—love a beautiful sunset, always changing, always the same, always too
brief. Beautiful Lady, I miss you. Share my sunsets
—share my love—share my life." All this while she
waits for Neal. Incredible, exasperating, beautiful
woman. "Let's give each other joy. There's not enough
of it in life and we have much of it to give each other.
I love you. Innocenza."

In the kitchen an obituary is pinned to the bulletin
board, a friend of ours who has died very young of
cancer—and beside it Sita has written her own name,
and "Alive, but for how long?" I pour my coffee and
reread her note. To love or not to love? To live together or apart? Never mind. "Let's give each other
joy. There's not enough of it in life." Yes, yes. Let's
give each other joy then—how much I want that,
to end the tussle of wills, the setting up of obstacles,
the turning away of the face or the back or leaving the
room, the withdrawals of self and affection. To give, to
have that joy to give. Am I worthy, able? This heavy
silent and depressed being of mine, how I must bore
her, weighted down with my convictions of futility.
To give each other joy. Longing already for the moment we'll meet in the streets of the city. The Chinese
New Year, the festival. Firecrackers and dragons and
parades.

This is the giddy time, her weekend. When the world
turns on its heel and goes carnival. Monday to Friday
are grim and efficient, early to rise and to bed, an im-

mersion in mediocrity and hated detail. Then for two
days each week life becomes romance. An artist has
no weekends, any day might be a workday or a holiday, but you are never off work, never free of worry
and the obligation of art. And yet any day might be
romantic; there is no schedule or division, only a con-
tinuum. But never mind that difference now. Or any
other difference. And all your tedious grief and whin-
ing. She waits for you, are you up to the challenge?
Can I smile, laugh enough, be light? All right, I will
try, I will meet her, try to set off this explosion, this
ignition she calls for. Joy. How well I know what she
means, that there is not enough joy in life. The very
scarcity and paltriness. And there's the fact that we
could, since it is there and possible, if we ceased op-
posing, we could produce this very jewel, this precious
substance that makes life wonderful rather than merely
bearable—by an act of will, turn our association with
each other into the good and the creative. As it was
before? In essence, but in everything else different, of
the present rather than the past, new as today is new,
this crystal morning. All right. Then dedicate this morning, this moment, to that hope.

All right, Lady, you've said it, what I might have
wished to say, longed to tell you, to propose. To set
forth as a plan of action. We are not finished, I think
we are merely starting.

Arriving late. Her instructions were off. There is
no hotel at Sixth and Market. Or rather no hotel likely
to house a conference. Only an old transient thing
called the Shaw. Hardly likely. I search frantically for
another clue. Realize I hadn't bothered to write the
exact name of the hotel, Hilton something, Sheraton something. Sixth and Market seemed clear enough.
Now it isn't, now it's an enigma. What a fool I am.
And she in her great goodness, her magnificent efficiency, had plotted this out for me so carefully, even
leaving a copy of the schedule of the conference. I
was appalled to see she had a workshop Friday night,
last night, what I had taken to be Neal's night. What

if she had dutifully gone to that workshop last night, the "seminar" Sherman mentioned, which I had casually defined as a fuck. And staying out all night? Well, maybe at the hotel, attending the thing wholeheartedly; parties were listed for after 10 p.m. No. Yes. Never mind, just find her.

The one clue, New Montgomery Street. The hotel's parking lot was on New Montgomery. Scratching through one-way streets and blockades and streetcars and the narrow lanes of Market Street and No Left Turns full of flea-bag transient hotels and filling-station attendants and parking-lot boys and motorcycle cops with inaccurate directions—cop said Post was next but it's not, it's Ellis, what will I do?—until finally and a precious thirty minutes late I find the Sheraton Palace. She is not in the lobby. Despair. Ask the desk. My eyes devouring each shabby sofa, each plush and stodgy armchair. And then way off to the left, so familiar, so unglamorous, so beloved. Her knitted patchwork vest, her camel's-hair coat, her long, lovely legs. To think that I have made her wait, when every moment was so precious with the new promise of her note, the bargain it had struck.

Her conference drones on inside. The ballroom, with its dais and tables and the foot-soldier fleet of folding chairs. She leads me inside. Like hell, like chaos, like tedium. The exhaustion of two days' talk on every face and body. "Shall we just go?" "That would be lovely." "There's a party as soon as this is over." "Well . . ." Uncertain what to say, willing to please her, to go to the party, to try to enter her mood. The conference is of the new journalists, there are some people I know here. "Let me just put my briefcase in the car." The few moments on the street already make us feel free. Forget the party, let's go on our own way, to Chinatown, the parade, our long-awaited dinner. She is feeling the freedom too, we decide to go off alone, ignore the party, the droves of people. A woman stops us in the street, an old acquaintance from Sacramento. It is an eternity until she releases us. Then finally, finally on our way. Fancy-free, two figures arm in arm, dwarfed by the buildings, almost skipping with the exuberance of having escaped, going off on our own, our adventure, our night on the town.

Everything is enchanting, delirious, infinitely pleasing. The drinks before the parade begins, the hundred foolish high-school drum-and-bugle corps, the majorettes, the clown. Even the fat sheriff in his limousine. She holds me, standing behind me, warming me in the cool night air, reassuring me. Even when my feet are tired from standing, even when her body leaning against my back makes it actually harder to stand, even then I am full of delight. As we drank she described the evening before, the sun setting when she was alone in the house. "It's the first evening I've been alone since you came." The solitude had made her melancholy, thoughtful. "I had a hundred Zen insights." She laughs, covering her face. I remember all my evenings alone there and say nothing. "Coming across Ann Scott's death in the papers, then watching the sunset. It went on and on. Where were you when the sun went down?" "On the freeway, coming back from the doctor's." "If you'd come back then, I would have canceled my engagement for the evening." Neal, I think, forgiving just as the snap of logic fits. "But it was a commitment and I had to honor it. Though by this time, nothing could have bored me more." I smile, feeling a little limp, confused. She turns the full force of her eyes on me. "It comes down to this, I don't want to lose you, lady. I don't want to lose you." "I'm so glad," hardly knowing what to say. Some voice in the back of my head saying, "You already have," and knowing it for the lie of mere revenge. I look at her, her beautiful eyes loving me, wanting me back. She has returned. For how long? Later, when I made a remark about my habitual inability to answer my letters, complaining that I'd really had trouble with the mail today, she misunderstood me, thought I had said "male" and meant Neal, she gratuitously swept him away, half in apology, half in dismissal. "Call it senility, call it a last fling." "I only meant the postal service, darling"—laughing to cover her mistake. And during the parade she held me.

My hand stroking her cheek. Suddenly aware of tenderness, the awful nameless pull of love, its desire to possess, consume. Lying next to her and painfully aware of it as I had not been all day, even that evening, entertaining friends, when we had laughed, flirting with each other, lovers laughing into each other's face at a joke or some gossip repeated by one of the guests, making the joke our own, special, private, intimately shared. And then we tired of them, wished them away. Longing for our peace and our rest. She is especially tired, hungrily wants sleep now. I feel desire stroking my thighs but do not disturb her, say nothing. Wondering if she intuits it. We turn away to sleep.

But I cannot sleep. Surprised by my restlessness. I always sleep so easily with her. One moment ago warm in the warmth of her body, content as always in the mere nearness of her and ready for sleep. Then of a sudden seized by a stricture in my chest, like smothering. I cannot breathe. Pulling for air. The suffocation of claustrophobia. Absurd, lying here on the low open bed, four windows around me—two looking onto the expanse of the bay and the city. What could be the matter? A terrible fear. The strangling is about the fear of staying here. If I stayed on past the time, if I settled, I would suffocate. Wanting to cough. Gulping for air. Hardly daring to move, not wishing to wake her. The friends who came by tonight, old friends from New York. I was gay, slender, witty, young, laughed with my head back, realizing I have not laughed for over a month, the whole time here. Laughed and went on laughing, enjoying it like some novel sensation. And now holding my breath, then opening my mouth to breathe. I cannot get enough breath. Turning once, cautiously, my innards screaming with some fearsome incoherent premonition of their own, the body taking revenge.

She wakes. "Would you like me to sleep in the other room?" "No, no, I'm terribly sorry." Lying very still now. I never thought this would happen, yet I would like her gone. I would like to read. To smoke. To stake out the black-and-white-butterfly sheets for myself.

My bed, my territory, my peace, my solitude, my own pursuits and space. I turn over on my back, stealthily. It will have to be better now, the breathing will have to improve. If I could just lie higher on the pillows. Memories of imagined asthma attacks at the university, damp spring nights dreading examinations. Nonsense. Years ago. Breathe easily and deeply. Get hold of yourself. If you don't beat this tonight, it might go on, become impossible to sleep together, surely you don't want that. Try, for God's sake.

Trying, lying on my back, feeling the lights of the city, which I cannot see, only feel. Their dim glow on the ceiling over the window hardly more than a vibration. Breathe. The breath constricted, painful in the chest. And beyond it mind and stomach in panic at the threat to life, the possible closure in the throat. If I could sit or stand. Ridiculous. This can't go on. I will go into the room across the hall, Pia's room, sleep in the cold, unfamiliar bed. Not force Sita to move. She lies beside me, asleep. Without waking her, clumsy but rising noiselessly, almost surprising myself for having surrendered the attempt, for doing what I so detest, banishing myself to the other alien bed. Not alien to her of course, her refuge. But to me utterly loathsome. Cold damp sheets, a musty room. Never mind, pick up the cigarettes by the bed, slip downstairs and get your book. And just as I am standing, she wakes. "I'll go over to Pia's room." "No, I'm already away, I'm up. You stay there, go back to sleep." But now she too is standing, ghostly in Pia's flimsy white nightgown. We are two ghosts on either side of the bed, a bit ridiculous, perplexed. But she has already outmaneuvered me. Her brief goodbye kiss. "I guess we're both restless. See you in the morning."

For a moment disappointed. Then relieved. Ensconced with lamp and cigarettes and book, reading Anaïs Nin to the last wonderful pages of the second volume, the death of her romantic life in Paris as a world war begins, the vitality of this bohemian world and the tragedy of its dissolution never more poignant and compelling than in those last throes, farewells, exiles. Conclusions.

At the faculty club. Lunching in the sun. Half satirizing, half appreciating the place. Its elaborately shabby elegance, the vast masculine comfort of armchair, the luxury of good wine at the end of a cafeteria line. Going to the lobby to buy cigarettes, I pass dazed old professors with their newspapers, jolly tables of young departmental hustlers. The world of academic bliss I might have had were it not for art—an old envy coming back, an old fear of the lonely future. So much drabber now, without her. Yet she is still there waiting at the table in the sun, its good warmth on her back. I feel it in my hair, glistening in the light, how pleasant as the sun filters into the scalp, down to the very vertebrae. We are leisurely and contented. She is reminding me of some annual dinner, Martin and his new woman friend are coming down to the city for it, will pick us up. I should be one of the party. Laura will want to meet me. "It will make her feel entirely in the family. She's already met the kids and Stanley and Neal." "Who is Stanley?" I ask automatically. I have never heard the name. "Haven't I ever told you about my friend Stanley?" "No. I've heard about Neal, but I didn't know there was anyone else." "Oh, I haven't seen Neal in a long time." I am bewildered.

"Stanley's a testament to the power of advertising." I look at her. "I put an ad in the paper. The kids said I was crazy. But I really wanted to try it, to see if there were actually any sensitive intelligent men left in existence interested in friendship and conversation, which was how I chose to phrase it." I watch her, feeling a curious pity but also admiration. Was she that lonely? Or this brave? I watch her, her mellow beauty, her ability to laugh at herself. "Box number of course, no name. And then the replies started coming in. Pia and Valerie and I put them all in the middle of the bed and read them out loud and laughed and laughed. Of course they were mostly just nuts. Illiterates. Horny creeps. But at the bottom there was a good letter just signed 'S,' which is how I'd signed mine. From a lawyer with several children going through a painful divorce. It was on university stationery with his department on the letterhead. So of course

I looked him up in the catalogue and in a few easy steps found out who he was. Naturally he had no idea who I was, just a box number and the initial 'S.' I decided I'd let him hang on the ropes a while, play with him, enjoy myself. So I called his office and left a message saying I was Serena—I swear at that moment it was the only other name beginning with 'S' I could think of. He called me back and I teased him—'I've got your number, I know just where you work and all about you.' So he started trying to find out who I was, went through the catalogue, played CIA. And couldn't come up with anything. No Serenas. Finally I gave in and agreed to have a drink with him. He picked me up at the house, and there it is, we've been seeing each other for months."

She smiles, the same half-bashful, half-willful, naughty smile she had over Neal. "He's just a nice middle-aged man, forty-five years old, who loves his children and sees them weekends. He's moved over here to the East Bay to a little apartment, and his kids think it's a great treat to bring their sleeping bags and camp out with him on the floor. He's shorter than I am and has a bald spot." The last, like the deprecations of Neal's youth, published to appease, to ease the hurt. Merely bewilderment still as she goes on to enumerate Stanley's virtues, the pleasure of his company, how delightful it was to introduce him to Martin, who happened to stop by once, how Stanley hopes he and his former wife can arrive someday at the pleasant friendship she and Martin enjoy.

Somehow the introduction of Stanley is tolerable, even interesting and sympathetic. There is more of the truth. Stanley is a new rival, another ghost of the nights of her disappearances. How vast, amorphous, yet overwhelming her mysteries, the pitfalls of her betrayals. It is terrible to add Stanley to what I fight against and am losing to, but at least the stranger is named, a real human being, an actuality. We fall to talking of the house, how the rent will be paid when I'm gone. Should we get a roomer? No resolution. And then to trivia. Suddenly she turned and smiled at me, and she asked how I liked it, did it make life more exciting, every day a new catastrophe around the corner? Teasing me. And then we fell into the quarrel. Her independence. Her right to her independence. Lovers of the past, her past, my past, whether they had interfered, whether it had been hard to bear—her material. Mine —that the time here so far had been very hard, the house full and alien, feeling her love so much diminished, the loneliness of these weeks and weekends, days and evenings, and for a clincher, that I was here for only a short time, a matter of weeks, and it mattered terribly to me how things went—it was only a short time, then it was over. Would I write her off so soon? she asked. I did not know how to answer. The sun beating down, the campus in green and blossom and springtime. The terrible contrast between us and nature, between us and the idyllic scene, the strolling professors, the carefree kids, the bicycles and dogs.

"After a few months you're going back to New York again. Then what have I left?" Of course. She lives here year round. She must have people around her, provide for herself. It is all sensible, reasonable. It's I who am unreasonable. "You yourself agree with me. You have all sorts of ideas about freedom." "I know. I don't believe in possessiveness. It's just that when you live with this it's so much harder than you think. I've never asked you to live with it like this, day after day." She looks away. "And maybe I just couldn't live up to my ideas," I confess, ashamed, looking down at the table as she gets up to leave.

We begin to cross the campus. "Do you suppose boredom is inevitable in relationships?" I ask, watching the professors and the kids, wondering if our differences are only temporary, commonplace. "Of course, relationships go in cycles. They grow and go through phases," she lectures me. "At one time they're very sexual, then it may die down for a time, take another direction, and then it may come back, flare up, die down again." She goes on and on, playing sage, but now I feel she is talking down to me. We pass a grove and blossoms and a tower. "You've just got to be made to understand that I am free to do what I like." "I do understand. I've been made to understand." My gorge rising at her tone. "And I can't see any reason why it should bother you if I see other people. Both of us have done that in the past." "But it was at a distance. We weren't living together." "There was Sarah, there was Bea," she insists. "How do you suppose I felt having to stay in a motel that night because you were with Bea when she came up from L.A.?" It is not till hours later that I realize she didn't stay in a motel, she drove back, furious, to San Francisco. How contrary she is. Jealousy then was natural, at least if she felt it. And I was flattered, took it as a sign of caring. "The times you mention were only two nights in three years. And you had them too—Brian, Hank. But somehow it worked. We did not have them while we lived together; we had our own separate places then," I argue. She is hostile, determined. It is her manner that makes me despair, just as it was her lying to me about Neal; if she had come to me and said, "Look, I want this," I could have understood, but it was the if-you-don't-like-it-go-to-hell quality, the bullying. How to explain the difference to her? Her voice is hard against me, negative, contemptuous. She is berating me for not seeing more people, having more friends. Suddenly I am very angry. The patronizing tone stings, hurts like malice. "I don't live here. I don't have friends here." "You don't even try." I keep silence, going along a fence and a sidewalk, the dirt hot and dry, the place ugly and without meaning, so angry I could strike her, nearly choking. "Look, I know exactly four people, only one of them is a friend, the other three are acquaintances. One of them I haven't reached yet, she's never home. The others I pursue all the time. Sherman I see whenever I possibly can. Susan too. Alta I just sat down with for the first time yesterday. Believe me, I try. I chase them." Feeling foolish saying it, but insisting she realize the truth, admit how alien I am here, that I am here for her, only because she is here. Something she has forbidden me to mention, since she's not interested in having any "guilt" about it.

But it is not the issue, trivial or continuous, that matters. It is her contempt, her ease in treating me like

a child underfoot who should go out and play, find
playmates. Or someone socially inept who has failed
utterly to adjust. We walk along beside the football
field. Still astonished at how easily she despises me,
still hurting. Astonished by my own anger. We draw
near her building. One hundred more yards and we
will say goodbye. I fight in my mind for the thing to
say, to do. Apologize? Say I was a poor sport, suffered
a jealousy that I shouldn't have, stand before her contrite, conquered all over again? I say nothing and we
part.

And the next night much the same thing. The suffocation, the rigid waiting. And something new: my
fists double up, a convulsion all through the body.
Anger. How could it be anger? I hardly dare investi-
gate the idea. Once this was a bed for sleep, reading,
conversation, lovemaking. I would sit up and read
half the night if I chose, it never bothered her, she
used to suggest it, encourage me to read, smoke, do
what I liked. But now I cannot even move, am afraid,
forbidden to stir. A prisoner here just as circumscribed
as in every other aspect of my life. The hour we go to
bed is chosen by her. I could stay downstairs, but
really I cannot, too fervid not to miss the few moments
of intimacy per day, moments when I lie close to
her, feel her warmth, her body, moments when she
might make love to me. Of course it is that, just that—
that she might make love to me.

She has turned away, ready for sleep. Is it a frustration merely sexual? I ask myself. Just as last night I
felt a moment's desire, then banished it as she turned
away. I supply all the usual reasons; a week night,
her job, tiredness. But tomorrow she is taking the day
off, we go to Napa. Never mind. After the quarrel at
lunch today, what could there be tonight? The quarrel.
After I left her, a curious thing happened. I went
home and answered all my mail, the stack of letters
I never answer, my reservoir of guilt, of inferiority
before her matchless efficiency. Attending to all my
affairs. I will not be a victim. Doing something for
myself. Then I went out and bought us a chicken.

Dinner was passable despite the quarrel. Afterward we read. Out of the evening there must have been one good hour. Lighting the fire I teased her, that I am the better firebuilder. Leaning over, I laughed into her face and my lips brushed her breast. Then I remembered I had a pimple on my chin and lowered my head.

I turn on my back, hoping to breathe better. Moving in stealth, surrounded by prohibition. No use. After minutes trying to slide up the pillows, to have my throat and shoulders higher. More air. The room across the hall beckons. My own space. A book. Cigarettes. I lie waiting to escape, to glide out in the dark, mind already lighting up and opening a paperback. She turns and shifts in her sleep, noisily, without fear, unconscious. I lie on my back again, waiting for courage or the need or the maniacal fear of suffocating to become powerful enough. But tonight more courage than fear, tonight it is possible, more possible to leave her, to rise and go. I toy with staying, beating it, afraid of the nights to come. But it is too desirable, the room over there, my privacy, my ease, and my interest. I lust after it. All that against the grave I lie in, the stricture in my chest, the futility of staying.

Slowly, carefully finding the cigarettes and the book. Then, in an instant, fighting the creaky places in the floorboards, in an instant more crossing the hall rug, pulling to the door, using a silk scarf hung on the doorknob to ensure against the sound of the lock. I am safe. Free.

All the way to Napa heckled by the past. Starting out grim and silent driving through Richmond's oilfields in my closed convertible. Our dull and speechless holiday. The weather gray and uninteresting, without promise. Every detail mocks the great high junkets of our early times. Other trips, other selves who drove down the road, top down, radio on full-tilt, going down to San Francisco eighty miles an hour with her hand on my thigh. Even in an open car I sat close to her, the sky around us shouting for joy—whatever the motorists thought, we were youth and intoxication, we were ev-

ery summer in the world, we had finally discovered
love, invented it. If ever I think of those early days, it
is often a picture of us in the car on some back-country
road near Napa. The hood just cresting a hill, trees,
even a cow. We are laughing, holding hands, and singing pop songs; dreaming aloud, planning where to eat,
telling our old loves and past lives, composing long, extempore paragraphs of pornography for a fantasy pub-
lishing house we have named Flaming Crotch. "We
must remember to bring a tape recorder along some-
time and get filthy rich." "All we need is a press,
there's no point making a whole lot of work out of it,
we'll just secrete it when we're horny. The world needs
a new pornography." "And we'll just toss it off on the
side, juicy tidbits when we can spare the time." She
would squeeze my hand, and the word "juicy" would
inspire us to flights, to smut and endearments and
laughter and the risk of the lewd and the tender
together.

Sita doing eighty on the highway, the magic road
from Sacramento to San Francisco and our great
golden weekends, the hills like green mossy breasts on
each side of the road. Her California, the hills she
taught me to love. Just as she taught me to live those
times, taught me food and wine and the sun of our
own Mediterranean—California and all it meant,
promised. For once not the tawdry of Hollywood or
the tourist's Frisco, but the real California, which was
always her self, those soft green hills, her ripeness and
beauty and wit and good nature and knowledge of the
world, teaching me this as she gave it, as she taught me
youth and how to be young, that it was a feeling you
permitted yourself once the lock was broken by love,
a rapture, a fine full air of spring.

And this other spring today. Three years later we
are the gray pygmies of today. Speechless for miles
with nothing to say. Forced comments on a house or a
car or a billboard. I turn and look out the window and
fight tears remembering the thundering sunlight of that
other time. Our bodies are dead between us. I sit on
my side of the seat as she drives now. It would be unthinkable to sit near her, it would never occur to her to

lay her hand on my thigh as she used to, or even to put the top down. I hear the psychiatrist's phrase in my head: "inappropriate behavior."

Then and now. It is this that sickens me each time, this disparity between what we were and what we have become. The suffocation of that joy. Even—and this is a more dangerous thought—the disparity between what we are and what we might be now if we had love again. Because it is all possible. Objectively speaking, we have everything: a car and a trip to Napa, a good lunch and the wine country. The hills begin to be a lovely green and the mustard is beginning to bloom in the fields. But instead, this heavy silence, this discouragement. Boredom. How bored she must be, driving with her eyes on the road, completely removed from me. I feel it too, thoroughly bored. But it is worse, it is grief.

Sita had suggested that we make a side trip to Jack London's house in the mountains. And it was there, after the photographs and first editions, after the artifacts of a manly life of boats and extravagance, fine jerseys and sails and old letters and handmade chairs, it was there we had our fight. Or as close to a fight as we've ever gotten—twenty bitter minutes in the trees by the parking lot. It had been my idea to sit on a bench in the little glade and recover from the efforts of literary tourism, smoke a cigarette, enjoy the pale efforts of the sun and the view. Never guessing what would come. Though of course I'd had my little plan. Given the scene, we would talk, would communicate somehow, close up the gap before it widened, get in touch, come together again. Floundering about for words, for a way to say it all, the feeling so urgent but the words so inadequate, especially the appropriate everyday words, the spoken language. To find the permitted conversational words that are not slang or jargon but still have the purity of simplicity. Meaning my overture to be almost a bouquet, a hopeful gesture of courting, probably a halting and feeble rigmarole meaning at the end only I love you, but meaning it with a fresh force, some novelty, something to catch her heart again.

And she astounded me with venom, with fury, an outraged female reciting her grievances, movement rhetoric, a feminist tract. A parody of our situation, hypocritical, dishonest. "This is some watered-down version of *A Room of One's Own*," I said. Hurt that she would see me as the enemy. "Exactly, that's exactly what I mean, that I need a room of my own." "Virginia Woolf didn't have lovers in mind but writers." She ignores me. "I want to be free of you. I need space. I had to show you that. I had to teach you that, whether you wanted to learn it or not." I look at her, amazed. Each word is a blow. "So you had to be taught. You just had to be made to learn. Even if it took something dramatic. And that's what Paul's room is about. That's what my staying out all night is about. I need my freedom. I insist on it." "Of course. No one in the world has the right to question that." I stand up, ready to go. I don't want a fight, I want peace. But there is no winning with her. And no talking, except to quarrel. She will have her freedom, well enough. She should have it, I am only sorry about how she defines it, that it increases as I decrease, that it needs to eliminate me in order to flourish. She walks ahead of me back to the car. I would like to shout at her—but there is no freedom for me. What about me? What do I get? You withdraw further and further, reserve a room for yourself, take lovers, and I get to wait for you, to see you in your odd moments, to come three thousand miles to be fitted in as a quickie before or after one of the real people, the men. Her back is angry, righteous, frightening. I follow it into the car.

We hadn't meant to have lunch at Juanita's, just a drink. It's out of the way if you're going to the vineyards, but some old impulse got us there to the big ramshackle house full of overstuffed chairs and roosters and mice urinating in cages, and Juanita herself like a great overstuffed sofa, fat, mean, cantankerous, as bizarre and full of antimacassars and old plantation decadence as the place itself. And wonderful, its very crudeness, the plaster saints, the run-down "antiques," the monkey that used to get drunk at dinner—how it all challenged and bewildered us that first time. After a look at the place, after the odor of the mice and the realization it was their urine soaking the newspaper in the big cage in the central hall that perfumed the whole rambling building, after one pass by the monkey, trying to climb my leg, we quietly took our bags and left. Fascinating place of course, but we just couldn't take it. This was no place to spend the weekend, even though Pia swore it was "pure camp" and I remembered Juanita from the years she had her houseboat in Sausalito, where Sherman took me on those first glorious trips to San Francisco to have hot cakes at all hours of the night with highway cops and pop stars and all the butter you wanted. No checks, just take what you want and declare what you ate at the door. But Juanita was a dim presence then, off in her corner trading obscenities with troopers and truckers. Now she was a huge presence right smack in the front door yelling, "Where are you going, girls?" We with the bags and all, caught dead in our tracks, escaping her. Even Sita's presence of mind slipped a bit at this, but we invented some innocent errand and drove hard to the next hotel. She'd stayed there once. A converted monastery, sounded just the right thing. But on inspection altogether too Protestant. Antiseptic, a Hollywood aqua chenille bedspread, a motel lamp. And that was it. The barest room I ever saw. We were ready to go back. Both of us as ashamed as we were amused by our cowardice. As if it were some special forgiveness we could afford, being so in love with each other, we could condone even this typical female shilly-shallying, this timidity before monkeys and mice and the bizarre in a house.

Back in our room, or rooms, for Juanita, conferring the favor of letting us stay all night, for which you needed connections, gave us a sitting room with a Victorian couch and a bedroom with a bed I imagined from a nineteenth-century house of prostitution, bed and bureau and washstand so redolent with sensuality, with Impressionist nudes washing in tubs, with Madame Bovary and the throes of romantic love in illicit places —back in our sitting room, safe from the mice and the rooster and the monkey, I could look out our windows into the flaccid and overgrown yard and realize that this room was every ruined plantation, the real dangers of sloth and heat and the past grown rank, probably beyond anything Tennessee Williams could bear. But how he would love it. It turned out that his friend came here often. It also turned out that the halls were full of tourists, and that after we had made love and she slept while I read for a class, they invaded the halls with their noise, their foolish trying of the door, their comments, their exclamations, the violations of their footsteps. So I put a sign on the door of the bedroom where she slept and spent the next three hours listening to them reading aloud in ringing tones, "Please be quiet, someone is sleeping." Listened like a dragon in its den, ready to spring, so fierce I was to protect her, my adored and sleeping lady, to protect her with the little power I had to protect, protection being always her prerogative to extend toward me. But here was my chance, this rare time when being younger I could be older, knowing less I could be wiser, the beloved I could be the lover.

That was the weekend of Sally Jean, our eponymous double, our mythic and joint alter ego. It began with the high-school yearbooks on the bedside table. Once between making love she read to me from these, her accent making the maudlin prose hilarious, the scrawled inscriptions, "To a great gal," entirely new and wonderful comedy. She had, through Pia, even mastered the idiom and could hold forth in it for hours. "Look, Sally Jean, you're just gonna have to keep putting it out for me, baby. You put out real swell, honey," her eyes beaming at me, her hand lascivious along my stomach. I had never seen or heard anything as amusing, as absurd as this impersonation. And called her Sally Jean too. We were both converted into peroxided American teens, gum-chewing, vulgar, horny, lazy, dumb. The perfect fantasy, the perfect charade and escape. Everything that we were not, a release into our antipathies, opposites, reversed identities. The mirror we plunged into for our most salacious games and roles and smut. Even the contempt in Sally Jean was flattery, the perfect assurance we were ourselves. Somehow the pretense in Sita-as-Sally-Jean patting my ass, her patronizing lewdness, "Sally Jean, just keep putting it out, baby," was the grandest compliment, the most intimate bond between us. Our secret selves. Selves no one would ever believe or understand. A code. Like the black and white sheets. Wonderful Beardsleyesque patterns splendidly drawn and printed; we both came to own a set and they were a talisman, fetish. "Remember me? I'm the one with the black and white sheets," she'd drawl. "If you ever get confused, just remember them black and white sheets, Sally Jean."

All so far away now when we enter the bar, the huge shabby bar where we used to drink before dinner, the great Rabelaisian dinners of Juanita, dinners of steak and roast beef together, dinners you could never finish and stopped eating somewhere in the middle, limp with exhaustion and defeated greed, dinners where a woman played the autoharp for us, coming specially to our table, spying us as lovers probably, suckers maybe, but came and sat before us and played us everything we liked. And Sita liked a song that asked, "Will you still love me tomorrow?" I saw in it her age, her fear that I would leave her, her surprise I did not gather the whole host of young women she imagined lurked or assembled everywhere for me to take them. There was a line in this song, "You gave your love so sweetly," that I felt always must be her feeling about me, about my coming to love her, about my docility and gentleness, a thing she had never expected of me, going by my reputation as a female Don Juan and bomb thrower, but a thing that completely disarmed her, and that by degrees perhaps, but very soon, I surrendered myself to her, so the words had a specific sexual or perhaps one should say amorous content, but against it was always the threat of time and her own age—will you still love me tomorrow? And the woman must have caught this and, whatever her notions of these things, been touched by it, for she sang the song over and over. She was near Sita's age. And I thought how foolish of them to worry. And I was right.

This irony, along with so many others today as we sit in the bar. Catatonic with silence, dying to strike up any pleasantry with the barmaid, the tourist couple to our right. I order a gin-and-tonic. Sita orders a Campari. I am pleased that she will drink, pleased that in our black mood she will do anything at all, speak to the tourists, charming them, or to the barmaid, democratic. Even take notice that lunch is in preparation. She suggests we stay. I had been hoping for more neutral, less haunted ground; some new place. She says she is hungry and the driving has made her tired. Well then, of course.

We sit in a little booth off by ourselves, usual Juanita collection of fifties frieze, the hideous made quaint through attention. Sita eats the main course, roast lamb. I made a mistake in not ordering it, choking down a gigantic tired assortment of breakfast things instead. We eat. We do not speak. There is nothing more to say, nothing to say at all. In time past we ate here and were happy, rapturously happy. And now are miserable. Is this all it is, I scream quietly inside myself, does it come to this? She eats her roast lamb with poised, polite bites, she asks if I would like a glass of water. In the midst of this insanity of decor and arrangement, of despair and loss and disappointment, she is a lady.

The moments spent in that odd little booth composed of some absurd tulle hanging for a canopy, some deathless pink armchairs out of the houses one loathed visiting as a child, and the great succulent dishes of food suddenly unappetizing, even nauseating, so that I wonder as much if I will vomit as over the bereavement of time, the terrible falling off—how do you have love and lose it?—how can it be there at one time and gone at another?—how if they loved you then, do they no longer love you now?—how does one stop loving? I never have. The moments like a funeral, a grim little mockery I imagine every hippie kitchen hand must see and find funny, Sita wondering aloud how Juanita can ever possibly make the profit she needs to buy the place if she feeds all these kids. The moments that are the worst of all. That little booth our coffin.

In front of Juanita's there is a round stone fountain. Sita took a picture of me sitting on the edge of it that first time we came up. I am wearing a black turtleneck sweater, rough wool that always seemed full of Paris and the art world—I used to call it my "existential" sweater—and a new pair of black trousers she thought particularly sexy. I am *tesoro bello,* I am the light of her eyes this day. I have taken off the smart straw hat I had been wearing and my long brown hair shines in the sun. I look very good. But to her I looked wonderful and she used to show people that picture with a frequency and fondness that made me nervous. "I took this picture of Kate when we were up at Juanita's one weekend, in Fetters Springs," she would say, showing the kids, showing the people in her office, showing friends. As if the little Kodachrome were some wonder.

As we go out we pass the fountain of course, the fountain where Juanita's police-like bellow stopped us, the fountain of the photograph. And beside it the raunchy little enclosure for the animals, donkeys and ponies and a few morose sheep, the usual untidy collection of roosters. Seeing the fountain, I steer us around to the animals and pretend an extraordinary interest in what mules eat. But finally passing the fountain on the way to the car, I see my ghost, a girl with shining brown hair in a black sweater gazing in ecstasy at the dead eye of the camera, out of faded paper eyes looking with blind miraculous delusion toward her certain tomorrow. I pass by as one passes a maniac or a corpse.

I had thought of it even before we went upstairs. Thought of it as you might contemplate the marvelous, a miracle, something you'd never be able to bring off or be able to do. Then doing it. Undressing in our room, growing sure I would do it, then panicking and heading for the bathroom as she undressed in Pia's room across the hall. But then coming to the door of "my" room, I watch her ensconce herself in what is at the moment "our" bed, and softly say to her, "Had a

lot of trouble sleeping the last two nights. I think I'll
go over there so as not to disturb you." Hearing her
protest as I reach the other room, safe, strong, miraculously strong. "Well then, *I'll* change," her voice calls
after me. "No, just stay there where you are."

Realizing that I forgot my book, have no cigarettes.
Ducking back to get a paperback. The book, but still
no cigarettes. Do I dare go downstairs for some or
will she jump in and replace me, forestall me in Pia's
bed, my gesture ruined, my effort turned to nothing?
For it is not merely that I want to sleep alone; it is
that I want to *choose* it, to have the power and initiative of choice, never mine till now. Finally not daring
to go downstairs but planted firmly on the bed and in
the room of my choosing. I will wait till she goes to
sleep. Then I'll go down. With cigarettes and book
and privacy and my victory. Meanwhile, just sitting
on the empty bed.

Realizing what it means: sex. I'd said to myself,
You will have to give up even wanting it. You will
have to go that far. Her insult from weeks before when
I'd told her that all initiative was hers, that she had
created a situation where only she could initiate lovemaking. And that this was unilateral, unfair, unequal,
without reciprocity. "You'll just have to learn to say
no," she said, laughing. "Time has taught me that if
nothing else." "You'll just have to learn to say no."
Like a slap. All right then, I *will* learn.

A tap on the door. I'm amazed. When she took to
other beds, I never dared to knock on her door. Why
didn't I think of that? But of course it would never
have worked. And I know already as she enters and
sits beside me that it will work for her. "Please come
back. You're beginning to make me feel like someone
who uses the wrong deodorant or forgot to buy the
right toothpaste." "You're not the first one to feel that."
But she is certainly not the one to put up with it.
Wheedling me now to come back. Her inconsistency—
that will brook no rejection at all and yet impose it
whenever she chooses. And makes it stick, terrible in
her irritation, her authority.

Utterly unaware of her inconsistency. Like a child,

having what she will. I can know all this and yet cannot resist her. "What can I do to bring you back? What can I say to make you happy? How can we start again?" When her voice says these things, I am helpless. Then she stops. She has already tired of wooing me. Just as I was about to rise and follow her. I look at her beside me. Her neck seems thick, she looks old. Her hair is in tight curlers because she is "going out" tomorrow night. He gets the curls, I get the curlers. I am tired. I would like to read. She is bored, it takes too long to court me. I wish I had a cigarette. "Come now, get your book and come back to bed." Why my book? She will not let me read in bed these days, or is this a new offering? I look at her, wondering if she plans to stay here and send me back across the hall. "Aren't you coming with me?" I say as I stand up. "Yes, if you want me to." Diabolic. She has arranged it so that I am asking her, inviting her to bed.

We settle in. The warmth of her snuggling against me. Then she turns away to sleep. I do not wait long for the stifling to begin or to escape it. Rising quietly, cigarettes, book, the short space across the room, across the hall carpet, and into my sanctum. Have I somehow kept faith with my resolution?

We meet on the stairs. Dark here even in daytime. Kissing, merely kissing hello. She smells of the sun, the glorious day outside, its light and urge in her hair her skin her lips. Our tongues slip into one another's mouth. I move in my jeans, surprised, not having meant to. Never expecting this. We break and meet again, mouths open, loins touching, warming moving heating.

And then it's over. She hands me the mail. We go upstairs. She has chosen the bed as the place to open and read the mail. I calculate my chances and look at the letters. A dull thing from New York about my loft, a boring letter to write in answer. The mail strewn around us as we sit on the bed. She begins to describe a demonstration at the governor's office. The reasons

she would participate or refuse to, the inanity of
driving up there without an appointment. I watch, only
half listening, listening instead to my senses. Will she?
Will she, when she finishes describing what she said to
the demonstrators on the phone, will she revert to the
scene in the hall? Was it a prelude, a promise? I have
forgotten all my resolutions, I am only waiting to see.
"Would you join me in some titillating . . ." giving me
her lips. Probably the sentence was supposed to have
ended in "lunch," but she does not end it. Our mouths
continue their own dialogue, the soft warm thrust of
tongues, sexual beyond sex or the sex of the genitals,
an intercourse of its own, preamble, overture. Wanting
to unbutton my shirt, her hand already finding its way
inside my pants. Hot for her, giving, wet, hungering.

The sun of early afternoon on us, our bodies in the
frank light of day. Waiting for her is waiting at my
desk, noon passing and losing hope. She said she
would be home at lunchtime, after some errands. At
one o'clock I'd given up. Then a car stopped, her keys
in the door, as now her fingers in me. Waiting a second,
then meeting her on the stairs, the kiss igniting. As now
she has me in sunlight, our old ease and extempore, the
sense of surprise, the unplanned, the spontaneous. Remembering one lunchtime at Derby Street, our frantic
and yet leisurely heat, a "quickie" she mischievously
called it, or even "chicken soup." Her delightful vulgarity, its miraculous contrast to the serene and stately
lady, even to the sensual woman bending over me,
sure of her power.

Taking her breast in my mouth as I come. Then
making love to her, the old disappointment. It was
there that it went wrong. There where the current shut
off. There as I stroke her legs and stomach and pubes.
There as we take off her clothes, wanting to quicken
the flesh, part the legs, breathe fire into her, drink her.
But she will not have me. Only the gentle friction on
her parts, only the moment's little spasm. Never even
entering her. And then she will take me again. And
again I am willing, but less so. Already the imbalance
depresses me, penetrates my lust, still consummate

upon the lovely flesh of her leg, its last crying wave, already despair enters my mind.

A minute after, the terrible disappointment. This really was a quickie. It does not stay on in euphoria, doesn't heal, comfort, or expand. The mind falls back at once to the sidewalk of reality, the smell of tar and asphalt, the ordinary. Letters on a desk. A letter from my prisoner telling me his appeal has failed again. "Shall we finish this off with some sandwiches and coffee?" She is already up, brisk, dressed, back in the world of offices and clocks. I follow her downstairs, disillusioned, remembering she had mentioned that she would be "busy" tonight, "an old friend from the South." At the time I thought that might merely mean dinner. Realizing now that she will be away all night, realizing it because the lovemaking preceded it. Precedes and follows all the nights out, the men. My rebate. Perhaps scheduled for last night. And last night I had denied her. And when I did come over to her bed it was too late or she was no longer in the mood. So this noontime flight is the alternate schedule, the substitution, the fill-in. How tidy she is. How just, how rigorously fair. My mind accepts it all, understands; my heart and stomach despair at the understanding. I have been had. Against all resolution, used. How much wiser if I'd kept the resolution, went without this. Its prospect so fair and sunny as we began. But afterward, seeing the shame. I have lost. Lost that little bit of pride.

And now the dining table, formal behavior, politeness, small talk. Shaken inside and calmly eating lemon yoghurt. She is quick and alert, in a bit of a hurry to leave. I am leaving soon too, a doctor's appointment in San Francisco, cheerfully forgotten during her visit. Finding my bathing suit and a towel, planning to meet Susan at the pool afterward, I look for her wicker overnight case which I usually borrow, but cannot find it. She comes back into the house, has forgotten her purse. I give it to her, going out with her to her car. Wondering if the overnight case is on the seat, if she has already put it in her car. Hating myself for wanting to look. Stopping short on the pavement, not doing it. Pre-

venting myself. "See you later" is all she says. No "I'll
call you tomorrow." Perhaps she isn't going to be out
overnight after all, maybe she's changed her mind. Last
night she had said, "I know a few things I can do to
make it easier for you, happier." Could she have
meant that, could she have gone that far? But I would
not have her cancel her freedom merely out of pity. If
only she would give them up, no longer wanting them,
wanting me instead. But not merely to please me or
propitiate. Freedom is freely giving. She has every right
to her freedom, I would never want to take it away. I
sit in my car after she has left. What is it I want?

And what could I have, anyway? She will go with
them. She will stay away nights. Well then, the rest of
the time. I will have that. Content myself. Yes, but if
she could only really *be* with me the rest of the time,
really be there for me, actually be with me when she is
with me—what would the other times matter? Why
should they? Any more than if she were away at work
or a conference. Absence is merely absence. But un-
fortunately it is not. It is time charged like air, poisoned. And when not absent, when present, she is the
dead or hostile being of Napa. I myself dead much of
the time, passive, a mere reactor to her moods, hot on a
staircase, nervous eating yoghurt. All initiative is taken
from me. I was so afraid even to put my hands on her
shoulders today as she kissed me on the bed, terrified
to presume, to begin, to brave misunderstanding or re-
buttal. I can hardly respond, carry through, keep up my
half of the dialogue.

A dilemma. Her polygamy, my monogamy; her activity, my passivity. This is not reciprocity, an equal
relationship, her much-touted adult and independent
business. By the very nature of the circumstances it
cannot be. Were I to have other lovers, yes. But there
are none. I know none out here. Beat the bushes to find
one? I don't want to, don't want to be so pushed. And
knowing no one I want, want no one. The circumstances of a masochist. Was she cunning enough to
contrive a situation where my recurrent ennui, or even
hers as well as mine with our bland "marriage" of last

year, should become "inspired" by masochism to go on being "interesting" through pain?

And to go on with this lame thing, this suffering, to go on how long, wearing me out how many weeks until I leave? And in New York having only emptiness, the complete absence of her. To go on doing this, spring after spring. Year after year. Her plan. And the alternative? To break off entirely. My plan. Then to have nothing at all. There is no winning.

She called in the morning, having stayed out all night. It had been the movies alone and popcorn, then a Japanese film on television, reading in bed. Careful diversions, carefully timed. Then the telephone as I'm reading the newspaper, calculating the hours till I see her. Her cheerful good morning. Aggressively cheerful. I am subdued, polite, not cheerful, tempered, trying hard for just that moderation. She would like to have lunch with me but she has an appointment. However, she would like to get together after work, maybe drink down the sunset at the Marina or go over to the city. Fine, I say. When she hangs up, I am sorry. Contrite that I didn't try to be "bouncy," with "Good morning, Lady," and so forth. By sounding merely ordinary, unenthusiastic, have I perhaps given her guilt, the thing she cannot, will not, abide? Was it absolute joy she wanted in my voice, absolute love, utter forgiveness, a total welcome? Were she given this, would she return to me in delight? And not given it, will she be surly when she returns, will the time assigned me turn sour? I can think of nothing else now, am obsessed with my mistake. An hour later she calls to tell me the political-science students want me to visit their class. I am bouncy, glad, laugh with her. She is coming home an hour early from work.

The evening began well enough with drinks on the Marina. "Look at the people," she said, "the black men are so much more exciting than the white." Obediently I look and agree that I, too, have always found black men more attractive. But she doesn't hear me, has fixed her attention on a chic black woman with an

arresting, elegant, thirties-style gown. Her attention
shifts back to the men. "Look, they are all in costume,
look at them, the one with the tiger's teeth around his
neck, the one in the huge velvet trousers, even the ones
with maroon polyester pants and white belts around
their big waists." I watch, wanting her attention finally
to come round to me but glad she is in a good mood,
interested, lively. At least we converse and do not sit
empty and inert. A black man stops at the table before
us against the windows. "He looks like a shark," she
says admiringly. He bumps against her chair and apologizes. She forgives him delightedly, flirtatiously. When
I look up a moment later, I find him staring at me. I
look down, confused, embarrassed. She listens to him
talking at the table behind her and decides his accent
is Jamaican. "A wonderful thing, a lilting sort of English," she says. I look out the window and find him
staring at me again. He seems to be speaking to me, his
mouth moves but I cannot hear his words. He stares on.
I am covered with confusion. I look down, feel foolish,
want to escape. Later she chides me: how could I resist
smiling, whatever he had said? I do not know how to
explain to her that he might have been a pleasant adventure were I alone. But that I am with her, and that
I want to be. And that he therefore doesn't exist.

After dinner we are given fortune cookies. Mine
reads, "You have a particularly magnetic personality."
Life's little ironies. I fold it and put it away. What does
it say? she asks. I answer in the Irish manner, by asking
her what hers says. She seems nearly as reluctant as I:
"Lucky in love." The mockery is rather too much, and
it hangs between us across the little restaurant table.
Maybe that was the turning point. Or maybe just the
way the weather had turned earlier. All day it had been
gorgeous, warm, tempting. But I kept on working, writing letters, waiting for the magic hour when she got off
from work. We would go to the Marina, watch the sunset, lovers in the thankful luxury of a Friday afternoon.
We had started off so bravely in the sun, so gaily, with
such anticipation. And then the weather changed. In
the space of ten minutes as I stopped off at a super-
market to buy an apple so that I wouldn't be drinking

on an empty stomach. When I came out of the store, the mist had already formed. By the time we reached the sea, it was nearly a storm. I was cold in my fancy Greek shirt, which an hour ago had seemed festive. Inside, it was already full. There were no window tables.

And she watched the men. Somehow that was bearable, "amusing," food for conversation. The dinner was excellent and we ate with zest. But somehow the "lucky in love" phrase was too much, too bitter. After last night, after all those other nights, Neal and Stanley and whoever the others are, even the men at the Marina, the shadows of men just at the periphery of our lives, strangers hulking and threatening from a hidden place in the wings, waiting till she approaches them, preferring them, stands and lies in secret with them, as she forays back and forth into my life. And you call that lucky in love? To sit there a fool and hear her say it. It was fortunate we were going, just leaving then for the movies. In another five minutes the darkness would cover me, my moods or mistakes or withdrawals, my exasperation or malaise. Fury, impotence, despair.

Coming home, I pleaded headache, told her I would read my way out of it. She had to get up early, had already set the alarm, and so went off to Pia's room to sleep. How eager she is always that if one of us is to move, separate herself, it should be she. That the controlling power of action be in her hands. That the room-of-one's-own decision be hers alone. I lie in bed, the charm of reading stale now, lonely here, my resolution exhausted. If she were to knock on the partly closed door, if she were to come to me now, how sweet. Coming into "my" room tonight, I stood by the bedside table a second. The phrase "confused, merely confused" going through my mind. What is it I want? Her fidelity? No, I would not circumscribe what she calls her freedom. I can't, have no right to. Then what? Not her fidelity but her love. Her love, having as many lovers as she chooses, only loving me as well? Something like that. Yes, sometimes. But tonight it didn't work. The rebate didn't come through. The ardor with which she usually returns from these men, the spill off from them or toward me, I'll never know, but always there is some quickening. Gratitude that I endure it? Guilt turning to sentiment? No way to analyze. Yet it is there. And I'm thankful, hungry enough to drink it in without asking.

But perhaps now I inquire too much. Perhaps I am bored or jaded. Cynical or sated, past hoping or starting again or believing at all. Yet if she would only come through the door, I would forgive everything, forget every moment but this, begin all over. She does not come. I do not go to her. And now the bay is misted, air and water the same identical gray. And I think of the weeks ahead, fewer than the fingers of my hands.

Undressing tonight, we had talked of going swimming tomorrow when her conference is over. "Call me," I'd said, "and I'll see if it's okay to bring a guest. I'm still not a member of this club Susan takes me to, but call and I'll see if they'll accept my application on a Saturday." "I won't have time to call, I'll be too busy," her voice out of Pia's room, snappish, impatient. I went to the door of her room and gently explained it all over again. "There may not be any phones." "But surely you'll break for lunch?" "I'm busy then too." I went back across the hall to my room, "our" room, partly closing the door, quietly exasperated.

As I read, the door rattled once, softly. I hadn't closed it firmly enough, the bolt wasn't in its groove. Thinking to myself, In a moment I will get up and shut it quietly without disturbing her. Then astounded to hear a rustle behind it, then a loud bang. It irritated her, and she had seen to it herself. But the vehemence, the violence. Like an insult. My face burns with a strange kind of shame. Sitting up with my book, feeling as if she had struck me. There was something cruel about the gesture, more cruel than anything she has done before.

When I look up at the door, I notice the balloon we bought at the parade. She had tied it to the outer doorknob when we came home that night, and with the slam of the door, it has ended up on my side. Wilted, shrunken, like a headhunter's trophy mocking me. Time goes on inside the room.

She is at one of her conferences. Another day drags by, another Saturday. She is bringing her friend Maud home to dinner and to stay the night. And they are late, hours late by now. The frustrations of waiting, of pacing the kitchen, checking the preparations for dinner, making myself ready. Because I am near tears and mustn't weep, determined to go through the evening with perfect stoicism. If Maud were to see anything amiss, since she's Sita's friend and her friend only, she would see it as a matter of my "being difficult," "giving Sita a hard time," "being a drag." They may well have discussed me in those terms already. Maud herself gives me only the slightest attention and, possibly for this reason, has bored me increasingly in the years I've known her. Because she is Sita's friend and not mine (as if it were not possible to be both), there is always a taut sort of politeness between us, always more brittle as her claims as Sita's friend begin to outweigh my own as her lover. I will be perfect. I have already prepared a magnificent steak dinner and I will be charm itself, the good hostess, the good sport. Meanwhile, I will withdraw utterly inside the realm where it matters. I will murder caring. And so this paradox, the happy home, the good dinner, the lively conversation; but inside I will have abandoned them both, gone away clear out of reach.

Do I do this to save my face or Sita's? For it would never occur to me to make a scene before her friends and I am just as eager to put on a fine show as she is. Our devotion, our discretion, our graceful and courteous behavior toward each other before others have been my pride as well as hers, years of it now, the joint enterprise of our relationship, the product of our two personalities merging to create a third, the "us" of each combined with the other, this remarkable and passionate friendship, so permanent and immune to distance or separation or time or differences in age, this image of ourselves we had projected to be admired, admiring ourselves in the process, the narcissism of love, this public self, the hardest thing to give up, this externalization of love, the bitterest thing to relinquish when the private love is dead. And so I will be perfect. And

I will murder caring. Both at the same time. For I have come to the end of something. And waiting for them, I feel it.

The dinner is splendid. Maud, who never eats, eats more than she perhaps should. I watch her finish her steak, feeling like the mother of the world to see her happy, forgetting that her lover is fatally ill, that her parents have spent three months visiting her, that she is in danger of getting fired again in her yearly crisis at the university, that she's maybe even had more to drink than she should. I also try to forget another dinner here last year, when she spent most of the evening in the toilet throwing up. But it is the Sita on that occasion that I want to forget. Sita with just that extra glass of wine, delightfully tipsy, cooking a roast chicken she continues to baptize in sherry, Sita in a silly and even rather ugly apron, huge, disfiguring, and yet in retrospect painfully lovable, Sita laughing and gesturing and being Italian and bending down her beautiful head to open the oven door one more time and baste that poor critter with wine, the rest of us too amused even to remonstrate after a while, merely enjoying her so innocent high.

Having eaten and drunk so richly, Maud grows sleepy and a bit disappointing after dinner. She sits on the couch and nods. I light a fire. In a few moments she is ready for bed. Sita and I stay up, deserted by our guest.

And I don't know just how it started. A chance remark I will probably never remember, but in a minute we are fighting again: the old fight, but for once I am fighting back. To my astonishment I hear my voice telling her that it's over, that I can't take any more. "I just can't stand it, that's all. I thought I could, but I can't." "Then what do we do?" "Call it quits." The still air in the room echoes the ominous words. I have gone this far without ever meaning to; without measuring the distance of the jump, I have said it. Part of me huddles its collar around its neck and waits in pure terror. Part, a part I never knew existed, keeps right on going. It is utterly silent in the room, the silence before disaster. "Would you do that?" "I have to. I can't bear living this

way. You are not *with* me any more." "Well then . . . "
She is accepting it, she is receiving my bloody little resignation and filing it away for the official stamp of my
departure. It was that simple. She never objected at all.
The air in the room so empty, so full of fear, as if a
murder had taken place. I have done it. I have said the
words I cannot retract. And it's over. Finally it's over.
"I'm sorry, darling, I'm sorry I couldn't take it. I tried."

"Then I will give them up." At first I don't even
know what she means. And then it comes to me—she
will give up the men. "I don't want to lose you." Looking at me with all her power, sitting above me and at
some distance on the sofa while I lie back in the pillows, looking alternately at her and at the fire. She has
tears in her eyes, her beautiful eyes, weeping, love me.
She will even give up others for me. At once I would
have her take it back; merely the statement would be
enough. And I hadn't even been thinking of them. But
of course, if she gave them up, it would be a new start,
the end of one set of fears. It is not that she loves
others, but that she doesn't love me—a significant
difference. But perhaps this is her way of loving me
again. And surely a gift. Such an act of caring, of
commitment on her part. "I don't know what they're
good for anyway, really, maybe I was just convincing
myself of something." Keep them, keep them, I want
to say. Give up nothing for me. If young men make you
feel young, if their attentions give you joy, have them.

While at the same time the serpent gloats, wants
them gone. And beyond that the voice of victory
flushed with pride that she would do this for me. "Don't
do what you don't want to, it would only make you love
me less," I urge, the serpent already winning. "I only
want it to go on, for us to stay together." Her voice
choked, moved, and I watch her amazed. For the first
time she has capitulated to me—because I meant it,
was serious, was gambling the whole stake? I watch
her, humbled by her humility, realizing that she is vulnerable, finally vulnerable. "It's three years, that's too
much to throw away," she says with this new weakness,
tragic in its frail humanity, moving me to a rush of
endearments for her, esteem, compassion, all the things

that first brought her to me. Now like a miracle, rising, rising even in her tears, rising and coming toward me, toward the great white polar-bear rug I lie on, the luxurious pillows, the firelight sealing us as I fold her warmth into my arms, her sobs in mine. And making love is wonderful, a discovery, all harms past, a new pact. The tears and anger leavening the tenderness we feel, the renewal. We have come that close to nearly losing each other, nearly parting in consternation and bitterness, nearly calling it quits and meaning it. And now to have it back. We lay a long time by the fire, and when we came we wept.

At my desk, to my right, these magnificent roses. Orange, actually orange. Perhaps fuchsia. A touch of pink in them, but really they are orange, literally orange. The most wonderful roses I have ever seen. They light the room, already full of the cleanest morning sunshine. This moment is a touchstone, I think. Fragile as the roses themselves; already one stem is broken. Hold back time, do not take them. Or this moment. A touchstone, I called it, a peak. The very perfection of it a kind of pain. Glowing like these strange vital flowers against the lovely brown of the worktable, the dark Japanese blue and white of the vase. My writing table. Having it again. Having my room again. The view of the city and the sea and the bridge. All restored. My first morning in a room of my own.

The roses are astonishing, the power and intensity of their color is such that it's hard to keep my eye on the page, to read for my class. The very fact of being rushed in the reading and of not being able to write and do my own work today, even this does not mitigate my pleasure, only increases it and my anticipation of tomorrow. The sun pours in. No other moment here will be as perfect as this morning. The realization itself a sorrow. Just as these roses go, roses that she bought for me yesterday as we were going to dinner in the city, buying them on impulse. And the roses radiate her, her gift—it is all her gift—the sun and the sea and the table, clean, waked, fresh for a fresh start in a fresh room. She has given it all to me. Given it back, restored it. All I took for granted last spring, having my room to work in, my warm cocoon of her love. How little I knew then what it was like to lose it. Spoiled, coddled, complacent.

Looking back on the ragged weeks. It is all restored now, returned to me, each piece falling into its place. Sunday afternoon while she plotted a trip to Mexico with Maud this summer—a trip I'll miss, being already in the East by then—I scrubbed the floor in what had been Pia's room and is mine again, while Pia moved all her belongings out. She and Dan have found a house in the city. She has taken a waitress job at a truckers' place in the Mission and does imitations of the customers. She didn't mention Emily, and when I asked about her return, Pia was vague. The new apartment has wonderful light, she said, her plants will love it. And I loved scrubbing that floor, waxing it, putting down the rugs. My own floor again. Moving my work-table back in, hanging some drawings. It is all ready for me. Finally, after all these terrible weeks of patience.

I read for the class, happy, excited, lucky in the insights and perceptions one hopes for in doing this work, falling into its method of thought but looking up every now and then to be astonished again, to savor the roses, their outrageous color, their pure loveliness, their so sensuous form, petal upon petal folding, vulva-like, some paradisaical vulva repeating its liplike crevice avariciously a thousand times. Each time I withdraw from the book I'm reading, make a note or look about me, the sunlight and the roses overwhelm

me again, pleasure so close to pain, joy so much a premonition of sorrow.

I will have to leave here. Suddenly it is neither rescue nor escape. Suddenly it is loss. For the first time,
absolute and irremediable loss. Finally I understand
her—"You will leave again in a few months for New
York and I will be left alone, why should I risk it?" I
had felt that too, coming here. That I would be gone
and without her so soon. Why invest again? Of course,
how unfair I am. Coming here and divesting her of all
she had built between her and loneliness: children,
lovers. The kids departed on their own, but the lovers
are made dormant by her promise for the few weeks I
have left here. Or until she tires of what she promised.

Her goodness has restored me to my room, my view
and my time and my roses. And her love, her attention,
are slowly turning back my way. And just as my full
resumption of place ripens, this moment of sun and
these miraculous flowers. Just then, I know it's ending.
Feel it coming, like fate, imminent as an amputation.
I stayed and gambled and am this fine moment winning. Losing, I threw and took the risk, and now see
another loss coming at me.

Only a few weeks and I return to New York. Just
yesterday, leaving Sherman's studio, I remembered the
roof of my loft, how pleasant it would be to put some
chairs out there, watch the sunset, invite friends over.
I'll buy geraniums, I thought, the thought almost like an
infidelity as I followed Sita down the passageway, surprised when she turned and kissed me.

Walking to dinner in North Beach, we passed a
flower shop and looked in the window. "Shall I buy you
a posy?" "No, please don't bother, darling," worrying if
she had enough money, anxious she not be extravagant,
but delighted. "What do you like?" "Well . . ." following her into the shop. "Pretty flowers for a pretty
lady." She laughs with the shopkeepers. Then I saw the
roses, their utterly incandescent color. Six for a dollar.
Why not? During dinner she put them in the water
glass. With each step of the way they became more
precious to me, more magical. The waiter admires
them. Coming out of the shop I was only flattered, but

during dinner I grew infatuated with them. She is tired, tired with that enormous fatigue of her Sundays now, one day to rest after a six-day week. I drive her home, protecting her.

The tiredness is possibly boredom. Perhaps she is already regretting what she promised. I would have her undo it. Perhaps she already feels unfree, tied. I long to undo what has been done, but am afraid to mention it, fear her annoyance at my inconsistency.

And the roses on my table, like a triumph. What if I never went home? Gave my loft to someone who needs a studio? Fumio has been looking for one for a couple of weeks. After the money spent and the months fixing it up, painting, plumbing, scraping floors? What if? I say it but cannot imagine it. The idea only a toy. The way people say, What if I were to get run over this afternoon? Because the loft is my self and my salvation, my only independence. But what if? And would she be imprisoned here with me then? It is what I felt last year and so did she, or she said so afterward. Yet while I was here she wanted me to stay forever, live together entirely, the "marriage" we refer to so bitterly now.

But do I owe it to her to stay? Having got it all back now, am I obligated somehow? Will I feel like a rat when I go? I had never had to worry about it till now—saw the time as the moment of release only, dreaded nothing but that it was a permanent break. And now I am by no means sure that it will be. I think of coming back next year. She thinks of it too, I am sure, though we hardly mention it yet.

To be happy now. To have joy. These flowers and this sunny morning. The class, which I'm truly enjoying now, and this evening dinner with my students, then to meet with Susan and Alta afterward. A full day. And the days ahead, days of work, swimming, the fine weather and the city. To be able, simply, to savor time as it comes. And yet these strange orange roses have already put the period on time, added the piquant note of finitude just at the moment they have signaled the top. I call her up to thank her, not really having the words, only the roses and my gratitude for being so happy this morning. As if the shock of their color, the bend of their graceful little stems, the crisp little green of their leaves were in itself her devotion, protection, tenderness. She does not quite understand but sounds pleased. How like a lover her voice can be, how like the very flesh of her body as it touches me.

Will there be another spring here? And if there were, what would it be like: January's coldness, new persons in the house, the unseen presence of lovers, the ghosts of men I never meet? Or meet only to suffer the more from. Or her lack of interest, the hostility breaking out so many times in quarrels and bitchery, her love's gradual diminution.

Who knows? You take your chances and so forth. I have thought once or twice of an entanglement of my own, if I were to meet some new person in the months away, some relationship that mattered, absorbed. But none do. And I am held here, Sita. By these roses, their small elegant pot, the lovely brown of the table, the sunlight over all and bouncing across the walls, the room mercifully transformed, emptied of Pia's hangings and plants and pictures and overstuffed chairs and beds. All gone. Mine again. My own room. And the great sweep of sea outside it, the span of the golden bridge. This moment having it all.

After my class is over, I'm in limbo with a few hours to waste. Was to have dinner with some of my students but there's been a mix-up: they thought it was next week, I thought it was today. Another student offers to eat with me if I'm "at loose ends." I keep face and mumble something about an appointment. Coming away from class high, excited, with the special enthusiasm that comes after a good class and then has nowhere to go. Neither have I. Or rather, that particular nowhere which is everywhere: home, the Mediterranean café, the Marina, the city. Home to my table and the roses on the desk, work a while before I go over to Susan's this evening. And then perhaps Sita may be home. Standing in the lovely campus evening, the rhododendrons in flower, the tulip trees, the scents of spring, trying to decide. I go to get my car. Rummaging for my keys, I realize I have forgotten to lock my classroom. Duty requires I hike back and do it. Coming out of the building again, still undecided between a café and home. The evening so fine, the promise of a spectacular sunset. But if she is home, if she stopped off there a moment on her way to her class in the city . . .

And she is home, her little gray car in front of the house like a present. I am thrilled to find her, carrying the whole burden of the roses and the morning, full of feeling. "I'm so glad to see you." "Well, I'm glad to see you too." She looks up from doing the taxes, putting her papers away, her mind in another place altogether. There is no echo to my mood, my clumsy ways to say it. She's spent her few moments busily, is now hanging out the wash. I struggle to help her, plodding downstairs and into the yard against the pieces of linen. Practicing phrases, hoping to come up with something, some arresting series of words. The small grass underfoot, the billowing sheets. While I hang one, she has hung all the others. I look around for more to do but she has already gone into the house. She munches cold chicken in the dining room. I eat cottage cheese out of the carton, watching her. "Do you have time for a glass of wine?" I'd asked when I came in, relishing the idea of a sociable little drink. "No, I'm in a hurry." Eating, she still gives off the sense of hurry. My gratitude, my love cramped inside me as I watch her. Later maybe.

And later she thwarted me too. Coming back from Susan's early, tearing myself away as soon as I could. Because she'd be home by now. I am even late. She may be in bed already, asleep. Planning to be stoic, silent, to slip in beside her and not wake her, merely feel her warmth. The front light on. Maybe she is still awake, maybe we could talk a little. Coming up the stairs, I know it all in the sight of the closed door at the top, the door to Paul's room. Now that Pia's is my workroom again, there is only the foam mattress in Paul's old room for her to run to for asylum. And she has done that. Sensible, of course, she didn't want to be awakened when I came in. And turning the corner, I see the rest. The lamp beside our bed in "my" room, the covers folded back, a note on the pillow: "Lovely Lady, sleep well, sweet dreams. I'll wake you in the morning." A flower sketched whimsically at the bottom of the page. Fragrant maternal sweetness of these notes, how ironic, almost treacherous. The room is lovely, inviting, empty.

This evening after she left I took the roses from the refrigerator (where I keep them in storage, covered like an icon, hoarding each precious moment of life), put them on my table, and sat a long time watching the sunset till it was dark. Even then I preferred the stars and the city lights reflected in the water to the room's bright overhead light, and so I lit a candle and went on sitting, merely sitting till I was hungry.

"When you're in a bad relationship . . ." someone had said tonight at Susan's, the phrase sticking in my mind. How easy, the time being past, to label it, to condemn it as hopeless, something you got into once, were well out of later. The pat little phrase comes back to haunt me. Susan and Alta both agreed. "When you're in one of those awful relationships, and believe me, I've been in plenty . . ." I nod my head; we are imitating women of the world.

And of course they're right. I said nothing of my own situation but I have read them a bit of my journal, since we are all reading aloud bits of our journals and they know very well where I am. They spied the wound and were kind about it. Probably would like to persuade me back to health. We are friends and fellow writers. A few generalizations about life and love and what is "good," what is "destructive," what is "hopeless."

But you don't understand, I want to protest, I love. It's because I love that I go on. Hoping. Trying. Delusions, romantic delusions, the phrase replies with its tidy view of life. But I want to live by my own standard, by love and the life of the senses. Or should one instead find refuge in a phrase—"a bad relationship" like that—and explain imponderables, explain passion this way? And the phrase sounded so convincing when Alta said it, so full of the conviction with which she had extracted herself, and would do so again if need be, tough, good woman that she is. You live by what goes far down, I could have argued, where you find energy, where you are convinced or can find belief, the faith of experience. But this is largely pain, they would have argued back, frustration, bafflement. True, or in this case true. But I have lived this. Deeply, all the way. I can remember it when I die—it is even a kind of dying in itself, or rather the losing of it is— because it was something from the beginning so sharply, so vividly and intensely lived, that the morality of "good" and "productive" and all that are irrelevant. But I tremble before their reasonable judgment and was afraid to read when it was my turn, hungering to communicate, to tell someone my plight, yet terrified to do so. And when they reply with good common sense, I insist upon my sickness, even arguing its value, turning it into a perversity, something clung to. Because it is mine, because it is my whole life now, my obsession. Sita.

Somewhere at the very bottom—the kernel, the heart—I suspect, of the problem is that love has failed us, failed us both. That we simply can't love any more as we used to, that it wore out, that it died somewhere, that fine aroma, that intoxication. And we will neither of us admit it. She chooses her mildly interesting affairs and a life of insecurity. I my angst and then my escapes to the East. And we are afraid to throw in, risk everything, and try making it whole again. Because we can't.

New York prevents me, anyway. Then it's I who broke the circle, taking a place in New York as long ago as last spring? Or was it she, deciding I had broken it by doing so? Was it she who broke it in Europe, those two terrible months during which she never even spoke to me? Tease the problem, find justice here or there—or blame or answers or riddles. It is not this, it is simple. Simple as the current between us, whether on or off; living together or apart; it can become in an instant alive or dead. If the current is there. But living side by side without it is nauseous, a moment-by-moment agony, something obscene when you compare it to the alive and living, the time of connection.

But isn't there something to be said for steadiness, continuity, security? If I had never left. If I had given up my town and my people, my studio and much of my art, the art world and its opportunities, my gallery. How much should you sacrifice? I sacrificed half. Foolish, probably not enough. Yet she doesn't consider these questions late at night.

But still it might have worked, this half-time life. If we had the current, if the lifeblood were there, it would have held us and the absences might have made it only the more exciting. Might. Might. Theoretical. Meandering. The real situation is her body inert in another room, and the closed self of this evening, the remote self of tomorrow's breakfast.

Her face in the light of two candles. I've done a London broil, striving for variety as meat chef. This one from a real butcher, not the usual Safeway thing. It's too rare for her, she says, "but it has a lovely taste." More wine and we edge toward what is usually a quarrel, but tonight we stay precariously balanced in a serious discussion. And then lapse into sentiment. She draws her chair closer. "And what am I to do when you leave? Does that ever enter your mind?" It had come up in the kitchen while we were cooking. "When do you take that trip to Puerto Rico?" I ask. "April twenty-sixth." "Then I guess I won't see you again; I have to speak in San Diego the twenty-fifth." And I'd been planning to go home to New York at the beginning of May. New York again without even saying goodbye? Suddenly the wall in front of me, the end. I look up at the cupboards, off to the stove. Her back is to me, preparing the salad. "How long will you be gone?" "Just four days." "Then maybe I could wait till you get back before I fly East." "You could spend the weekend in San Diego, it's beautiful down there. You might even want to go down a few days ahead." She goes on in her California tour-guide manner. I listen, incredulous. Can those last days together be so unimportant to her that she can cheerfully pack me off to look at scenery instead? As always it is so hard to understand the brisk managing side of her, the capriciousness.

Is it caprice now, her hand on my shoulder, asking about the future? "We have a lot to discuss here. Your belongings. The house. If you're coming back. All of it." One candle gutters. Her eyes by the light of the single candle, so very beautiful, so full of feeling, tenderness. Compelling. "Maybe if I had a connection that could keep on supplying me with underground classes at substandard wages?" I tease her, opening the way. Wondering, as I do it, if I want to come back, so unsure myself. Yet part of me assumes it now; I will come back, I will always come back. It will go on, it will always go on. "You don't seem very eager," I say, nudging her, sorry the very instant I do it, not having meant to, wanted to. "I don't want to push you. Not until we both know what we want." "And the fact is, we don't," I conclude. We smile. A wan, hopeless smile.

"Now when I think of leaving, it makes me very sad. It hadn't been this way when I first came. Things were so hard then that leaving was rescue. Now that we've come closer together I dread the time I go back." "It will be very lonely here without you." Her eyes telling me this, canceling the others, the friends and lovers and diversions. "It's very lonely in New York too, damn bleak in that loft a lot of the time." "Maud used to tease me, that when I came back from Europe last fall I almost systematically started surrounding myself with things and people and activities." Her hands move, describing the things and people and activities, moving them around the polished surface of the dining-room table like small wooden counters. "Maud used to tease me that under it all I knew just as well as she does that there's the house wine and there's champagne. It's that simple. You're my champagne." Laughing. "And you know my extravagant tastes." Her eyes, mischievous and full of light, snapping in the warm glow around her face. "I'd be able to forget for days in a row, and then when I'd be dressing or walking to lunch, I'd suddenly remember. I have felt the greatest tenderness for you, more than I've ever felt in my life for anyone." She puts her lovely head on her arms, her white sweater gleaming around her shoulders in the candlelight. Utterly beautiful to me. I sit drinking wine, loving her, admiring, telling her my admiration, adoring her in words, words I am normally too shy to say. Emboldened a little by the wine, by our closeness tonight, our final ability to talk. Even to talk without argument or bitterness. We are lost in our situation, hopeless as the distance between our worlds, a whole continent, three thousand miles, two radically different ways of life.

There is the art world and my need of it, which she saw when she came to explore it at Christmas; a small foreign child she was while I dragged her through slums, through the Village and SoHo, exclaiming softly, "Now I see, now I finally see where you live." We talked of it again tonight, the sense she has of being excluded there, her hatred of New York, her love of California. "But if I went to New York, if I arrived at your door, the door of your loft, you know you couldn't stand it." "I think it would be super," I say. "No, you don't. Four days maybe, but not much beyond that." Wondering if she's right, if I want New York to be alone in, free, my own place.

But wanting while she goes off to telephone Maud, wanting simply to admit how empty and alone New York really is. Wanting to say that Dobie, for example, is just a nice guy to build bookcases or go dancing with, but that's all. That only twice was I drunk or dumb enough to sleep with him and it wasn't any good. That even Dobie prefers a platonic friendship out of some dingbat romantic notions of his own. Wanting for some crazy reason to tell her all, to show her the utter barrenness of my days there, admit even that I'd been sleeping with Ruth and that it is nothing but guilt and disaster and that when I go back I won't do it again, that the whole thing with Ruth is a species of crime because she loves me and I do not, cannot love her, maybe—the terrible thought again—as I am Sita's crime because she cannot love me. The old analogy; as Ruth is to me, so am I to Sita. Wanting to tell her New York is solitude, that there is no one and nothing there for me. And yet not saying it. Shyness? Self-protection?

She comes back to the table to talk again and drink wine. It could work, she says, hard as it is to live our lives together only half the time. It could work. She wants me to come back next winter. We talk late and until we are very tired. As she was undressing in Paul's room, where she keeps her clothes, I found her and my arms brought her to bed with me.

During the night she escaped, but I did not mind, waking to a bit of a hangover to see that it's barely dawn. Coming back from the toilet, I walk softly, crossing the treacherous floorboards before her open door. "Come here." I stop like a thief in a pantomime. And then dive into the warmth next to her. "Snuggling"—surely the most pleasant thing in the world. Scrunching further and further into the mattress as we struggle closer and closer warmer and warmer nearer and nearer, our bodies like a letter fitting into an envelope, my legs over her legs, our hips sliding against each other, her arm tighter and tighter around my shoulders, my face nestled more and more firmly into her collarbone. It is bliss. The simplest and most primitive bliss. A childlike, sexual, friendly, animal bliss.

A garland of her notes. Notes left on the pillow wishing me sweet dreams, notes that Susan had called, or that she'd be an hour late, notes wishing me good morning or good night. Each with its caricature flower drawing, its old-fashioned and ironic salutation of "Lady." How many notes that start with "Lady" these three years, the word half courtly, half mocking, given what weight of tenderness by now, what smooth slopes of eroticism beneath the growth of familiarity. I have saved them, saved every scrap of paper she's ever given me. Letters. Notes. All the visible proofs of her love, even of her existence. It began when I first met her. I could never bring myself to throw away anything from her hand. Almost as if I knew from the beginning that one day she would be only a memory, a series of relics from some strange lost love, the beautiful older woman who had loved me once. Like a full rose that had bloomed once in my life. Even in those early days the sense of fatality, the telescope vision, seeing it already from the other end, from afterward. Why, when it is so present now? But now it's only a present suffering, the bitter ending of it, not the delight of then. Now it is an hourly humiliation so unlike the past with its light quick moments of intoxication. Now in contrast to them—a disappointment so sharp it is a kind of mortification.

Yet her voice on the phone this morning was humorous and caressing. She thinks she has sold one of my drawings. Real money. We are both pleased. "I'll take my usual commission," she teases me. "I'll let you take it out in trade," I counter. An old joke, her joke, a joke from the old days. "Would you like me to apply in writing?" "That will be satisfactory. But I must inform you that carbons are now required, because of the demands on the property." "Would Xerox be an acceptable alternative?" "Well, since you're an old client . . ." "Old? The oldest! Would you like a statement from my doctor to that effect? Or certification that I'm free of contagious social diseases?" "You have fleas." "No, they've left." "Really? I got bitten twice last night. You see what happens when you abandon me?" "They couldn't resist your body. Succulent. It's that succulence. I'm beginning to feel it way over here." Hearing her voice, loving it. Mellow, capricious, sensual, teasing, its urbane shuttle between her office and its bureaucratic realities and our own private and forbidden pleasures.

The past like music flowing back. How the telephone would ring on my desk in Sacramento, a desk crowned with the flowers arranged for me in the big shallow black bowl. I would be reading for class. Those long, rich days of reading and thinking, getting up only to walk the floor and pull a few dead leaves off my plants, waiting for a thought to form, for a note to be made. Rooms full of flowers and the sun and quiet. And her call, her voice Italianate and full of trills, like bubbles running up a glass, a voice full of invitation, ideas for dinner or explorations into the countryside. Or late at night a voice Indian and full of longing and desire, sadness and distance. When I answer the phone in New York and she says her name, she always says it as if she expects me to have forgotten who it is. Cross-country calls these three years. Her voice hurt often, lonely often, rarely reproachful. You fail love with distance too.

Or do you merely say "a bad relationship" and dismiss it? As a carriage is hurled across a typewriter and on to the next line. Are people like used cars that you trade in, the object being efficiency or health? Health, surely, that's the model for such phrases, the psychiatrist's "well-being" as measured and therefore imposed by the "objectivᵒ" observer, authority. Or do you stand by the thing you have made, experienced, created with hours of friendship and lovemaking and talk and boredom and companionship and quarrels and enjoyment and the power to remember?

But I do not have the fixity to carry this off, to cleave, settle. The courage of matrimony, its complacency. I am more romantic, believe more in the nostalgic than the everyday, have more faith in the music of the past. To say, "Here it is, I stick by it," is impossible for me. I stick by nothing. Or rather only that which has the ring of music, experience which leaves a fragrance behind it. I can envy the honest stolid matrimonial everyday, its commitment to the banal in exchange for security. But I cannot live it.

Let it always be an affair then between us. The way she laughed at Christmas, watching me cook dinner, sitting in my only chair in my big Mexican sweater, throwing back her head when she said it: "Let's always be having an affair. Wherever we meet, however many times a year—let it always be an affair." And I was excited and flattered and a little challenged, perhaps even made a little nervous by the idea; yet it struck me as perfect. To go on year after year with no more safety than the hazard of that. Perfect.

Of last year here, last spring, our settled time, I remember almost nothing. Only that it was comfort. That she brought me out of suicide. Separation from the man I'd lived with so long, the studio I'd had so long, then an almost fatal depression. And then I came to her. The place was reassurance, here I took the first steps back to living. And then walked off to New York. Clear away. When I joined her in Europe that summer, last summer, the balance had already shifted. I was no longer beloved, cherished, covered by her passion and nestled in her affection. Her passion of the early days, the great protective affection it ripened into. All gone. Only the steely resentment of a stranger, the nightmare of being in a foreign country with a woman who despised me and seldom spoke. And next the stranger when I came here this time. Now melting slowly back into the lover. How to trust it? How to take the steps, permit the folly of believing again?

I have never doubted the past, the Sita of then, a woman dead now. So full of love, of eagerness, of extravagant gestures to please, to surprise, to delight. Nothing was too much trouble, too far, too long, too expensive, too troublesome, too tedious, too obscene for intimacy, too silly for words. This garland comes from that time, the ghost who composes these notes knows the old music. Speaking to me on paper, she speaks to someone who was, and is no longer, but in the act of writing comes alive again for a moment, the one I was when she loved me.

I watch her face as she talks to me. Animated, entertaining me, talking for fun, for the recitation of it. A string of wooden beads around her throat, how I love the skin on her throat as I listen. A light flannel blouse, pearl-colored, handsome. Her hair curling around her face, its gray almost pearl-colored like her shirt, shimmering in the early-evening light. A story about a woman who arrived without an appointment and stayed all afternoon. Sita performs the bore who showed up in her office. "You won't believe it, but this woman is actually named Dr. Doctor. She's not a medical doctor, only a Ph.D. Might as well have been an idiot, took up two hours of my time and managed to say absolutely nothing. Silence. Dead silence. Just sits there. One of those moment-to-moment talkers, you know, the kind who may manage a whole sentence in an hour. But she'd come to see me because she wants me to give her a job teaching something she calls Assertiveness Training for Women."

She is laughing, waving her arms. Her beautiful features are lit with amused malice, with the delight of her impersonation of Dr. Doctor, varied with one of a dead body slumped in a chair, which alternates with her own vivacious account of the interview, her hands flying in Latin articulation, the rings on her fingers sparkling in the twilight. Her gold ring slaps the table for emphasis. "Dr. Doctor did manage to tell me a story. How she'd gone to a store, an art-supply store. And the man ahead of her had gotten a piece of cardboard from the clerk. When he offered to pay for it, the clerk said it was free. Dr. Doctor said it took her five full minutes to get up the courage to ask for a piece of the free cardboard too. And this woman wants to teach assertiveness!"

I know exactly how Doctor felt, have been Doctor all my life. I ought to take assertiveness training too. But instead I say, "Maybe she should give it a little whirl as a student before she starts teaching it, whatever it is." "That's just what I suggested—very tactfully of course." Sita beams. I merely enjoy her. Unable to judge, uninterested in judging; for all my sneaking sympathy with Doctor and the Doctors of the world, I am enchanted and beyond morality watching her. "Then at a quarter to five—she didn't leave and she didn't leave—I said I just had to get out my mail." Running into one of her silly puns, "You know, though Doctor didn't, that I keep a little male under my desk and at five I trot him out." Her smile lush on me, mischievous, sensual. "If you keep him on a leash coming home, he may even do his duty," I say, grinning at her, the word "duty" catching up with me as I say it, like some nightmare prediction.

"I think I'll put cinnamon in the coffee," she says, stretching. Should we go dress yet? I wonder, not wanting to yet, cherishing her mood, her company, bored by the political cocktail party at which we must appear soon. "Cinnamon. Do you like cinnamon?" she asks, being cinnamon as she asks it, aware as she says the word, repeating it over, smiling its syllables out, aware she is cinnamon itself, its very color and flavor. "Do you remember those little red cinnamon candies, red on the outside, cinnamon on the inside, do you remember them when you were little, how hot they were?"

Her mouth imitating their shape, their supernatural hotness. "Hot, hot, hot." She laughs at me. I smile and appreciate. Just the way she says the words is sex, playfulness, eroticism, every form of coquetry, the word warm in her mouth. Is she this way with them, with men; was she this way with every lover, with the men of the past, the husbands and the lovers? A great flock of birds rises into flight. It is that time of day. The bay sparkles with the last light of all.

I put the coffee cup away and rinse egg off the dish. Morning. The time of facing your soul and starting to work. There is the old manuscript upstairs in its manila folders, the record of the year of the plague, the death book. Supposed to be working on it, but instead I indulge myself with this notebook business. This account of her and me. Really of her. If I could make an account of her. A tribute? An act of love. Fix her on paper. But it's complicated, sheer adulation is tedious, false, fictitious. If you are honest you have to tell things they later regard as unflattering. With lovers you don't merely love, you hate too, you disapprove, you recriminate. You're unfair because love is unfair. And this whole notebook's unfair probably. And inaccurate. Too close, too intimate. It should be described as an experiment in charting and recording a relationship. Day to day. No one's ever done that. Surely not of two women. Which is just what makes it risky. Risky especially for her. Risky for me too; on behalf of the great generalized hostility of the world, I have here perfected the instrument of its revenge. I have lodged its loathing in a ball inside my stomach.

Last night I had dinner with Christiane Rochefort, the French writer. Susan had introduced us. Christiane is middle-aged, and a writer of fiction in the great tradition. I liked her Parisian art world toughness, her gentle, aging woman's face, soft as her cashmere scarf. I liked her and she was kind to me. But we are of different generations. Under her prodding—"What are you doing now?"—I told her I was keeping a journal. "I kept a diary once," she said, making a face, "but it was not literature." I mentioned my two unfinished manuscripts. "Aborted manuscripts," she said. "One can never do anything with them." I don't believe she meant to be unkind; she was merely relating her own experience. I listened, hoping she might not be right.

If Sita were someone else, and if I were someone else, if we had the cover of fiction, would our experience be more worthwhile, less disreputable, even more "real" to readers? Or would we be only a "story"? Robbe-Grillet caught something of jealousy—the gut reaction, the sweating palms, the obsession. Yet in his novel there are scarcely any personalities at all—only counters for the exposition of that emotion. And I think that was what I was after at first too, with all my "process" propaganda. But personality could not be suppressed. Hers anyway. I am too fond of it, too involved, admire too much not to want to convey it, every detail of her life is sacred, fascinating to me, my only fear that I will not express it sufficiently, fail to do it justice. A person always so much more than you can get on paper.

Meanwhile, I am left with my doubts, my notebooks, my hopeless task, its obsessive desire to record, study, analyze, preserve.

Turn it to fiction then. Since you're so fond of thinking you are at last drifting that way—out of the suspect waters of the personal, the autobiographical, the experiential—and into the safe harbor of fiction. High art. Didn't you tell Susan the other day that you were at the edge of fiction because you were describing a phenomenon even more than persons, doing an event, the end of love, just that essence, that moment, that experience, that process, process for its own sake. Using the first person, but the narrator didn't matter at all, could be anybody—it was the process that mattered, that held the stage. Blah blah.

So in fiction then, thinking in fiction. I could turn myself into a painter. Repress my writer self. Even my sculptor self. Just say I paint, am someone who paints —not drawings, mind you, paintings in oil. But then I almost become Sherman in my mind, someone who paints in oils. Blue denim shirts, Grumbacher brushes, tubes of Winsor & Newton, that old six-dollar cadmium red, I remember it well—probably up to twenty bucks by now. Oil, the smell of oil paint, the time of painting, the slowness of oil, all the times you light a cigarette and stand back and look at the canvas, the time of day, the pauses in sunlight, the body time, the long daylight hours. A painter in oils. Someone else, not me. Like me, but not me. But less and less like me as she becomes someone else, a fantasy self. Sherman? Or someone else entirely. She keeps becoming Sherman. No, let her become someone else, someone you don't know. But then I don't know her and stop knowing about her. Characters take on lives of their own. Which is why they can have plots and murders and unexpected events, events unexpected even to their creators. Christiane Rochefort told me that one of her characters died apparently of his own volition in an automobile crash several minutes before Christiane could prevent it or even decide if she approved of the idea. But I am writing of something experienced, something known that particular way. Not imagined, not fantasized, but known in the gut way that you know a stomach cramp.

But try, try being a painter. It would be so convenient. Noticing once or twice I have almost written down "painting" for writing, canvas for manuscript, carefully guarding my writing table to be flexible enough for later revision into easel, studio for study, etc. Little points here and there where I protect my identity so it might still be switched. Little points of dishonesty or self-preservation or malleability. And I walk around the house thinking all the time of other names for her, different streets, towns, places. The disguise of fiction, the defense of it. The nuisance of my give-away geography, New York, California. But it is just these two points at the opposite ends of the continent which compose the situation, are its very essence—how do you deal with them? Not wanting to. Wanting to just go on and on writing it as it happens, keeping a record of time and experience, perception— however imperfect.

And it is so imperfect. Holes everywhere. Whole passages unwritten, key events never set down. Laziness, inability to record accurately, well, completely. Like a shoulder badly drawn looks so awful, so awkward. And the vulnerability of intimacy, how do you rifle it, expose, betray to strangers? Even the solitary page?

The phone rings, 9:30 a.m. I wake to discover I am still dressed and stretched out on the sofa. Sherman's voice telling me she's called the restaurant. They have the notebook. She'll walk down and collect it later today. Gratitude for her goodness, shame and amusement and surprise at my present situation. How did I get here? Coming home from our bachelor dinner in town, Sita gone again, a quick trip to L.A. which will bring her back this morning, another mysterious trip to L.A.—when I questioned her she asked if I needed proof it was university business and offered to show me papers—of course I was ashamed. Ashamed again to wake up on the couch and remember I have lost my notebook. I had worked all day for the class, which left me only an hour to write before going out. Wanting to write. Not even wanting to go to town. But then, dressing, I had; had suddenly wanted the city, bars, restaurants, the night. Thinking all the time that I would go somewhere, some café, afterward, write—better yet, come home and write. And then in the street late at night in front of Gino and Carlo's, drunk, the bars nearly closed, standing in the street saying goodbye to Sherman, realizing I'd lost the notebook.

And last night I told Sherman I was writing it, that it was a process of something struggling for life or dying, that I was keeping track of a process. "Good," she said, "do it." I was surprised. Here was sanction. But Sherman's an old pirate of an artist, she'd understand. Does losing the notebook mean I must tell Sita? Picking it up this weekend, the errand of recovering it—does this involve me in revelations? And would her knowing predict events, subject life to control? All the old questions. You should have gone into them before.

What am I doing on the couch? The down of remembering. Coming home already nicely lit—and playing records. Wanting to hear music. Alice Stuart, Roberta

Flack, Nina Simone. Every song that had ever mattered between us, that replaced her absence. More
wine, maudlin after finishing the open bottle of
Riesling. Dancing even. All by myself dancing around
the living room. Having wanted to dance at the bar,
but Sherman was having none of that and there was
no one else. Sherman's Wild West bar empty and sinister tonight because the bands are all downtown playing a concert. Atmosphere of a place where nothing's
going on. Only our long-chinned talk of loneliness. I
remember telling her how much I had loved Fumio,
that I would go back to him even now. "She knows
that, she'll never forgive you for that." Then switching
and telling her the other side of it, how he used to ask
me every morning at breakfast what I wanted for dinner. "Don't you see that could drive someone crazy?"
She nods. "I not only didn't know what I wanted for
dinner at that hour in the morning, I didn't even know
if I wanted to be home for dinner. I just knew that I
hadn't worked yet. Just that I wanted to work and then
I'd think about it, when I was ready to play. But I felt
trapped."

In the morning light remembering this crap. This
sludge of sentiment, half-formed, two-faced, partial
truths, bad faith. Bitter or in tears over this love or another, all gone down the wind of my own errors. And
lost the damn notebook too. Has its humorous side,
and a headache you can count on. Get up and go undress in the bedroom. Be ready when she comes, wait
for her in bed.

Earlier than I'd expected. The key in the lock and
her steps, then silence. Looking up to see her just as I
feel her weight softly on the edge of the bed. "You
came. You came back." "Of course." She takes me in
her arms. "Forgive me, darling." "For what?" "For
nothing at all." At once she launches into tales of the
tedious dinner party last night, the hosts who wouldn't
drive her to the airport. "Toddling about at six having
to take a cab. And I had only that ten dollars I pinched
from the food money. The cab comes to six dollars. The
limousine to two-fifty. I was terrified I'd never get my
car out of the airport parking lot. If the limousine had
cost another dollar, you'd have had to drive to Oakland

just to rescue me from a seventy-cent parking charge."
Her arms enfolding me. We sleep again. The whole
weekend is ours.

The whole weekend. Two long mellow days. On
Saturday I draw her from the nude. She reads a book
and does her hair while she models. An almost irritating cleverness at entertaining herself while the process
goes on. I do drawing after drawing of her back, the
pose most convenient to her other pursuits. Each time
I fail. I imagine her sneering at my poor and inadequate
efforts, for I cannot capture her today. I try other poses
too, the lovely sinuous line of her side, the slender belly
and loin and shoulder, the superb fruit of her breast,
its brown berry in profile. "Do you despise what I'm
doing?" I ask her finally, confronting her for a moment
in the bathroom. "No, of course not, I love it that you
draw me, no one has ever paid me such a compliment
before." And then I believe her again. It is like that, the
up and down, the on and off of faith.

This weekend which is to give so much. The only full
weekend for a month. Next weekend she is off with her
committee to their retreat. The following is my trip to
New York. No, not the end, not going "home" (already it no longer seems home), but a short visit of a
week, a book tour that my publisher has asked me to
make. And when I am back in California, it will already be the end of March. Then there is only April till
I leave. So this weekend is precious, promised to me all
week ever since she first mentioned it last Sunday, taking just as she gave, by telling me the retreat followed
it. I made a face but accepted and spent the week in
expectation. We had even thought of going away,
Sutter Creek, the gold country. But we didn't call
ahead early enough, the inn was nearly full, there were
only single beds. Sita put her hand over the receiver
and grinned, saying, "I'm not driving eighty miles for
a single bed." You can have that at home, I'd wanted
to say, but held my peace. And now the weekend, its
weather uncertain, the bay gleaming one hour, beckoning us out and to the city; glowering an hour later.
For a while I have her, then washing her hair claims
her attention. Or a newspaper or the phone. Her mood

is elusive, shifting, her attention so hard to capture.

I had promised to take her to dinner in the city, but as we drive along she decides instead on the Marina. Eating dinner at four-thirty in the afternoon, how odd it seems, even ridiculous. She is delighted, however; we'll get to the city with plenty of time to park before the concert tonight, we'll even have time for a walk on the pier. Solomon Grundy's big windows frame the sea, the mounds of Angel Island, Buena Vista, Treasure Island, the three great spans of bridge: Bay, Gate, Richmond. Our kingdom this, and the sailboats and the city sparkling way off; this is the panorama and the place she had stretched out for me from the beginning, this the sunlit world of California, this for the city-rat eyes of a downtown New Yorker.

Always she won me this way, over and over this glistening spread of water and seagulls and island and city and bridge and sky. Clear and immediate as the sailboat whose canvas nearly touches our window. Of course I loved her world, it being she, she being California itself. No poor American thing belonging to smug blond children but to the buoyant and vivacious northern Latin, the Mediterranean great lady who spread it out before me, nobly and affably displaying her jewels, pressing them into my hands. Half of her. And the other half, the South American Latin, dark, even Indio in her long patience, also discovered it for me. The "brown wren," this one calls herself, having believed most of her life that she was homely, slighted. Just as the other woman in her has always been beautiful and known that beauty, reveled in it, flirted with it, rolled it like a Sienese banner of silk unfurled and snapping in the wind.

Sita across the table from me now. And her world spread before us in the sun. We are very happy. I can feel the moment, even remember it ahead of time, the curse of foreknowing that, even as it is sweet now in the mouth, warm along the arm, it will be some cold New York nightfall bitter on the lips to remember. Some time after she is gone from me, some solitary hour closer to death. It is this, this foreknowing of mine that makes it impossible to live in the moment. And the dubiety, the lingering skepticism.

The man at the table behind us sermonizes his wife and his son and his daughter-in-law on gift taxes, inheritance taxes, the value of his house, his boat. We grimace at each other, hating him. "I'm going to ask Martin to put my boat on the lake this summer. I can stay at Maud's and use it on the weekends," she says. I tease her for having sold the boat to Martin though she goes right on using it herself. "I'll pay the dock fee," she says. We both smile. Suddenly I realize I will not be here this summer. The little pain of it, just as when I heard her discuss the trip to Mexico with Maud, or her drive cross-country. In a few weeks I go out of her life again. The bay spreading at our elbows. The man behind booming that he can give son and daughter-in-law thirty thousand each without any taxation. Sounds awfully high, wonder if he's right. "Now, the house is worth eighty thousand of course, get that without any trouble at all." Must be some house. "Course your mom and I gotta pay taxes on the eighty grand, you know that." I wish he'd stop shouting. I wish he'd shut up. The figures of his self-importance booming through my efforts to concentrate on Sita, the little time left in our lives. "Now, that's the gift tax, you can work it around real good if you know a good lawyer." Motherfucker, why don't you shut up, you're poisoning my lunch.

Lunch, I'd call it. Dinner, she'd call it. We rally each other over the word. I try again to tell her of my love, telling her over and over lately, because she keeps saying she never did feel loved by me. "I was a way station, a provincial outpost between one person or another in New York, because New York was all that ever mattered to you, all that was real." The sea stretching away at her hand and her beautiful face that has courted me so many times and does no longer. "This became real. The first time I came I was out here just for a while, remember, a temporary job. New York had been home, after all. Anyone would see that all this was beautiful, but you made it take hold." The old confusion between the two places. And soon I go back

to New York. But already this scene, which was
merely landscape at first (and New Yorkers are suspicious of landscape), now begins to replace the broken
buildings of my slum, erase them.

The hurt I can feel even in my cunt—the fear of
losing this place. Then the old questions. Can you have
both? Love both? Can people live in two places? Students always live in two places, at college eight months
of the year, at home during the summer. Can people
really live in two places? Or is there an attrition of energy, some loss of attention? The artist in me is terrified of this, that my concentration will be dissipated,
fewer works produced. And then there are practical
matters, the opportunities of New York, publishers and
art dealers and events, and the collective energy of
other artists.

"Finish so we can walk on the pier." The man's voice
is booming away behind us still, his investments, his
taxes. I don't want to finish, I want to block him out
and go on talking of love. The honey of its words,
wanting her to tell me more, and again in greater detail. I want the sweetness of these moments to go on
and on—the sea and the bridges, the islands and the
city, our enchanted scene, familiar, beloved, paradisaical. "Why do you want to leave—just because of that
boor behind us?" "No, I want to put my arm around
you when we walk." Disappointment gives way to
pleasure. And when I didn't understand how the sun
dial on the pier worked, she laughed and showed me.
Walking away with her arm around my shoulder, still
laughing.

Sunday morning. Waking in terror. She is all I have
against the world. Against failure. Death. The disappointment of my work. Manuscripts discarded, unfinished, useless. "What's the matter?" she asks. "I'm
scared of life, scared of work, scared of death." And
for once I can tell her that my life was always a surprise once, full of kinks and turns as a subway tunnel,
not knowing the future, the where or the what in store.
"And that was always good. But then last year it
turned 180 degrees, and when I'd gone through the

suicide trip and losing Fumio, it all seemed suddenly a straight, flat highway with just death at the end of it. Like the lights of some town, just how far away you couldn't tell yet, but it's flat as Kansas and death is the only thing ahead." She holds me, comforting. "Do you worry about us too?" she asks. "Of course." "What can I do to give you assurance?" I tease her: "What do men and women do? on these solemn occasions?" "What they do is jump out of bed and get married. Shall we get our crazy friend Frieda to marry us in that gay church of hers?" "Really!" "I'm serious. Would you feel better if we made some pledge to each other?" I close my eyes against her collarbone.

Pledges are just what I dread. It is just that certainty, like the flat black road surface to death. And yet, and yet the surety of there being someone in the future, in age? She goes on, her mouth above my head, repeating the line from Browning at the end of a play on television we saw the other night, "Grow old along with me! The best is yet to be," Laurence Olivier leading Katharine Hepburn off into senile romance. I had been strangely moved; she had gone upstairs to weep and I wished she had not left the room. How odd we are and at what cross purposes. How we fail to guess or communicate even over a television drama. A month ago, the pledge she speaks of—which terrifies me now and which I sedulously avoid replying to by keeping my head down and smiling and remaining silent— a month ago it would have released me from hell.

Sunny Sunday morning. We make love over and over. The weekend indolence I have coveted for weeks. But it did not begin this way. Finally bringing myself to say it out loud, the disappointment of yesterday, of the other days stretching back and back as I lie now in her arms, listening to her tell me she loves me. "We don't make love, we aren't lovers any more." "But of course we make love." "The last two times you've made love to me you haven't even bothered to finish. And you never let me make love to you." "I haven't felt comfortable." Thinking: Is it that you need a man, prefer that, require that, that six inches of flesh—feeling defeated.

"I haven't felt comfortable because there is no time, no energy. But now there is." Taking me and letting me take her. Over and over in the sun of the morning. Taking me and giving herself to me to be taken, hand or mouth, tongue or finger. Lapping the sweet juice fresh between her legs, the flesh like fruit in my mouth, the ineffable sweetness of her little mound or pouch of flesh, sweet as my hand reaches it, its swell, the soft hair under my fingertips, the nearly painful sweetness of it, this ridge at the base of her belly, this crevice between the thighs, its thrilling and terrible sweetness to the lips, its sweetness to the tongue and mouth. I am insatiable, still thirsty for her after she has finished, wanting to go on mouthing and licking and beginning again. Taking her over and over in my hand or mouth, my tongue teasing to enter her as she opens wider and wider, stroking the dear desired triangle even after she is done, stroking to another heat and spasm. And wanting more, still more. The delight of having her again, taking asking and getting, opening her thighs to kiss again this sacred spot, this mystery, my mouth on those lips, the source, the source of her. Forgetting the denials, the refusals, the rejections, the rebuffs, desire turned away, turned rancid and bitter. All forgotten now in the joy of having her again. It all comes together, contentment and triumph.

After breakfast she calls to me from the couch: "Come and join me in here, those dining-room chairs are so uncomfortable." I settle in with my newspapers. "I've been thinking about it and I get the impression those people in New York who handle your books aren't very good." It is rare and lovely for her to be interested and I'm flattered, though a little confused by her taking up my career. "I really think they're pretty good and they do save me having to do it myself." "But how do you know they're not just dragging their feet? I know more about public relations than any of them." New York, the world she hates, fears, and could not conquer and manage as she does here. Talk of New York brings her to Fumio and the woman he lives with and into the dark backwaters of the end of my marriage and the nervous breakdown that came before. "If it's any comfort to you, a lot of marriages founder after something like that. They snap under the strain."

Today we talk about the breakdown. We usually don't. She was with me, stood by me through much of it. I thank her now, realizing how rarely I have, how the whole memory is so bitter I habitually avoid it. Hoping to avoid a quarrel, since it is hard to remember what they—my elder sister, my husband, even Sita—did to me, hard to forgive their naïveté, stupidity, bad faith. Perhaps that's the wrong order, for it was naïveté more than malice. But the capture, giving me over to guards and jails when I was confused and afraid, having me beaten up in a parking lot, wrestled to the ground, tied, trestled, bound upside down into an ambulance. That they stood there and watched, when any of them, especially my sister and Fumio, who were kin and legally empowered, could at any moment tell the huge two-hundred-fifty-pound guards to let go, lay off her, not to hit her any more, to stand back and let her be: We'll talk to her, she's just scared. I looked up at each one, pleading, and they did not move.

"Don't you understand?" I ask her. "Anybody that scared freaks, but if you give them some room, talk to them . . ." "We didn't know what to do." "Yes. And you'd started machinery you couldn't control any more and you couldn't stop." "True, all through the thing. And whenever they wanted to move you from one place to another or get you to do anything, they sent me. They realized I was the only one you'd listen to, the only one you'd even hear." She stops. We look across the room, embarrassed, in pain, even to remember is painful. But she keeps on remembering, how this or that friend tried to make me see reason, how Frances, for example, a psychologist friend of ours, wanted me to go to the country for a week. It goes on and on, the old reproaches, the number of occasions when I was impossible, incoherent. "You were like someone on speed. Amphetamines. People who take amphetamines are like that." "And I still don't even know what happened, what caused it. Pressure?

Michael X's case, trying to prevent his execution? Teaching? Filming the music festival?". "It started a month earlier when your other sister was here. Then it kept on escalating through June. You were a wreck when you got back from that trip to England." I want to tell her that I was fine in England, worked like a whirlwind for Michael and was probably effective. Just exhausted and overexcited when I got back. "No, it was when Fumio came out West, to visit, right after that. Having you and Fumio in the same place. It made some strange, terrible pressure. Some awful enormous incoherent guilt for loving both of you. I think I couldn't stand it. I think that's what made me jump the rails."

Silence. "But I'm sorry for what it cost you, for what you suffered too," I say, looking up at her. She is sitting on the arm of the couch above me. "We've been through so much." "Sometimes that makes it harder," I answer. "Or richer." There is tension and silence and then other words, the coming back together after exploring the terrible, the wounds and mysteries, the reaches avoided, proscribed. "And what do we have when you leave?" she asks. "What do I have, anyway? It will be lonely here." "New York is lonely. There is really no one there for me, eating alone, living alone, no job even to go to, no 'colleagues' and that sort of thing. I'm lonelier there than you are here, more isolated; I know fewer people." "What do we have when you leave? What commitment do you make? It's not fair . . ."

Odd, even crazy that she should talk commitment, she who had shed me permanently a month ago, replaced me, leaving no room even at the edge of her life. Then it was I who wanted to talk commitment, to hold her to the letter of some past agreement. Fair—the word makes me wince. Surely I didn't mean to be unfair. "Look, Sherman told me you'd decided you were done with me last fall." "I was finished. Yes, that's true." "Well, not having been informed, I arrived anyway, fell out of the sky in January to find there's no room in the commune. But I stuck around. The kids bicker and split, all on their own and with no help from either of us—you to make them stay or me to make them leave. But one day Valerie and Pia just start pulling each other's hair and it's all over. Then . . ." But the next thing is hard to say, the gray figures of men between us. "Then you're still a mile away and I can't reach you. You're wrapped up in other people and your conquests." Exchange of wry little smiles. "But somehow you decide to look me over again, somehow"—my voice changes—"you began to care for me again. How I don't know. Why I don't know either. Lady, you dragged me around Europe like an amputated limb. Then you dumped me. Now you've changed your mind. When will you change it again?"

I lie back and relax. The camellia and the note beside me on the pillow. Her infinite sweetness in writing this, finding an old envelope because she couldn't find a sheet of paper, wishing me good night with a flower. She is asleep in the other room. I feel no resentment at all for that any more. I am late tonight, having dined with my students and having had a wonderful time. One student got drunk and was very tedious, a layer of hostility under her compliments, but even that didn't faze me.

I could live here, I think. Getting to know enough people so it even seems possible to live here. That student who showed us slides today is really a brilliant photographer, such an air of strangeness about her pictures—"Fictions," she calls them, people in the most ordinary situations yet surrounded with an odd stagnant air, a vacuumlike atmosphere: a girl in a barren room, a floor lamp photographed all by itself, a man with his head deliberately cut off by the camera's framing, couples whose very postures speak volumes of anxiety. It would be nice to know her. And there are others. I tote them up. A few other writers out here whom I should try again to reach. Yes, it would be possible.

Everything is possible in this satisfaction—stretching out, lighting a cigarette, deciding not to read. I

should finish off that manuscript on Japan I was working on out here last spring. It wasn't "interesting"
enough, I'd decided, leaving off in what was probably
the best passage, the time after Yoshiko died and
Fumio and I first fell in love. Too painful to write so
soon after breaking with him? Or was I merely interrupted by the return to New York, the trip to Europe?
I could finish it. My life a mess of unfinished manuscripts. "Aborted manuscripts, there is nothing you
can do with them."

And the other manuscript, the dead folders that sit
on my desk. "My season in hell," I snarled tonight at
the drunken student who was needling me to know
what I was writing. That black murky junk still on the
desk, the year of the plague, the job I'm ignoring completely in favor of this stuff, my "microscope," I called
it tonight, refusing to tell the student what I'm really
doing, though she has a whiff, I suspect, from Susan,
who's also a friend of hers. "What did Susan tell you?"
"Just that you'd read from something new and that
she'd liked it." "Everyone in the world must be keeping
a journal this spring," I'd said, dismissing it.

But it's true. My students. And their students. Janice,
the student who got drunk, has a class of senior citi-
zens and *they* keep journals. Virginia teaches black
teenage boys from the ghetto, and they keep them.
But mostly it's women, the new women, the new
women writers, the new sensibility of women finding its
way onto paper now. Fervid, secretive, then abandoning all secrets. But I find myself still caught up in se-
crecy. I have still not told Sita about this notebook.
Close to it so many times, with oblique references, half
disclosures. That day at the faculty club. Yesterday
over dinner out in Sausalito when she told me what
name she wanted to have if I ever wrote about her.
Suddenly, apropos of nothing: "If you ever write about
me, you should call me Sita. Of all my names, it's the
right one."

The camellia she has left for me on the pillow. If I
went to her, would she mind, be angry? Wanting her,
wanting to lie next to her, to feel her warmth. Only
that. Gratitude, a new kind of affection, friendlier than

anything I could feel in the bad days, the weeks past. Liking—realizing that I like her now. And couldn't like her then, not when she gave pain. How to be sure even of this? Love in one or a dozen of the senses of that word: longing, desire, the need to possess, need of a hundred kinds. But this affection now, this liking is different, elusive, tantalizing. If I lie next to her, I will know what it is that I feel, I will satisfy something. Not afraid to go—which must perhaps be some signal it is out of good faith? Quietly, ever so quietly. Not to wake her. Treasonous floorboards, the rustle of covers. Moving slowly with the patience of a madman or a mother or a friend. Then the warm, waterlike ease of the foam-rubber mattress, the current of gently heated air, the assurance of flesh giving off heat, the full balance of her weight next to me. In her sleep her foot reaches out to touch mine. Like a kiss.

"Commitment," she'd said. The word was a stone around my neck when she said it. But doing the grocery list I add glasses, hardware, rings for the bedroom curtains, so they can be closed easily and the morning light will no longer hurt her eyes. I will fix the door Dan and Paul removed so cavalierly, losing the hinge pins in the process. The bookcase? She wants a bookcase for the front room, later Paul's room. And maybe it can again become what we used to call it, the library. All my books are still in the hall closet, where they were stored while the kids lived here. Gradually, step by step, the place is restored to me, to the two of us, to me and the Sita who is with me, rather than the Sita who was with them. Should I build her that bookcase? Time, money, tools. Buy one? Commission a carpenter? Commitment is building a bookcase. When I came here I certainly had no such intentions, came and found the place gone, full, occupied, given away. I wanted to run. And decided to stand my ground, fighting for space, fighting the ghosts of men I never saw, or saw only once, sitting across the room from Neal. Stayed and am winning.

How contrary I am. It is just now that I'm scared and want to run. Commitment? Do I lose the future,

its unknowns, its possible adventures? And otherwise?
To be an aging woman living alone in New York, solitary meals, a body going toward death. Grow old along
with me, she'd said. Hell, I don't want to grow old at
all. I never want to die.

New York. Publications. Exhibitions. Will I lose as
an artist, staying here? Even staying part time? My
friends, others my age, running on ahead of me. And
this age, this decade, one's forties, the time when the
most work is done, the prime of maturity. But it's not
merely that which would elude me. More. Love affairs,
parties, encounters, a fistful of experiences never had.
In loving her do I lose the world?

How contrary, how irresponsible I am. Wanted her
when she was gone from me. She returns to me and I
want to run. And stand still not out of integrity or faith
but out of cowardice. I don't dare tell her I am afraid
to be caught. She was right after all to withdraw. Her
instincts were sound. "She goes away," Sherman said,
"because she can't stand being the victim of her feel-
ings for you." I stood by and waited till the children
were gone, till she had given up the men. And now I
leave? Now when her eyes turn toward me, all others
being gone, departed, forsaken or forsworn. I stand in
the kitchen ashamed of myself.

A trifler then? But I never meant to trifle. The thing
catches me on every side like a machine out of control
in a Chaplin movie. When she is cold it is my fault
somehow, when she is fond it is my responsibility.
I fear having her on my hands, and I am afraid and
ashamed of that fear. If she knew? She would be furious, would never forgive. Her superb mad pride would
take her off at one leap. But I can no more forgive
than she can—and it's just that, the failure of faith,
the wavering in loyalty, the shallowness of character in her that could have sworn love so persuasively
in the past and then grew so fickle, so rude, so sullen.
For all my patience, all my doormat masochism, there
is a current of rage in me, a strand of malice that can
never forgive the defection.

I am someone in a fairy tale transplanted to a beautiful kingdom every year. A place of springtime and

sun and flowers. But one year I arrive to find my queen or fairy godmother or princess or whatever completely obdurate. She no longer loves me at all, no longer even remembers. Then slowly, by infinite degrees, I warm the ice which surrounds her. She comes to life. She smiles and loves me again. And then I say I cannot live here, prefer my winters and my darkness and my shanty at the bottom of the mountain, and tell her that the paradisaical kingdom is not enough, is not habitable.

This is ridiculous. So what is it I miss, then? My solitude? The very thing I fear. My independence? For with her I lean. And since she cares less she is always stronger. I depend, give way to her superior force and personality, her facility in decision, her efficiency, her certainties. I who have no certainties. So it is always an unequal relationship, even when it's happy.

What else do I fear? Coming back, coming back each year. The waiting, hers as well as my own through the intervening months. The attention always stretched to someone far away, not seeing those who are close, the things that are near, the day-to-day. Other relationships never really form or take hold. One is always coming from or going to the rendezvous.

She mentioned the loneliness ahead of her, the empty summer. I don't want to inflict that on her. It isn't fair, just as she said, it isn't fair. Not that she'd be as isolated as she says. The men would come back, or other men. She'd take lovers of course. But they would be temporary, marginal, tangential. As mine always are. Or else they would take hold and replace me. And then I couldn't come back. And I want to. Mostly I want to be able to—to have that door open. The way to the sun.

Each winter, to have that escapeway clear, each winter as the depressions of my winters settle in, the apathy, the longing for suicide. To have her older face waiting for me in the place of the sun, her serenity, her ease, her comfort. Making love once in the old days on Derby Street—the time I was mad or beginning to be mad—late late at night, having exhausted her, exasperated her, and now insisting on this act too, my face along her thigh, the soft hair of her pubis on my lips, I understood it. One of those impossible insights that I loved in madness and the others hated so. Comprehending at one bound the myth of Demeter and knowing that she was Demeter, that the fountain between her thighs was my own youth and I Persephone, who had come to her in spring and would come forever, for she was my youth, older than I and yet my youth, my ever-recurrent spring, and spring itself only a metaphor for the source, the waters, the hidden river, the tunnel of life between her thighs.

Lady, how I exasperated you. How I fail you still. Wanting. Not wanting. The moods and vacillations, the morbid speculations of a love as contingent as this, as voluntary and unsanctioned and insecure. She must feel the same, has felt the same. But doesn't speak it. Nor do I. Silent all those crucial moments on Sunday when she asked for a pledge. Sly I was, and pledged not. Afraid to lie outright. Yet as much as I can, I suppose I gave it. Yes, and I know that it is being leveled at me now.

St. Patrick's night she got drunk, a rare occurrence and even a little funny, though she herself wasn't funny, she was angry. Bounced up and down in bed and almost yelled at me, she who never yells. "How can I know you won't go back to Fumio? Can you promise? Can you promise that if he wanted you back you wouldn't just go back to him and live with him there in New York?" "He has no intention of having me back. He's delighted to have me out of his hair." "That isn't what I asked you. I asked you if you could promise you wouldn't go back." "No point in it, it will simply just never come up." At this juncture she burped and I had to smile and didn't actually take her seriously. As I didn't earlier, about Molly. The day before Molly had come to the house to interview me. I liked her as well as the attention—that somebody was taking me seriously as a writer. Molly has a nice Irish humor, a dark and roving eye, a cap of curly black hair. Young, but I rather fancied her. Under the cover of her questions she asked if I were in love. I hedged a little, the question was too complicated and more than I felt like divulging. I was probably flirting with her too. Nothing important. Molly can play the fiddle, would be at the neighborhood bar on St. Patrick's and invited us to come and hear her. A rare thing a real fiddle, the jigs and the reels and so forth. So we went. And it was very lively, Sita got tipsy and jigged away. But there was one odd little moment. A young woman sidled up to us and asked, what would I like to know about Molly. "She's a good friend of mine and I can tell you anything you'd like to know." I'd nothing to say whatever, but Sita said, "Do you really think she's going to ask with me sitting right here beside her?" It was absurd. I was embarrassed, even humiliated by both of them. And yet sharply pleased that Sita could still be jealous. After all the broad hints that I should find my own "interests" now that she had a few going. Perhaps she was merely annoyed that it was said in front of her. Or annoyed because she's given up her men. But it was lovely still to see her jump and pounce again. Bullying and proprietary as her jealousy had always been; unlovely thing that jealousy always is, it was lovely somehow to have it back. As for Molly, I haven't given her a thought since then, except to make certain not to be home when she came by to pick up the copy of the interview she had sent me.

I go to dinner with Sherman the way other people go to their psychoanalysts. Perched on a bar stool at the Tivoli, gazing at the collection of old light fixtures lined up above the bar, odd Chicago art-deco stuff, always mysterious, hypnotic over me while we sit here talking,

going on about art and how to live our lives. Always
the brave pretense that art matters more, that we put
it first. "So what if I just folded my wings and settled
down to live in Berkeley, California? After all, it's not
the art world finally that makes New York home."
"Oh, that fucking art world." "No, you don't understand. If I folded my wings and settled here, how can
I explain what it is I'm afraid of?" "New York has
energy." "It's also lonely as hell sometimes. Look,
what I'm afraid of is that there might be fewer books,
that there might be some book I never wrote." "You
said yourself you can write here. She's supportive of
that, at least you're not sabotaged there like I've always been. They see me paint, they watch that day
after day." Little gestures of painting, a big clownish
grin. "And gradually, they come to figure out how
much it means to me. And then—oh, unconsciously,
mind you—they start hating it." She breaks off with
the usual dismissive wave of her arm. "Hating it, man."
Turns. "But that's not your problem." "No, I would
write if I stayed. Maybe. But there might be some
book lost, some book I'd never meet. Some adventure,
I can't explain. And no sculpture. There's no place to
sculpt. I have a show scheduled next December. The
gallery's in New York. My studio's in New York. I
hate sculpture, it terrifies me. But . . ." "You need it,
for some damn reason you need it. And you need
this"—she slams her fist into her palm. "Yeah." "You
need that, that goose in the ass, that stimulus. That's
New York." "It's not that simple. I go nuts in that
loft some nights."

We drink and Sherman accepts the homage of the
regulars as they come in for a drink after work: like
an old and acknowledged master in her big denim
jacket, her beautiful head, the cropped androgynous
hair, her ringed fingers holding a glass or gesturing, the
majesty of her height and age and courage; everyone in
the quarter knows her. I go on explaining to her wisdom, "It's that if I stayed and settled and didn't go on
I'd never know what I'd lost, what book or sculpture
or drawing—I'm not even drawing here and I used
to draw two hours a day every day in New York. You

know what I mean, all those discoveries of living alone, whatever adventure or love affair or growth or change. Instead, it would be settled. You can stay in one place and start seeing the end. I don't want to see the end. I don't want to know what's ahead." "So it's New York. Gotta be." "No, it's not that clear-cut. If I leave her, there's no one I'm close to in New York. And it means giving up that nice warm living-with-someone thing." We smile, acknowledging all this.

"I love living with someone, Sherman, I've done it most of my life. It's good. You work all day, then they come home, dinner, a fire, sleep together." "Yum yum." She snaps her ringed fingers, grinning. "Look, Sherm, that's life, just life. Just for the sheer living of it." "Like most people." "Yeah, the lucky bastards, none of this garbage about making art. Just enjoyment. Take it as it comes. When the sun shines they roll up their sleeves and they can feel it." "Bullshit. They're frantic. All they do is wander around having to score. They gotta score a car, some sex, a game of pool, a permanent, a job. They gotta worry about what's on TV or if the kids' school can teach 'em to read. They're driven. They're just as driven." "Maybe you're right; let's order another drink." "Of course I'm right." The laughter of comrades.

"I keep thinking of age, of living alone and being old. And not having kept this when I had it, of having thrown it away." "You're really morbid." "Hm. But you know what? It's better now. She's come back to me in some strange way." "Only to disappear for the whole weekend again." I defend, protect, explain, produce reasons, commitments. "I think she really didn't want to go this time. The committee bullied her into going at the last moment." "And how soon do you leave and go East?" "Beginning of May. But there's this little trip next week. Just a few days. Then I'll be back to stay all through April." "You can't be both places. You just can't. No way." Her arm wipes out the possibility in the air, one of her most definitive dismissive gestures. "I don't see why not. I don't see why I can't live here six months a year. She thinks it could work too." "It hasn't." "No, when I came back this time it was a nightmare. But it doesn't have to be that way." "When you're gone she entirely regroups." Neat gestures of her hands making boxes on the bar top. "Rearranges her whole life, substitutes. I don't blame her." "I don't either." "So when you come back, there's no room any more. Why should there be? You can't have it both ways." "So it would appear." "You don't believe that though, do you? You think you can." "It might be possible if we had some fine and special understanding and really wanted to live that way, wanted it enough." "Crap."

Her body bringing me the phone. "Call Marguerite, she's in the hospital." Sita's body: elliptical, pear-shaped, Modigliani. The lovely lines of her hips and ass disappearing now in the frame of the door. How many times I have drawn these lines in my mind, with a brush, with the eyes opened or closed, remembering or imagining or recording on paper? Does conscious-ness of an experience change it? Writing is so much more problematic than drawing, full of moral pitfalls, ambiguity, public responsibility. If you record a day of your life, does the decision to do so change the shape of that day? One of Doris Lessing's days in *The Golden Notebook* is fifty-four pages long. It's com-plete; the rest are summaries—the "impression" of a day foisted artfully upon the reader by providing a few details. Fiction is made this way—as lineal per-spective gives the illusion of three dimensions in draw-ing. But does the selection of a day—that you begin by knowing you must remember and observe—really af-fect it? Do you change the balance, distort the truth? The period itself, its choice and selection, does that not in itself constitute a kind of misconstruction, and the rest follow subconsciously?

What do you leave out, what do you falsify? What do you mar by the imposition of a pattern? Recently I was sure I was recording a natural pattern—decline and fall. But where am I now? I read de Beauvoir's *The Woman Destroyed* the other day and was trans-fixed—she had already done everything I had hoped or intended. Her story went straight as an arrow to the murder of a relationship and the woman dependent upon it. There, I thought, that's it exactly. And it wasn't. For days I felt a special anxiety because I was not following that pattern, the tragic tangent. What I thought was the pattern. I would have imposed it on the notebook, but I could not impose it on events. Instead she returned to me, turned and returned. Would I have preferred the expected, the reasonable shape and continuation of events? Preferred some trite and "logical" pattern I could impose on a notebook? Wanted a notebook more than a lover, preferred a bit of scribbling to life? Or did the pattern only seem inevitable and rescue from it arbitrary, temporary, artificial, more cruel in the end?

This notebook business. The keeping of records. Good for an occasional *cri de coèur* maybe; but when it becomes bigger than what it recalls, takes on a life of its own? When the time comes that it has to be owned up to? I stand accused. Trapped in my own device. I have even told her I was writing the notebook. It seemed only fair to do so finally, not knowing what to expect as I told her, perhaps even expecting her wrath. She was only amused, regarded the thing as a hobby horse, a waste of time, an evasion of real writing. She was witty, teased me about it charmingly.

When I came here and things weren't as I'd hoped, I could have just gone away quietly, someone with any pride might have. And no notebook. I realize now that I may have stayed to write it. To experience and then analyze that experience. I'm reminded of that morning in the dining room after she'd been out all night, the night we'd come back from Mendocino. I'd decided at Mendocino to stay in California, a decision that was almost immediately invalidated by her departure for the night with that exit line about calling from the office. I was pacing the floor in the dining room, just before I went to meet her the next morning, and the course had to be decided on finally, since that should have been the first day of class. Pacing the floor and remembering the damn deer at Mendocino, remembering them, just then and even in the state I was

in, writing a sentence on those deer and saying to myself, I will stay, because if I leave it I will not have
had the experience and I want to have had it.

On Valentine's night when we drank the Asti, I
wanted to drink it in bed; my notion—frivolous, silly,
vain—that it would be such fun to intersperse the Asti
with sex, imagining taking a sip and then going down
on her, alternating the tastes. A bauble of course, a
fancy, some bit of ingenuous decadence. Harmless
enough. But written out—what does it make? Lessing
says that when Joyce wrote about Bloom crapping on
his pot (I believe she says "defecating"—perhaps a
different activity), the passage shocked, which was
ironic. Because it was precisely the opposite of his intent. Joyce had meant to rob the words of their power,
of course, talk us into accepting our own humanity in
Bloom's outhouse. We don't get much closer.

I don't even defend what I do, though I should. As
long as writing is perceived as magical, it will be so.
And as long as it is magical, it will be given an aura
of reverence—of which the charge of exploitation is
but the obverse, the analogue. And the defense that
you wrote this to understand, merely to understand
your own experience, even to select your own experience and then to study it as it occurred—nonsense too.
Your methods are too imperfect yet to understand anything well enough to justify making an issue of it. And
what after all is your own experience? How do you
possibly separate it from that of others? And you
stayed—remember—you chose to stay. In order to
have this experience. And to have the record of it.

Or is that the most specious bit of silliness yet? Was
the notebook just the last and most pathetic ploy of
all—to stay. The course being a bit tottery just then
and you needed a really ponderous reason so you could
go on suffering in love—pretending it was work, telling yourself you were staying, not in the forlorn hope
of recovering Sita, Sita dead or a stranger or disappeared on you, but you were hanging around here because really you were doing this "for yourself," and
so forth? And anyway, are you ever even going to finish this notebook? You go to New York in a day or

two and you haven't written in it for five days. You hate it now. You loathe working in it, put it off from hour to hour. You will never be able to fill in all the days you left out. Your opening is weak and would fail to prepare the reader—assuming there were one —to enter into the characters or the situation with enough information and impressions. The day-to-day business of course is unspeakably tedious, inherent defect of the journal as a form. But the fact is, you have really lost interest in the project. And the more she returns to you, the less you need it. The notebook was only useful in her absence, a poor substitute. But of course she comes and goes. And there is no assurance her return is permanent or even real. What if I let the notebook slide to find only at the end that she had eluded me too? And the time was past to recapture her even on paper.

What then if I have neither Sita nor the notebook of Sita? The shape of her thighs, the ellipse of her hips, the delicious handful of her ass, the hunting spring of her long legs, the almost solemn line of her spine and vertebrae, that little saddle of flesh at the small of her back. The line, the line of her hips. That outline. That ellipse.

A dark little counter overlooking the airstrip. L.A. The beginning of the trip. The writers' conference already behind me, with whatever fuel it provides— tidbits imbibed and already spent, devoured, and the plate empty. I'm scared of this trip. Scared of going home. Scared of the cities I must visit and the media, the public, being examined, making a fool of myself

on the radio. A glass window into the night. Landing
lights. A gin-and-tonic ordered and on its way. Thinking the thoughts of great blank glass windows, neon
lights, the cocktail-lounge mumble droning behind me,
thoughts of airports and strange towns and unsteady
hotel nights. Thinking of where I am on the dirt road of
my life: the self, rising high on each airplane's wings,
looks down and sees its double bent over, hiking along,
a dot on the artery of time. Spotted, pinpointed. Where
am I now, the time running out?

She is always on my mind, hovering behind the forehead, an echo coloring all, even the conference moments, its applause and camaraderie, encouragement,
late-night talk, laughter, all those other women engaged
in the same strange process.

Waiting room. Kennedy in the morning after the all-
night flight. A Hasidic Jew in a great long beard and
round black hat. I am home. I will see Ruth. Have
breakfast with Fumio. If I can reach him. The phones
on the Lower East Side have been out of service for a
month now. A fire at the telephone company. Strange.
It is all strange. I will see Second Avenue again, climb
the five flights of stairs to my Bowery loft.

The skyline at dawn. And at the end, at the bottom,
the fear finally reached and discovered, I see the loft.
White. Empty. Unfinished. The furniture I still haven't
rewebbed, the wooden arms and legs of chairs and
sofas still undone. The pillows I never ordered. The
rugs I haven't bought. Can't afford. The green of the
bedspread quilt. The plants piled up by the windows
where Ruth faithfully waters them.

No, it isn't really the unfinished quality, the fact that
there still isn't even a cabinet for dishes and groceries,
or the great cavernous space of its white walls a hundred feet long, not that either, or its fine high white
light. It's the emptiness; that it's empty. Alone, solitary.
The life before the life with her. For a while the new
life after the ten years with Fumio. The single life instead of the life with her. And this odd, unlooked-for,
accidental, even unnatural return for a few hours. (I
land at six and leave for Washington at 7 a.m. the next
day—will sleep only one night in my bed and for a few

hours this morning before going to find Fumio and Ruth.) Like some bizarre trial. A taste of the old life, the new life beyond the one in California. Life alone versus life with another.

I like them both. But living with another hinders, limits, impinges. And being alone has so many empty places, bald spots, with an uncertain and possibly terrible future.

On the wan Bowery pavement, the two big suitcases to carry up the five flights. Trembling to see it again. Anticipation. Anxiety. Passing the third-floor studio without even opening the door. The hundreds of drawings in there, like corpses laid out in a mortuary. One suitcase and then the next. But I must, I simply have to open the door to the fifth floor right away, can't go back down for the next bag, must rest, must see it again. Confront the specter. My home.

Looking both ways up and down its length. It didn't seem all that huge, only empty. You could fit the Berkeley house in here easily. And be civilized in the meanwhile. My heart hangs fire while I check for catastrophes. No broken windows. Only later do I discover the pane is missing over the heater vent, fallen aside. A day's work on a ladder, but I have no time or energy now. Bless Ruth; the plants are thriving, the mail is neatly piled.

The morning is coming, rose light into the east end of the loft illuminating the kitchen. I never see this light when I live here, am always asleep at this hour. Lovable, it becomes my studio again. Romantic as the day I found it. The new life it would represent. Now dubious. The place does have potential. But so unfinished, rudimentary, little more than a cave whose walls I've painted, floors I've done. The expensive mystery of plumbing installed in the bathroom and kitchen. And there a glass sits on the drainboard where I had left it three months ago. Time like a hammer falling, the old agony and terror of time. Life running out and what have you achieved, you with your fancy and extravagant studios? Some drawings. A manuscript you didn't finish. That good red lobster painting on the dining-room wall, the blue and green one in the bathroom.

Using the toilet, then reaching for the brush to scrub away the months of rust in the bowl. No brush. There is one in Berkeley, there is one at the farm, there was one in Sacramento, even one at the old studio on the corner, now torn down, just a hole in the line of buildings like a vacant tooth, my studio for fifteen years and now destroyed. All the damn toilet brushes I have bought and here there is none. Maybe the third floor? Forget it.

Go back and see the rosy light of dawn filling the kitchen, illuminating the great still white walls. Brick, pure, freshly painted. Tomorrow the tour begins. There is only today in New York. Sleep a while, then see Fumio. Have dinner with Ruth. Don't go to bed with her. Keep your promise and don't give in. For her sake, don't start it again. No time for others, and anyway, there are so few others. Here there is Fumio, who is mine no more, fights me off, transcends me. And Ruth, whose adoration I cannot bear. Always I tell myself, There are so many in New York—old friends, art-world buddies, movement women, the nebulous circle of friends and acquaintances. But they vanish when I name or invoke them. You don't call New Yorkers on the spur of the moment. So it will be just the two. Ruth is waiting. Fumio may be hard to find.

Coming in, I met Carey, the hippie kid on the first floor, and he said that seventeen thousand phones were put back in operation yesterday. But mine's still out. Fumio's probably is still out too—our slum is bound to be the last restored. Sleep then, and when you wake, find him. Terrified that I might not, might spend the day, the single precious day, hunting him down from studio to apartment. The apartment he shares with Bonnie. No, I can't call him there either. I had no way to tell him when I'd be coming, no definite date till the last minute, and then no way to call. No way to guess then how absolute the need would be when I arrived, how he would stand out against the little figures who are almost enough to get by on most days here. Enough for dinner or a drink. But when you come from far for a visit, it's only the people who have mattered long and hard who are enough.

Like Sita. Have I come all this way only to miss you, to measure the distance, to see my brave beginnings here, my solitary artist life grow gray and pale and pointless? What am I deciding now, knowing the stop-over here was for deciding? And not just to hang up some clothes and beat out a few wrinkles before the media ordeal, closing my eyes in dread of the next four days. Lying down in my own house. Back to the real self, the self that knows its guilt by looking at its un-answered mail on the desk, the self below that one, which knows how few pages were written here. The restlessness of evenings, flights to the roof to see the sunset. The days were not so bad. But when you see the last sunlight go off the buildings. Then. Times I missed her most, will miss her; times you miss someone, the lover, the friend, the person to eat with as dark comes and hunger and the terrible loneliness of this city's nights, the nights of life going on to death.

Before I lie down, once up to the roof to see the morning come, no longer the great rose of dawn it was in the kitchen but an ordinary day. Already at seven, the sun well up. A good day for New York, but after the first light, almost banal, each building in its place, the Empire State, the two silver sheaths of the World Trade Center like twin cigarette lighters. But with some new upstart blocking the base of one of them—did they build that piece of crap since I left? Pacing the roof. This summer I'll put down wooden skids, steal some of those loading platforms they use in the warehouse dis-trict. A deck made out of them. Trees. Geraniums. Outdoor furniture. Parties here. And paint the third floor. Build my worktables, get tools, make it ready for the sculpture show in December. The overpowering list of things to do. If I dare. If I can make it.

There's something unpleasant about talking to Hiro, even beyond the fact that Fumio isn't there, that I've climbed all these stairs in cold fear and he isn't even there, so now I'll have to try phoning him at Bonnie's with the hateful possibility that she may answer the phone. Asking her permission to speak to him. Hiro's embarrassed—he remembers too. The time when we

had moved the stuff out of the old studio and up to the
country and at the end of the day Fumio sprained his
back but still insisted on going back to Hiro's that night.
He wouldn't stay with me. It was the first time
or maybe the second that he refused to sleep in the
same bed with me. We never have again. Ten years
and then late one night, late, when he is hardly able to
move out of the back seat of the van, the bastard insists
on walking five blocks, though he is right next to his
own house. Or what had been. The condemnation
order still gave us another week. But he wouldn't come.
I begged him. Because if he didn't come with me I
knew I'd try to do it again that night. I had the night
before—went to sleep with the two-inch pipe wide
open, the gas so loud it almost kept me awake. But I
meant it; woke up in the middle of the night, heard it
still going, the huge dangerous stink of it, and went
back to sleep. This is your chance to change your mind,
I thought. But I didn't want to back out. I knew just
what I was doing, though the akvavit helped. And then
I woke up at seven and it was moving day and I was
still alive. Everything else was over, the marriage, the
old house, the old life, my chances of sanity or work.
And he stood there on the sidewalk, probably even
aware of what I'd been up to. But he wouldn't come in.
His face distorted with the pain in his back. And for
that I was sorry. But it was also the first time I'd ever
been able to see him suffering or even unhappy—this
adored man—with a part of me merely standing and
watching. Not caring. Not all that much. He'd stopped
caring entirely.

The next morning I called Hiro's to see how he was.
Hiro was clearly embarrassed. He should have been.
A friend for ten years now lying to me. He "didn't
know" where Fumio was. Of course he was at the
apartment, Sakai's old placé, which they used as a
hangout. And probably with Bonnie. Hiro claimed not
to know the number. I was stunned. Surely Fumio was
a friend, surely I could check on his health, whomever
he was with. Hiro's voice tentative, hideously self-
conscious: "I don't think he wants you to know the
number." I was humiliated. I was now a woman whose

husband instructed his friends to keep his whereabouts secret from her. We had come to that.

Today Hiro's face and manner seem to recollect all this as he so very politely tells me Fumio hasn't arrived yet. The telephone at the apartment over in the Village is working. Do I know the number? All graciousness. Yes, I know the number, thank you very much. Hiro, whose paintings I used to baptize with six-packs and long arguments about art. Such a good friend once, such a stranger now.

I walk along Great Jones Street toward the Village, looking for a phone booth. How odd to be using a public phone, to be calling Fumio, calling him at another woman's house, making appointments with him. Fortunately it's Jack, his apprentice, who answers. And then Fumio's peculiar little frog-like voice, half adolescent, half old man. He agrees to breakfast, though he's already eaten it, is probably on his way to work at the studio, isn't relishing interruptions. And at Sandolino's he's distracted, bored. The perfect Sunday breakfast place, I'd thought, with fantasies of lazy mornings and the *Times*. But instead it's packed, impersonal, the management rude, dismissive. Fumio makes it plain he finds the place a drag.

We walk back and climb the stairs to his studio. Half the objects in the room are from the old place. That chair, the bureau, the maple table we ate at for ten years. I cannot look at these things without tears. When we broke up we were casual about the furniture, each picking what we liked, the other too depressed to care or even notice, let alone argue. In the few days the city gave us before the building was to be torn down, saving the sculpture was the main issue. Both of us lost many pieces. Furniture was unimportant. For over a year I hadn't even known where much of it was. Whether given or thrown away. Now I see one familiar object after another while he makes tea for me, being kind, patient, polite. That high stool we used to have in the workshop. That battered old pan we used to cook artichokes in. The little wicker stool. How nice to see it again. Then, unexpectedly, this thing, a shabby little stool I used to sit on when we had guests, because you could pop right up from it and into the kitchen. You almost squat rather than sit on it, but it was always my favorite perch. This little stool, this ragged funky thing suddenly a vise squeezing memory, every moment of those ten years contained in this humble object. The seat of it some unusual, unidentifiable kind of wicker, the legs simply four little black pegs. How many martinis consumed on this, my throne? How I argued here and held forth on this thing, how I dispensed drinks and coffee and opinions. Popping up to get someone more ice, loving to have guests about me. Fumio too, for he adored people and was a delightful host. The beautiful rhythm and balance we had in entertaining people together. All the hundreds of people who came to that studio those ten years. Gone.

Even when he shows me his new sculptures, my eyes keep examining the edges of the room and finding new reminders. He seems utterly oblivious, something I'm thankful for. If he noticed he might see how down I am, how helpless before him, how depressed in my very soul, how without hope as an artist. I do not want him to know that vulnerability.

And at the end he is very sweet, giving me a pair of wooden clogs he bought in Sweden. The six months in Sweden with Bonnie. Never mind, he has carted these unwearable shoes all the way home for me, remembered them in one or another shopping bag and several moves, and kept them on hand just for when I might visit. And a drawing too. A pair of lamb chops, a study he'd done for a wooden sculpture that he says never did work out. "But the drawing's not so bad." His old habits of understatement, criticism, rare praise. Looking at some others, I see a flower drawn just at the edge of the paper. And beg it from him, feeling no guilt whatsoever since we always swapped; last time he came to my place he picked out three things he liked, a series I'd called "Samurai." I said they were for him, meaning that I'd thought of him. "Thank you," he had said, quite pleased, and so of course I gave them to him. This little man sitting across from me, ten years older than I but looking still a boy. "What will you do when you begin to age, pass him off as your son?" my mother used to tease me. But it didn't last that long. I couldn't keep him. Strange self-contained little person in his tight shoulders, the dear flesh around his neck showing at the throat of his shirt. He wanted only to be rid of me. And now he is. Our leave-taking as polite and futile as the day has been. Does it come to this? I want to scream. But say nothing. And going down the stairs I swallow and refuse to cry.

Ruth had left me roses by the bed. She knew I'd be coming today, and when I call she says she'd be delighted to have dinner. We meet at a restaurant over on Barrow Street. But in person she's a changed and rather unfriendly presence. First, there's the hassle about the mail. "I find I resent doing this for you any more." "Sure, I've already notified the post office. They'll forward it from now on." "You owe me money for postage due." "I'll write you a check." "The plants are getting to be a nuisance." "I'm awfully sorry." Why remind her that it was her own idea? It would have been easy to ask the woman downstairs. "I've bought some automatic feeders for them so I don't have to bother coming over." "Fine." "They were expensive." "Just tell me how much and I'll include it in the check." "My analyst thinks I shouldn't see you so much." "That's nice." "She says I'm obsessed with you; it's destructive for me." "Probably right." "My mother doesn't think I should model for you any more." "Does she know what went on at our sessions?" Anything to tease her out of it, restore some semblance of friendliness. I will miss Ruth, whose great body I have drawn thousands of loving times, the cheerful sensuality of those long afternoons. "My mother thinks I should concentrate more on my own work." "A good idea." Ruth growing up as a sculptor, no longer the student, the kid I used to lecture and exhort and berate into taking herself seriously as an artist. "And I won't be able to work as your apprentice on your next show."

One blow after another, Ruth, who was too staunch, too convenient, too good. Ruth, who decided to fall in love with me one day up at Columbia when I was making a speech, Ruth star-struck and determined, hunting me down over three years' time. She begged to help me

on the last exhibition, wouldn't take no for an answer.
I said there was probably something undemocratic
about having an apprentice, but she stayed anyway,
worked like a demon, learned. But it has always been
wrong. Her infatuation, her obsessiveness, her maniacal
patience, her services, her dogged devotion. I had been
"picked." But had no part in the picking. Ruth loved
me, it was never my idea to love her. I was located
and decided on. Her adoration always seemed unjust to
me, imposed upon. At terrible cost—the guilt and
recriminations that settle on me when I reject it. There
is something selfish and predatory about Ruth's selfless-
ness. But when she showed me two years' worth of writing, up at the farm, two years of writing with myself as
its subject, I relented. Flattered. It was good writing.
The summer I was mad and Ruth seemed the only
friend left. Ruth to play her guitar and her Israeli
folksongs and model and take photographs. A nice idyll
until Sita came back and Fumio decamped and things
got serious. But Ruth saw me through the hard days
too, the suicide times, the homeless months after I lost
the studio. Just friends again rather than lovers. Until
that night last October when I got drunk having dinner
with Hatsie and I called her, roaring and sodden and
said, Just come over and fuck me, and the good soul
did. That morning they pulled down the old house, but
I was too sick to get up and watch it go out the window.

And now I sit across from her, having wronged her,
determined not to sleep with her tonight. Don't wrong
her again. For you it's a good lay, friendly sex. For her
it's different, she's in love. And angry. "My analyst has
helped me get in touch with my anger." I hate this sort
of talk and am at this moment trying not to get in touch
with my own anger. It's getting to be a pretty tedious
dinner. Come home to New York and you come home
to nothing. "I think we should be friends." "So do I,
splendid idea." "I take it things are better in California now?" "Quite a lot." I have even used Ruth as a
confidante, called her once when I was very depressed
and told her how badly it was going. Meanwhile, she's
freed herself. I watch her unwrapping herself from me.

Good. Good that she's getting her own studio, that her
analyst has taught her how to balance her checkbook
and stop taking money from her parents, that her stomach ailments are better, that she's finally finished that
portrait of me and can go on to something more promising. Good that she's growing up.

But the process seems to require losing her even as a
friend. Perhaps it was not my friend she wished to be.
And yet she's been the deepest, staunchest friend at
times. Now she's become this irascible alien. We order
dessert. Rhoda, who worked on a film with me, is at
the next table. She comes over, and then takes off,
having hardly said hello. I nursed her through a crack-
up last fall; but tonight she seemed hardly able to remember my name. Ruth is a hostile presence across the
table. Suddenly I feel lonely the way New York makes
you lonely. What's the point of it all? I wonder. People
are like sharks here, no one ever does anyone a favor
without a huge price tag on it, you think you
have friends here but you have nothing, you go
around hanging on to the memory of this place and
your bloody art world and they are nothing but a pile
of shit.

Ruth walks me home but pauses a good ten feet from
the door. We say good night. As I climb the stairs I
realize that her coming up with me was never an issue.
I think of her walking up the Bowery alone, her back
and shoulders in an old blue peacoat and wonder
whether she feels as righteous and dejected as I do.

Now Sita again. Framed in the door. How small she
looks. How dark. And how young her hair, nearly its
own brown again. Lively as a gypsy, my old Chiquita,
some adventurous caller from another world. It all
goes away, the bad day in Boston, the good day in
Chicago, the chill of New York—all disappear. We
feel stealthy as she slips in the door of my hotel room.
"This is the craziest place in the world." "I've got New
York on the line, I'll be right with you." How it all
goes wrong; first having to come out of the shower to
deal with the maid who wants to get the room ready

for the night. Why not, this night of nights, when Sita comes to me air freight from San Francisco on a university errand cleverly scheduled so we can rendezvous in the midst of my tour, a stolen night of our own.

The Beverly Hills Hotel had been just a name to me; some dotty motel L.A. pink-stucco thing probably, the ubiquitous vinyl monster beloved of travel bureaus. Not the marvel that greeted me, rumpled, out of a taxi before the haughty eyes of women in long skirts, still more haughty doorman. Hollywood, the real Hollywood, with stars and starlets off to a premiere. On closer inspection just overdressed Los Angeles. Humbly past the desk, the labyrinth of corridors that lead to my seclusion, my luxury. I examine the room—excellent furniture, a balcony we've no time to use, alas, a swimming pool far off. And room service, an elaborate and compelling menu. Order up champagne or wait? What guilt attends it?

And now this gypsy at my door, more precious than ever, this co-conspirator of mine. But why does everything go wrong? The maid turned out to be undoing the bed, which to her surprise I bid her redo. The yellow silk of its coverlet is our tablecloth, our drawing room, our very house tonight. The maid sulks. I feel remorse. And then the blamed phone just as Sita knocks on the door. All should have been in readiness. At least I showered. And at last I am off the phone. At last she is in my arms, laughing at our naughtiness, our intrigue.

"I have no idea why I feel so wicked." "Neither have I. Let's order everything on the menu." She looks around the room. "I love it. I have a real affinity for the expensive." "Isn't the furniture good for a hotel room? That green chair, for example?" "How will we ever get that lovely armoire out of here and onto an airplane?" She sets down her wicker case and comes to join me on the bed. "Speaking of airplanes, I've got one at 8 a.m. Do they have limousines?" "My dear lady countess, limousines are a thing of the past. Let's see if they have taxis." Already she is going from me. The morning so soon.

"Should we make love?" I ask her uneasily. "This is

making love," she says, sipping champagne and stretching out. "We will—slowly, gently." And till then we talk, a feast after nearly a week's hunger. Every detail of the house and the garden and friends and the tour, its prickly interviews only whimsical now, jokes to present her with, all that had been forbidding, humiliating. The good things too, like that woman reporter from the Chicago *Tribune*. "Hey, I met Mary Travers of Peter, Paul & Mary." "What's she like?" "A right-on lady, reminded me of Nell. So did Shirley MacLaine. Good tough women, troopers, actresses." The champagne excites us—we could talk forever, kissing, embracing, breaking away, showing off, amusing, reassuring, rejoicing, trumpeting our happiness.

"When I got here, you won't guess what was hanging from the doorknob of the room. A pair of women's underpants." "You're putting me on." "My first thought of course was that you'd arrived ahead of me and were leaving a calling card." "Where do you get these depraved ideas?" "I assumed it was some sophisticated little joke of yours. An invitation of a sort. Naturally I accepted. And besides, I didn't want the bellboy to see them. On checking, however, I discovered they weren't clean. And that the odor was not the correct one." "So?" "So I threw them in the wastebasket." "They call this a good hotel." "I think they belong to the couple next door, who seem to be out." "Unless they're in there listening to your every word."

But they aren't, we are safe in our joy, private in our delighted reunion in Nirvana, in a state of frivolity remote from any reality. It will evaporate. As soon as we check out in the morning, it will never have happened. We will only remember, have only the tintype of the mind. But solid now this moment, like that beautiful green silk chair across the room. I will carry it in my mind like an emerald of remembrance. Sacred, holy, to be invoked on high occasions or in the hardest need. Like a licking stone carried in a child's pocket.

We have already passed the dinner hour. Must settle for supper. "Pity, no chocolate soufflés with Grand Marnier." "We'll have to make do with Cabernet and filet mignon." We are obscene in luxury, rotten with

decadence, resplendent with vice. And happy. Also
exhausted. Falling asleep as we come finally into each
other, our flesh all good-willed exhaustion, sated merely
by the touch of her breast, the infinite sweetness of
her downy hair, the soft triangle between her legs, the
sharp hot joy of her finger finding me, parting the hair
to reach the lips, enter and, entering, seal all; finish
we never did.

And a few days later she meets me when I land in
San Francisco. Home again. Drinking at Señor Pico's,
looking out over the bay, how splendid our city is, how
glad I am to be home. Juanita's has burned to
the ground out in Fetters Springs—Sita has clipped the
article from the paper for me. It is a piece of the past
gone, snipped as with a scissors, excised from time and
place. Even this one elegiac note doesn't matter as we
watch the perfect sunlight on the bridges and the islands. For dinner we go down to Fisherman's Wharf,
to a tourist trap with nasty waiters. Sita is exhausted,
nearly falling asleep over her seafood. Only exhausted
—or bored? I run into dread again.

She came to my class. Appearing magically in the
hallway near the door, wearing my own gray jersey
and the string of wooden beads. "I'd like to sit in, unless it cramps your style." Why didn't I say that
it would? Because I never suspected that today would
turn out to be the one day the students would just
sit woodenly, refuse to answer, shy away from discussion. The book we've read is Violette Leduc's *La
Bâtarde,* and of course they're afraid of its lesbian passion, of its immediacy, its personality. My comments on
style and technique collapse around me. I start to sweat
and can smell it. A circle of silent, embarrassed women.
I panic. I have run out of notes, out of things to say.
We're in a windowless basement room. Thirty women
on hard plastic chairs. The bright fluorescent light. Li-
noleum tiles. The week of the tour gave me no time to
prepare and the book is huge, enormous. But I've read
it many times and have just spent six careful hours
reviewing it today. Even if I were unready, alone I
could wing it. Or face the first defeat in solitude without

her face coming at me from the right side of the room, a seat set back just near the door. Seeing her face, the gray jersey, the beads, the gray of her hair and her glasses swimming into my terrified vision. Her face calm and kind, encouraging, never meaning to destroy.

It was disastrous. The class that is my hope, my joy, my consolation. My own thing against the heavy encroachment of love. Teaching, which I'm so proud of, so good at. My high dinners after class, with group after group of students vying to entertain me. Our buddy sessions around the coffee machine in the ten-minute break. Why are they letting me down so? These women whom I try to turn into writers, whom I urge into life, now sitting dumb and forlorn. And Sita watching. There is no energy at all in the room, none in the circle of our chairs, none whatsoever in my body. Where is Gretta today, with her psychopathic babble, talking until the others revolt? I could use her. A few others monopolize the little that gets said, but they are repetitious, haggle over trivia, harp stupidly and subjectively on the author's personality. The rest abide in stony silence. They give nothing, offer nothing.

My love looks on. This is my celebrated class. And I cannot take hold, give direction, and command. The little talk dies away into silence again. My eyes grab for the notes on the page. What else did I mean to call to their attention, dazzle them with—the passage on tearing up her father's photograph? No, skip it, not important enough in this vacuum. The use of the adjective, Leduc's superb qualifiers—the "charity" of a lover's shoulder blades. But it elicits no response. The technique of personification and apostrophe? No, I've mentioned that already. On a good day I could get some thirty minutes of mileage out of that. But not now. The clock drags.

Okay—face it: what do they think of the portrayal of lesbian experience, the erotic content of the book? Did it shock them? Laying the groundwork by mentioning a previous class, the class in Sacramento, how hard it had been for them to discuss this. Embarrassed silence. One admits she was shocked but can go no further. One found it "very erotic," "lovely" even. And falters. We switch gears to the great act of betrayal in the book, the incident in the room of mirrors, the brothel where Violette has brought Hermine to try her or to break her. I say I find this passage shocking, gratuitous. Evil. They don't. The one who has been glib with Proust for an hour finds more Proust. The rest don't find anything at all. I glance again at my notes —I have run out. There will be an eternal silence. Desperately I take another tack. Someone had just mentioned one of the passages from childhood, how Violette, while out walking with her adored grandmother, occasionally permitted her attention to stray away from her companion, a thing she describes as being "unfaithful." "I would pick up a stone or a pebble and then run after her and give her my free hand. When the stone or pebble was warm I let it fall on something soft: the grass or sand. Then I could breathe with the satisfaction of having had an existence of my own." I pounce upon it, how the word "unfaithful" here, so strange and extraneous to ordinary usage, is indicative, even typical, of Leduc's sense of sin and of the absolute in love. I see Sita gather up her jacket. In a rush I turn to the problems of registration, part of the reason she is here. People attend the class who are not registered. Others whose registration is somehow imperfect due to the process of canceling and then rescheduling the class, attend and even write essays, though their names do not yet appear on the roll. I labor through this, hating the police aspect of it, the bureaucracy. But solve it finally, even pleased with myself by the solution. I look up to find she is gone.

Walking toward the house, I accept my failure, knowing beforehand how it will be to live with that all week. Who can know the love of a teacher, its ups and downs between Monday and Monday, its symbiotic existence upon a group of strangers, its hungers and thirsts and deprivations? The tragedy of a bored or empty lecture, the victory of a set of essays or even of one clear and perfect illustration. I'll tell her that it was their off-day and mine too. A fluke. A pity we hit the wrong time. Say all this to her lovely brown eyes, with the windows of the living room open to the early-evening air flowing serenely past us as we huddle together on the couch, our arms warm, our heads comforting each other's shoulder. She is kind, kindness. "They didn't get the book; it scares them." "It wasn't so bad." All the usual flagellation of self-hatred dissolves. I forgive myself. And I realize I am divinely happy, a happiness saved from a thousand destructions. I will believe her, believe in her. I will ask no more than this. To be in her arms, to feel the soft gray jersey on my cheek, the fine spring air from the open windows.

There is no purpose even in writing this notebook any more. I have decided only to live in this happiness. Lose a manuscript? My work? So what? Supposedly so precious, actually nothing but the bottom line of survival. Merely living is better, living in this enormous comfort and this breathtaking peace. I have arrived at rest. The air so clear gold going toward the rose of sunset. We cannot bear to part from each other. I will go with her to the city for the evening class.

It's over. I should throw the notebook away. It's to no purpose any more. Quit it. Junk the whole project. Whatever end it served no longer exists. Yet the pity of leaving off, dumping it. Another abandoned manuscript. This on top of the Japanese stuff, the death book that will never be a book. The wrench of giving it up. On the trip everything surged toward the newest book, the book about the murder of a child. I had been longing to write about things outside myself. And I was confident again.

If I stop this journal, is that a sign of coming to rest? Of committing myself to her, leaving no out, no outlet? Or would that be only another failure, another submission? Or is it peace? To stop examining, reporting, recording the bloody emotions. To stop prying. To have a life so fine, happy, somehow *holy,* that it will bear no scrutiny, would resent the third eye of an interloper. To live merely for living. And then what do you do with your life?

An hour ago she telephoned: "I'm looking at four daffodils and wishing I were seeing your face through them. Someone in my office just handed me these flowers and I wish you were here to complement them. I've missed you all morning." The singing of her voice, its amorous ingenuity. That, or the hard little scrabble with words? What do I care? What do I care, when living itself goes on so perfectly?

I will have a party for her in New York when she stops off on her way back from the conference in Puerto Rico. It will soften the separation, soften my going back East, because in a sense she will be going back with me. This will be her second visit to my loft, and it's now much further along than the rough space she saw last Christmas. It will be her second visit of many, for we will share our cities now. Each time she comes to New York she will admit, on my account, to hating it less, learning it all over again, like a new city. Downtown, an artist's city, not the dull rich lady's city of her old days, the world bordered by Bonwit's and Saks and the Biltmore. And each time I will make it magic for her, pore for days over the entertainment guide, take her to the shows in SoHo, the right streets in the Village, the restaurant she hasn't been to yet, out-of-the-way museums. Each time it will be that much closer to a balance.

So I will invite all my friends—or rather, the best ones, the ones that matter most, are dearest rather than "interesting" or "famous" or "impressive." They will meet her and know her. She's accused me of hiding her, has complained that I have never introduced her around. This will be in her honor then. All of them will be called to admire her, to appreciate her—all these tough New York types summoned to pay her homage, see her fineness, render their approval. I am pleased and excited by the idea, compose new invitations in my mind each day.

The idea of her coming to New York, her idea, how clever it is. Nearly erases my departure from California. We will merely part for three days, only to meet again in my town, my world. I would not have wanted it that way before, was even a little uneasy when she first suggested it. Once I had just wanted to leave. The gesture of leaving California and going home, the gesture I had been trying to make for months. The gesture of walking out. And part of me still held to that, I suppose, when she first mentioned it. Saying goodbye in New York seemed to cancel my gesture and its inference of independence. How insidious she is, I'd thought, listening to her outline the plan—that she could stop off in New York on her way home from the conference in Puerto Rico—how insidious to have taken even my leaving away from me. Because this way, of course, it is she who will be leaving me. After the magical week she outlines: "You know what a wonderful time we had last Christmas. Well, it'll be a whole week this time, not just four days. A whole week just to do nothing but make love and drink champagne and admire your pictures and your beautiful white walls and go to the theater and sleep and not worry once about this damn job . . . but after that you have to put me on an airplane and send me home." Always that moment at the end, that moment in Kennedy. Watching her leave the Christmas she came to my farm—wanting to scream and run after her, tear at the arm of her mink coat and at her smart cocked hat and never let her out of my sight. So close to death that Christmas. "All I can remember of your loft is that lovely green quilt on the bed and those huge white walls. And I think that's all I'll need," she goes on, outlining, arranging, selling me the idea. Of course, of course, to have her in my home again, to show her more of what I love—funky things like Second Avenue below St. Mark's, but would she ever understand it? Always like a child, nearly wanting to hold on to my hand when I lead her through my slum, her eyes huge and appalled, intrigued perhaps or astonished that anyone would actually live on the Bowery by choice. When one could live in San Francisco, in Berkeley, California? Walking very close to me, and I am always surprised and a little amused at how foreign and insane and squalid it must be to her, keeping so near to me, a countess on Second Street amid the wine bottles and the bums, the debris and the wild dogs at the corner where some old derelict is squatting, too poor to feed the mangy beasts. Sita climbing the five long flights to my loft on her lame leg; tenderly I wait and carry things for her, carefully I arrange life so there are only a few trips. Sita lighting my dingy corridors, my empty spaces, my dark unpainted studio on the third floor. I will sit her down like a patron, show her drawings, not just spread out the portfolios as I do sometimes for other artists, everyone just squatting on the floor or sitting for hours on their haunches. No, she will sit on a chair like a patron. She will become austere as she sometimes is, grave and judicial, a snob; her ancestors commissioned pictures for five hundred years and one of them was a Pope. The idea delights and intimidates me. Will she understand my pictures? More important, will she like them?

The idea of her coming to New York has hold of me now. Once I wouldn't have wanted that. But that was before, when I merely meant to leave. And it would be the end. Now it is no such thing. I will be back. We have arranged about the rent and she is looking for someone to share the house with, someone to rent Paul's room. If no one satisfactory turns up, I'll just go on paying my half until I come back. Extravagant, and it becomes more and more so as time goes by and my little pile of royalties runs out, but worth it: the house is mine now and will go on being mine. And I wouldn't want her to have to put up with someone she didn't like. We will go on. The future is all there now, each winter I will come here to her; each summer I will go back, but she will come to me. She has the month of August for vacation this year and she is now talking about driving cross-country to be with me, come to the farm, go up to the Cape. If she flies (and I will find her the money if she hasn't got it), then we will have more days to be together. And during the months we are apart until January, there will be trips, conferences, speeches—we'll manage this, the prospect amuses and delights us. The permanent "affair" she teased me about: "There'll be years and years of our rendezvous in different cities, all those hotel rooms, lady, we can make a career out of it." She had sat in my big Mexican sweater when she came to New York last Christmas and watched me make dinner and laughed, throwing her head back. "We should have a permanent affair, it should go on for years. Maybe it should always be an affair for us. We're better that way." But we even talk now of the time when I give up New York and settle in California. We look at houses out of the corner of our eye.

Once I wanted just to leave when May came. But now of course it's entirely different, because she is so different, so good to me now. Like the frog, for example. At breakfast the other morning my cigarette fell out of the ashtray and burned a hole in her favorite blue tablecloth. It seemed past repair, and I had nearly been afraid to confess. And then last night she came home with this absurd embroidered frog. Seems all you do is iron it onto the fabric and you have a delightful readymade patch. The frog touched me enormously, it seemed a symbol of all her goodness, her kindness to me, her patience and gentleness, a goodness beyond what we mean by friendship or even the maternal, something almost Buddhist in its endless warmth and care. That was Sita as she used to be, a Sita whose love was at first so expansive and generous I feared for it, terrified I should in some way exploit or abuse. "I saw a future of indulgence in her eyes," Leduc says somewhere about a woman who loved too abjectly. I remember quoting Sita the passage, dragging the book over to the phone once in Sacramento. "Look, there's something I want to read to you because I never want to take advantage of your goodness." And she was a bit amused and said yes, she would certainly watch out for that sort of thing. I was warning her, warning her of herself and of me. And yet I think I never loved her quite so purely as that moment. Protecting that infinite tenderness and sensitivity and kindness which were at the very heart of her love, the love that I loved—goodness I suppose it was actually. Even virtue. Or what virtue would mean if it were a word still permitted to have meaning.

And so to celebrate this frog and my starting the new book—the book about a child who was put to death, which I have talked about writing for so many years— we opened champagne and lolled on our cushions and drank toasts. The evening sun filled the room and I think we have never had it so good here. The time is itself now, doesn't need to be compared to other times, as it used to. In the future it will be a time to be compared to.

At dinner Sita was tipsy, and made a long, long speech about politics, about her responsibilities to Latina and Chicana women. Which seem to preclude her being a known lesbian. Because the Latin community is so conservative, prejudiced, Catholic, macho, reactionary. All of which together is too powerful to be ignored. I am silent and admiring and entertained by the La Pasionaria aspects of her performance, and so charmed by the refrain of "You are my life and my love, but still . . ." that I probably do not listen carefully enough to the rest. Was it her fears of the world that swayed her toward men when she drifted from me, the ease of being "straight," the convenience, the political convenience, the social approval? Listening, I drink in all her wonderful and extravagant professions of love and almost ignore the rest. "Who's requiring you to tell the Latinas you're gay?" I ask languidly, wondering after all what the fuss is about, assuming that she is really just enjoying the business of posing as the heroine of her people tonight, the proletarian Chiquita whom I adore, the Sita who harangues money from the city council for the *conferencía femenil,* the Sita who has spent years in civil-rights groups. Once we attended a drug workshop with Pia during which everyone made some statement about themselves. Sita announced to them that she was "Pia's mother and a lesbian." The last identification seemed so gratuitous I nearly laughed, for whatever "lesbian" meant to the wrecked young people in the room, it was scarcely a word that applied to the beautiful, early-middle-aged woman they saw or to the Sita whom I or anyone else knew. Somehow she has always seemed to be a woman who might love another woman, or had, or did even then, without being what the world imagines is a lesbian. And so I listen with only half an ear now, sure that she does not really have to face this issue in real life but that she is experimenting only for herself in saying it out loud—that she would not want it known, that it could cause her trouble, hurt her reputation. Or rather, that it would render her ineffective with the Latinas who are her special constituency, make it impossible for her to help them, render them services she is dedicated, and uniquely qualified, to give. All very strange since in the past I have been far more discreet than she, scrupulous largely on account of her job. And it was Sita then who would laugh and say, "But of course they all know we are lovers. How could anyone not know by now?" Proud of it, a bit proud of me, her "catch" once. And now I listen to her, gradually dumbfounded by what seems to be coming through her sweetly disheveled fulminations, her revolutionary posturing, and it seems to be fear. "So if I have to, I'll deny it." "Really?" "Don't you see, I can't afford to be open about it?" "No one's kicking you out of the closet," I tease, to reassure her. But it's disappointing, the coward's way. It's not like her.

In the morning she couldn't even remember what her speech had been about or how I got her to bed. "With smiles and the fondest patience," I say, kissing the back of her neck, the coffee-brown skin, the softness of it, the delicacy. The sun shines into the room. Again these days of happiness, the sun, swimming each day, great roaring dinners with a fire afterward, again these days perilous on the rim of love, of joy balanced over fate, days of happiness even when things go wrong or a student of mine is in trouble and arrested in a fight and Maud calls that she has finally lost her job, or a letter arrives from Italy reporting that Pia has borrowed two hundred dollars from Sita's brother there.

"In all those years I lived in shacks and worked for the damn water company and starved and brought up two kids, I never asked them over there for money." Sita bitter and scornful, her honor dashed, her heart broken by Pia's guilty malice when confronted, a child caught at wickedness turning spiteful, calling her names. Martin has come to dinner to report that Sita is still not living within her budget. She is still in debt for the kids' extravagances during the time of the commune. He is grave and pessimistic. She cannot afford to

go with Maud to Mexico in July. But she will bring
him around somehow; Martin enjoys playing curmudg-
eon and shaking his head, and the dinner is as mellow
as old friends.

There is still peace, even happiness. For the first time
I am sure I am able to comfort, that merely lying next
to her at the end of the day I am strength for her. And
the happiness winds around me like a cocoon. The
rhythm of workdays—the swim in the afternoon, our
drinks, our dinners. Our weekends. Our every precious
day until it is over. And the new book growing, its
pages growing from eight to eleven to fifteen. As I
swim laps in the spring evening, I find an idea in one
lap, a method in another, waiting for the time I must
give up imagining and begin research on the events the
book will be based upon. The evening sun glinting on
the water, the pool on the top of a long hill, and far below the bay and the bridges and the towers of San Francisco, spread out like a faerie city, mystic in the curve
of the shore, the twist of bridge floating to Treasure
Island, poised for a second in invisible space, then
floating again to the mainland and the crown of spires.

These are good days, these are the best, an oasis in
the desert of the past, the past I less and less remember
or even believe in, her voice angry and impatient when
I do—"If you're going to start hassling me about that
again," she'd said, when I made a face that we'd have
guests this weekend and because there's a meeting on
Sunday. And I learn to keep patient, to trust, to accept
less than all. One odd moment listening to her shower,
wondering if the banquet at Santa Barbara, a farewell
for a university official, a man retiring but already condemned to death by cancer, the banquet which means
staying overnight down there, wondering if it means a
night with Neal too. And cease to wonder. Listening to
the sound of the water, her sound, her lovely body
glistening through the room a moment from now. There
are only moments. Live in this one. The happiness of
these days.

This notebook, the narrow-lined one, will contain
the final entries. It's late April and the experiment will
end May eighth in New York at the close of that last

week there together. Even to write down those words makes me feel weak. The entire experiment was a failure. Abandoned any number of times and particularly lately, the last week or so when I find I only make lists of moments over a weekend. "Maud here. A meeting in San Francisco on Sunday, I looked out at the bay and wondered." Or hungered or yearned or some similar tedious and repetitious emotion, too vague, too diffuse, too challenging or insufficiently challenging to put into words.

Yesterday she cleaned her desk. Always admirably efficient, she completely rearranged and updated all her papers in an hour. Then she told me, as we sat close together on the couch, that she had saved every letter of mine, even valentines, along with six inarticulate poems I loathe and am in dread of ever seeing again. "No one had ever written me poems. My three husbands never even saw me. I was a body washing dishes and raising children. They never saw me. But you, you've written me poems, you've made drawings of my body. No one ever said it was beautiful before."

To hand her these pages. Some proof, some testimony of love. Inconclusive. It is as much a testimony of hate, uncertainty, ambivalence, indifference, boredom, resentment. And if it convinced for a while, it would pall soon. You can read and be pleased and then put aside. Easily, very easily. It would constitute no way to hold her. Even the fact of obsession, still more obsession exhibited—this would necessarily cause her to stiffen and reject. Nothing is so odious as unsolicited adoration.

Then say I did it for myself, since it is just whatever I wanted to bother putting down on paper. And of course it was here that it broke down altogether. Because I never *got* it, never got it at all. Not even such a simple thing as the air in the bathroom when I look at the walls and remember she wanted them painted after the fire they had here during the commune. Now there isn't time for either before I leave. Not getting something like the blue-and-white Greek bedspread in the bedroom, all it conveys of our cohabitation, our intimacy, afternoons when the sun falls on it and she is gone. And I think of afternoons the sun will fall on it when I am gone, when I no longer exist for her. Or the riskier and more difficult atmosphere of the front room, Paul's old room, the so-called library whose bookshelves are yet to be built; guest room, space for a future roomer, scene of her nights away from me—its foam mattress on the floor and a chintz quilt she has thrown over that, the pillows at all angles, her sunlamp aimed from a lamp onto the mattress where she bakes herself listening to country music on the radio.

Hundreds of things that will be gone soon, maybe forever. Surely forever from this notebook or my attempts to place them with any permanence. Things I scarcely understand myself but will miss like a cry of pain. The sight of the kitchen when there are dishes to wash and I would rather write, the sight of them somehow baffling me—as they would never baffle her—until I pull myself together and remind myself I do after all know how to wash dishes, even understand by now where they are supposed to go, where each thing is to be put away after all the changes of the commune. The commune gone now, buried like a lost civilization, and I have wangled my way back into her heart. Yes, and leaving now. How can she forgive me? How, for that matter, can I forgive myself? Doing it, leaving, I know not even why.

True, my sculpture show must be done in New York. But that's late, next fall. And I dread it and hate it anyway. Cancel? No, it's a necessary recovery of the self. Stick with the new book? You can write that anywhere and might do better writing it here, in a settled life. But I know I want to leave her. If only so that I can stop writing this damn record, a record begun as consolation for losing her love. Having regained it in some measure, writing about it has come between us, forcing me to escape for a while just so the notebook can come to an end.

And the end too, how feeble. Seven days together in New York. I do not even leave her. She leaves me. Gets on an airplane at Kennedy, disappears down a chute as I have seen her do how many times. She has arranged it thus. But what we have instead is amor-

phous, as amorphous and inconclusive as life. There
are no solutions, resolutions. Only the repetitions of
the rise and fall of the heart: rejection, then a little
less rejection, then acceptance, then rejection again—
subtler and more malicious. And on the other side,
vacillation again. Followed by dread, the old dread but
a little smaller; dread of life, either alone or together.

First we went to Grundy's for a drink. We were on
our way elsewhere for dinner. Even as it happens, I
know it is to be remembered, pressed in the book of
the mind, uncovered in other places where remembering it will hurt, will tear in the New York evening, will
haunt me in age if I lose her. But what was it like? We
are two bodies in a car on a long coast road. I feel the
line of the bay in my heart, my fingers tracing the water
and the sand and the road itself. The bay in the pink of
the sunset, the sun itself a fire falling, heaving down
upon the hills, heaving itself to extinction each second
faster and farther. The line of the bay, the sheen of the
water nearly alive with the strange powerful light on it.
Cars have stopped to watch. She pulls over. For a moment or two we stare at it mutely. "It will get harder
and harder to live in New York." "Maybe you'll have
enough of the Bowery someday, enough bums, enough
cold, enough suffering." "Sixteen years might almost
do it." I laugh because she is teasing, just as she did in
the parking lot leaving Grundy's. We were going some
place new, a restaurant on the water over in Oakland.
The bridges and the sea before us like thunder. "Such
a beautiful place to live," I said. "Well, of course it
doesn't have all the advantages of the Bowery. Picasso
succeeded without living in New York, Colette, de
Beauvoir. Even Dante." "Turn off the engine, we've
only got a dollar's worth of gas." "All part of the adventure." We are silent again, looking to the sea. Suddenly she starts the car. We pass other cars that have
stopped, others willing to drop everything to gape at
the moment. The sun plunging farther, nearly touching
the hills. Great eternal force. "Where are we going?"
"I've got a great idea. A surprise." "Where?" "Back.

What we had is the best, why bother to explore?"
"You're right, you're exactly right."

And so we went back. I cannot explain how this
little episode, a bit of indecision and then inconsequen-
tial decisiveness over something as trivial as where to
eat dinner, I cannot explain how it mattered to me,
how it portended. Or even what it portended. Yet it
seemed to put a seal on things, a curious kind of commitment, a vote cast. And for more than our favorite
restaurant. For the notion of us perhaps. And yet I
don't think she felt it so deeply as I, was probably not
aware of anything but the power of the scene. And
that power was probably something else. A landscape
is something different to each person who sees it. And
I expect she did not see it as us, or feel it as a crisis.
She did not even think of it as the last time. I think
not, no, not at all. When we were home I saw her
come out of the shower, her beautiful body almost old.
Going down on her, trying to make love to her.
"My body lets me down," she said, and then a long,
uncertain discussion of the menopause, if it can affect
a woman who's had a hysterectomy years before. Then
she talks of the insecurity of the relationship. A few
days ago she said that if we were either of us to fall in
love with someone else, it would hardly matter if we
were together or apart. "If it were going to happen, it
would happen anyway, wouldn't it?" I say New York
is my independence and that I'm swallowed here now,
now at any rate, and that I need the city, need to be
away. She turns away from me: "Maybe we never
could have learned to live together, anyway." I stay
awake, sipping wine, reading and rereading the page
of a book. A medium despair—not like the old one.
But the next day an ongoing anxiety.

Pictures of her. If I should lose her, against that
time, to have some copy. Sita in the doorway of my
study, an apparition in an orange bikini. Wonderful
she is, brown, young, slender. "Have you heard about
the banana scandal?" Eating one as she asks, playing
herself, playing Chiquita Banana. "Very slippery
case really." I begin to laugh, but forget what I have

been typing, an essay about the Iranian political prisoners, my last sentence a description of death by torture, one of the cases documented by the London *Sunday Times.* "I'm serious," she says. "It's in all the papers. United Fruit's been giving out all this payola. It's been going on for years." "Your usual South American government, the expression 'banana republic,' for example?" I grin at her. "Under the skin," she intones mysteriously and tweaks the edge of her bikini. I forget the prisoner, forget my rage of a moment past, reading and transcribing horror in another place, and I sketch the words as she goes on, trying to catch them, to etch them on my brain, scribbling on the back of my draft of the essay. It is like trying to sketch her body, always she escapes me, evades me, slips past the fingers of my pen. Engraving her on my mind, on the backs of my eyelids, in the black spaces behind my eyes, so that if I close them someday afterward the brown body in the absurd shreds of orange cloth will be there, will always be there, even though she goes back to her sunlamp and I return to my prisoner.

It is an hour of the day when I am usually careful to absent myself, having lately chosen it as the time to swim, the hour or so just after she comes home from work. She had let me know that she would like more time to herself, a bit of time on her own after a day in an office full of people. And though I wait all day for the time of her return, a day entirely alone, it seemed only the simplest kindness to be away when she returns, one of the things I could do to please her, an opportunity even. There is so little time. The parting is so soon, only days now. She spends the time in the most mindless and lovable bliss under her sunlamp, listening to cowboy music. Perhaps it is the combination of all these mad details, the banana, the terrible suffering of the Iranian political prisoner as he dies, six months ago and several thousand miles away. According to the *Times* report of January 19, 1975: "He was placed on an electric oven and burned in his sacral areas. His wounds were not treated for a long time and the smell became unbearable to all. He was half paralysed and he was taken to court and shot soon afterwards in this

state." Perhaps it is nothing but the reality of her lovely
body in that doorway where it stays now, where it will
always stay, her patter of wisecracks and her whole-
hearted adoption of American vulgarity. Perhaps it is
all and nothing of that, but a step beyond toward the
forging of an icon, her gesture of tweaking the edge of
her G-string, that particular insouciance, which cannot
cancel but maybe balances the agony of the prisoner,
maybe assures one that both these phenomena exist in
the world. This man called Asgar Badizadegan: "He
was slowly burned by means of an electric fire while his
hands and legs were tied to a bed. He was so badly
burned in the lower lumbar area that it reached some
of the vertebral bones and he fell into a coma . . . He
was then transferred to prison hospital and underwent
several operations. But he can no longer walk, only
crawl on all fours." I have been enraged all afternoon
by this and her appearance is a kind of sanity for me,
reminding me that there is also sensuality and humor,
bikinis and country music and the lazy early evening,
the time when work is over and you have a drink and
the light grows golden and ripe like a swollen belly
pregnant with the bloody sunset within it.

But there is always the jarring note of where I am
and where she is, where I was when she came in, my
mind absorbed by horror and injustice, her saucy bikini
mood so free it seems an impertinence. We quarreled
later, perhaps this set it off, perhaps the thing festering
for weeks already. Pajaro Dunes, a place where she
has another one of her tiresome conferences this coming weekend, our last weekend. I am to come with her,
smuggled along, as it were. But we are uncertain,
afraid she might get in trouble for bringing me. When I
bring up my doubts again, she says, too easily, "Why
don't you just stay here, it makes no difference to me
whatsoever." We descend into quarreling: I confront
her with my greatest fear, that by now she feels contempt for me. She denies it in an openly contemptuous
way. As I leave the room, she fires at me: "It has nothing to do with me at all. You are simply a person who
doesn't like yourself very much." That last phrase
burns my ears all night. Because it is true. True here,

anyway. I have despised myself here day after day in a manner I often thought I couldn't bear. And yet I bore it. She is right, perfectly right. But what makes it so? Is this to be a permanent state, this forgetting of normal self-respect? What is it about this love that destroys the self? When it was reciprocal, mutual, joyous and fresh, I lived in a shocking state of self-esteem. Hubris even. And now, loving and unloved, I fold like a broken tent. No pride, no personhood. Get out. I've got to get out of here.

I close the door while she brings the car around. Pajaro Dunes. The deep-blue walls of this little room facing the sea, the weathered driftwood outside. How I have come to love the remarkable cobalt blue of the walls of this little cottage, our place for two days. Two days which she spent waiting on other people, the tedious conferees whom she served as cook and waitress. The enormous task of cooking for thirty persons here to elevate their minds with Gestalt psychology. The psychologists exceedingly important and knowing, the conferees enthusiastic suburbanites exalted by their status as clientele, and Sita and I the drudges who serve their dinners. I am small enough to feel resentful, but she is generous, gracious, the camp cook and matriarch. A countess who can wait on the noisy herd and never move a muscle of her disdain.

During the free moments we walked the beach and fell in love with the sandpipers and the terns, the tiny, quick-legged birds that keep hurrying mindlessly toward the water as if in pursuit of food or magic, something that never seems to be there. So they fly ten feet away and begin again, the very image of yearning patience, the persistence of these saints of hope. The scurry, the unbelievable speed of their little feet, their nearly invisible steps, the twiglike legs spinning as they rush. Over and over and again and again; a little movie of love. Impossible and imploring.

Some of that in myself. She was elsewhere much of the time, even when she was with me. Wanted to walk the beach alone, wanted the solitude of sunning herself, her body stretched on the porch, ripe and mellow but forbidden. Two of your general California underfed teenage specters sunning themselves next door, no more than five feet away. The gray of the weathered buildings, a resort compound composed of a thousand cubicles, the bleached wood and deckboards speaking of Provincetown and Eastern things I love. Then the mirage vanishes and you remember it is new and California. Which is why the little apartment is such a break. It's not really old, of course, but the furniture is antique, oak pieces from another time, a bottle of wine to greet us, and those wonderful blue walls.

I would like, in some inarticulate and puzzled way, to thank it. It was our last home, our last place. Soon it will all be over, all be gone. Only a few days now till she leaves for Puerto Rico and I for New York. So this was the final landfall. And then too something happened here, a strange minor miracle. I think I had her, finally. Not that it carries over. Making love to her Saturday night and she cried out as she hasn't in a long time, perhaps never, that way. The animal intensity of it, the glory of moving her so. Not, as I say, that it carries over. Indeed, the very distinction was that it happened and then ceased to happen, stood for a moment and then disappeared. The occurrence was the very proof of its never having occurred. Maybe it was just good sex, the pleasant fulfillment of lust, the orgasm you give yourself because you are merely taking and the other serves you and serves well. Or perhaps what I saw is the joy she has with another, with any other, with all the others. For I did not feel it was for me. "That is how it should be," she had said, almost as if she had forgotten and was reminding herself. Yes, of course, I thought, would that she wanted it so always, responded, pleasured herself this way every time. And yet I was not there with her, not really, did not ride the waves of it along with her, did not feel what she felt as she felt it, as once I did. So long ago, Sacramento. Did not even have the rapport and connection I usually have when I make love to her, however stunted and remote that can be at times. No, she was somewhere else and I did not really feel I was her instrument, only a friend nearby, delighted at her luck.

It winds down. And now I must let go even this odd little holiday with its blue walls and its ocean, where the incomprehensible, perhaps even solitary act of our love was enacted. It was as if she shot past me. Even as I was supposed to be reaching the goal and giving her the pleasure that would bind her to me, cause her to be possessed by the particular gratitude of the flesh that cements a pair of lovers, bolting them together in memories so intimate and intense they can never quite forsake them—even then I felt her pass me. Not the usual passing beyond of profound orgasm, where for a moment all life and persons, even consciousness itself, is dimmed or goes out in something near fainting. No, not that, but the passing beyond of someone moving ahead and away, like the wind of a fast-moving car overtaking. And I never saw her go out of sight, she simply vanished.

And now in another world—how other—she is waiting, perhaps even annoyed by the delay, as I linger wanting to say goodbye even to the sink, to the glasses, to the table where we drank the wine and she told me of Rio, the lights at night, how many miles of them along the shore when she was a girl there, the animals hanging from the roofbeams dripping blood onto the dust of back yards, blood for the voodoo. "And do you still believe in it?" I asked. "Of course," she said—another Sita, another from the one crying out in the little bedroom, and another still from the testy, middle-aged woman waiting impatiently behind the wheel of the station wagon for me to drag seven bags of leftover groceries up the hill and into the dull tailgate of the mediocre university company car, so that we can sit and be silent all the way to San Francisco and the house on Indian Rock whose rugs I hated so particularly yesterday.

The magic disappears, evaporates, is left behind. Doors close on rooms with blue walls and the white of nearly New England windows, the sea is gray and waiting for the rain that will come today at five o'clock. And the room remains behind as the door closes and you see the warren of other cubicles up to the right and the walk off to the left, and beyond the communal garbage dump the car waiting, its totally pedestrian color. Paper bags of groceries. Ahead. Forget ahead a moment. And the time coming. A long time. More than you'll need. The deep blue of the walls, the clean white of the woodwork, the light in the little bedroom, such a yellow light, almost the light of vigil lights, the Catholicism of our childhoods, the yellow, strangely yellow, shrine-like quality of that light and then its darkness and then her cry. What did it say?

All the way to New York, seeing the continent crossing through the windows of the plane, seeing the time there in the sky as it passes, taking me away. A spring of instinct screaming, Fool—you have left it. Your happiness, what you had of it, by the end you had something. No, no, she comes to me there in New York, Sita in New York in three days, she has promised. Cheerfully ignoring the color movie and the headsets of canned music. Not reading or writing either. Outside the little window, Wyoming, then Kansas, Indiana, Ohio. The long way, the full distance, and that one terrible voice mocking me, You had it and you left. Other times—the Sita who put you on the plane for New York that first summer when you went home for Fumio's show. The fondness, the doting, the almost astonishing pain with which she saw you to the helicopter in Berkeley. "The way you looked going off in your straw hat," she said later, "I could hardly bear to let you out of my arms." And Sita seeing me to the helicopter the last time, when I went to New York for the book tour, Sita bored in the waiting room, fidgeting, wanting so badly to leave before the 'copter even arrived, but too sporting or conscientious, or aware she was being watched, dutifully lasting it out.

No, these things don't matter. The first trip back was after all the first; she may have worried I wouldn't return. And the last time she knew it was merely for a week. After all, people get used to each other. Her boredom is surely no news to me now; conquering it, that's the news, winning her back, courting her with my city, my friends, the party I plan for her, the theater, the restaurants, the right streets, just the right streets, certain parts of the West Village. Barrow Street and Morton, Grove, strolling there in the evening, the sense you get of the life in those places, the romance of other people's lives, strangers with books that go up to the ceiling, that is part of the charm of New York; the avocado trees that grow in the windows where painters live, I will show her how if an avocado grows it's sure to be an artist's studio. I will take her through the loft district and make my little speech about how in these few square miles, these twenty blocks or so, all the books and paintings are made for the whole country. And she will smile and squeeze my arm and call me a provincial. And what if she doesn't come?

Leaving the house at Indian Rock, I buried little notes like Easter eggs sown in secret places, notes she'll find in drawers, surprises. Notes beginning, "Lady, I love you, so I snuggled up against your bras and stockings, waiting for you to find me." And when she finds them, I will be already gone from her. Don't even think of it. Or the last days at the house. Sita already gone to Puerto Rico and her friend Walter installed in the house. That she would give the house to someone else, turn it over to a housesitter while I was still there—as if I were a piece of furniture—an arrangement she announced at dinner a night or two before she left. I had just told her how I liked the Bay area now, loved San Francisco. And she informed me that Walter would take over and that it was more convenient for him to move in on Friday rather than waiting until after I had left. Arranging it all without ever mentioning it to me beforehand. If it is not convenient for me to have Walter and his son underfoot while I pack, it doesn't matter. I heard her in a helpless kind of fury. Already I was displaced. After Walter leaves in July, there would be another roomer. Walter would be no threat whatsoever, she assured me. "Though of course I don't plan to be celibate; I'm not that kind."

I should never have left. Should have stayed and guarded what was mine, stood sentry over the house, my car, my papers, all that I left there, had begun to make there, the students, the friends, it's madness to go back to New York. I had everything there, was a fool to leave, the claustrophobia seizing my throat; turn this thing around—I've made a mistake.

But no. No, she's there. She's East already. She's coming to New York. I go to join her, not leave her. I will see her in only two days. Just enough time to get the loft cleaned and ready.

That night, as I was washing out the refrigerator, I heard the doorbell. Odd, I thought, no one knows I'm back. A wayfarer, an artist buddy wandering by, needing company or a drink or having a nervous breakdown; all the reasons people don't call beforehand. Or a nut, a drunk from the street. I lean my head out the window into the quiet and comfortable rain—I am home, no one can harm me, I am making ready. "Western Union." And already I feared it—but you fear other things, your mother's death or something happening to a friend abroad, or just someone who's decided your telephone is broken. An honor or a catastrophe. My hands shaking with that particular fevered hurrying as I walk up the stairs trying to open the envelope, my legs tired already from the climbing, my forehead hot with dread. But even then it was almost entirely a surprise: NEW YORK TRIP CANCELED. SCHEDULE CHANGED. LETTER FOLLOWS. SITA.

An hour later I still cannot believe she has done it. The traitor, the bitch, the liar—and in that asinine telegramese. "New York trip canceled. Schedule changed"—what I had based my life on torn away in that smug business language. "I'll call you from the office." More of that. Who is she there with? What stud of the moment has caught her eye, who is she fucking, what anonymous male encountered on an airplane, in a dining room, at a meeting; whom does she ogle and then offer herself to? I can hear the come-on, "Perhaps you don't find older women attractive?" And of course he does, of course by now it's a point of honor that he does. As she unfolds, becomes her beauty her charm her wit her fascination, removes the formal self, the cold eyeglasses, the efficiency, becomes the Latin, the woman of passion and feeling and sensibility. Do you read them Neruda too? "Body of a woman . . ." "No, it sounds better in the Spanish," she always said, her mouth kissing the words, *"Cuerpo de mujer, blancas colinas, muslos blancos."*

Stop, you will go mad. Call Puerto Rico again. The operators are out on strike. Call them until they answer, call Bell Telephone. Screw their damn telephone strike, screw the Statler Hilton, get through, grab her by the hair with your voice, seize her, don't let her get away. Lies; if she lies, say nothing, get her back. Finally, at three in the morning, her voice: "I've just been writing you." I close my eyes and stop the tears by main force, just as I stop seeing that hotel room and whoever is with her. "Sita, what are you doing?" "But, darling, I've been weeping, I'm so bitterly disappointed. I'd wanted so to come." If she weeps you may not call her names, only a friendly little "Maybe you met someone there and would rather stay?" "No, no, nothing like that, they lost my provost's film at the airport, I've been three days tracking it down." Long, involved, expensive descriptions of her troubles, the nuisance of the provost's film, the odyssey of recovering it, the further nuisance that she is obliged to bring the film over to Florida to show it to a conference there. "Which is why I thought I couldn't come, but now I think I can manage a few days with you. It will only be from Sunday to Thursday, would you like that?" Of course I'll take anything, forgive anything. If only she comes. Then it is not over. Because it had seemed that the telegram killed everything. Walking away from the phone, saved now, I tell myself surely that was exaggerated,

surely there will be January when I come back to live
with her again in California. Surely this is an ongoing
thing, don't jump to conclusions, don't foresee death
and the void. Like last week, when I came home
from shopping for dinner and she said Maud had
called from Sacramento, was in a terrible state, her
lover's illness, losing her job; she must go up and take
care of her tonight, drive up after dinner and stay
over. I made a face, I suppose, though I said, "Fine,
that's probably necessary." And I remembered I
needed something else at the store and went back to
get it. When I came home she had disappeared. Simply vanished. No note, nothing. Then I remembered
that going out I had slammed the door. This was my
punishment then, that she had not stayed to eat the
dinner I was making but had gone straightway to
Maud's. But at first I did not even guess where she
had gone, I only stood in the house with its engulfing,
paralyzing emptiness. Like the first night she went off
to Neal. The same desperation as now. But never
mind, it's fine. She's coming.

And so she came. Coming from Florida on Sunday
night. Everything is ready. I have bought furniture,
scrubbed, laid in provisions, wines, champagnes,
steaks, lobsters. Walking into the lower level at Eastern, I see the flight sign and at first don't understand
it. Flight 42 from Puerto Rico. I look at the telegram
again, the second telegram. FROM FLORIDA FLIGHT
42 9:40 P.M. It can't be. Did the airlines make a mistake? Does the flight originate in Puerto Rico and
stop off in Florida? I check. No. Flight 42 is a direct
flight from Puerto Rico. I sit down. I am a little dizzy
with the idea that she has lied to me. That she has
lied perhaps over and over. That her story on the telephone was also a lie. She never went to Florida at all,
stayed in Puerto Rico the whole time and would have
stayed there until it was time to return to California
if I had not caught her in her hotel room and—what
—shamed her into coming? And now she goes on lying,
when she gets off the plane she will go on saying she
has come from Florida. If I let her. She will lie and

lie and go on lying, divesting herself of that fine integrity she wore like her pride of birth.

"Did you come from Florida?" "Yes." "The plane comes from Puerto Rico, the sign says so." "Then I came from Puerto Rico." "What did you really do?" "Stop bothering me and help me carry this thing," the provost's film, a great stupid plastic can of it. I help, still asking, still wanting to know. But there is no knowing. "I was supposed to bring it to Florida but they lost it again. Just carry it, I'll explain some other time." And crossing the road—"Don't ask me questions, just let's enjoy the time together." And I realize there never will be any explanation. She will never admit that she lied, nor will I ever force her to. From now on I must accept what I get. She lies and will go on lying. And I will know it and have to keep silence. It changes things, changes them completely.

But there is still the time ahead, the four fabled days. When there is no more truth, when you no longer trust someone. And they know it too, know that you are someone to lie to, and are therefore despicable. Yet they forbid you to ask, forbid you to brave them and call them liars, demand instead that you acquiesce, pretend that the lie is not even there to be seen, or that answers given you are not even there to be heard, humiliated by. So pretend that you are deaf and dumb and merely carry baggage very carefully across the airport road. And when she seizes you and embraces you and says that we must have a lovely time and not quarrel, nod and turn before the tear on your cheek is discovered. Then get the car. And tell yourself a thousand times until you have memorized it and can really act on it . . . this didn't happen. All that matters is that she's here, that you have her these four days. Now, only now. Begin from now. Picking her up in the car in front of the terminal, loading the luggage, taking her hand at the stoplight. Now it begins.

And so she came. And we spent the four days, the week that had melted and shrunk, spent them at the theater, at a dull serious play uptown and an uproar-

ious farce downtown, and I loved being with her. Even
at *Equus,* which bored me so much I went to sleep. But
merely being with her, sitting next to her in a theater
uptown where I hadn't been since college, even that
had a curious charm. And laughing at the wickedness
of Off Broadway, the audience yelling and standing
to cheer, all the boisterous homeliness of it, that too.
And the party, and giving her to my friends and the
two of us dancing and showing off, the particular
harmony and compatibility of that moment, even what
she wore, a soft pale-rose wool shirt, and how I loved
her breasts in that shirt, the lines of her torso and hips
as she moved in the dance. How shy she seemed
then, shy and somewhat reserved; yet the next day,
walking uptown with her from the Modern along Fifth
Avenue, she said, "How nice it is to walk with you
uptown," and I laughed and said, "Here we are in full
view of all the best places, not just Rizzoli but Tiffany
and Cartier and right over there is Miss Elizabeth
Arden, where you used to spend the whole day getting
done." "In another life." She smiled back at me. And
her arm was in mine.

Quickly the moment came again at Kennedy. She
got out of the car very fast and gave her bags to the
porter and waved me on. Was it because she did not
want to say any more goodbyes, the way she did not
want me to make love to her the last night and left me
in despair, then making love to me after she had refused me herself, making love to me almost insultingly,
just so much kindness. Or was it only because she
loathes goodbyes? I rolled over on my stomach, wanting to cry, and she took me from behind. Just as now
the porter removes her and the cop waves me on bitterly, vehemently. Over and gone.

Then two weeks later she called. Early in the morning. The phone reached me still half in sleep, trying
to make a pot of coffee. Her voice pronouncing my
name: never the crisp English syllable, but a sound all
her own, plaintive, today even ominous. Already I'm
scared. I had not recognized her at first; understand-
ably it made her nervous and angry. But she goes on

to the weather, almost as if she'd lost her nerve. Then: "I have something to tell you . . ." "Can you hold on a moment?" I lean over to turn off the coffee. Going to find a cigarette. I'm really scared now. When someone is three thousand miles away and reaches you on a machine, you are at their mercy. And my life is wonderful now, the work goes well, I am happy living alone, my friends come round me, Fumio is kind again, I draw every day, the manuscript speeds along. What if she reaches out this long way and disturbs my precarious peace? And there is good news too— I will see her again in a few days. Unexpectedly, I had gotten a free ticket to the Coast to speak for the Iranian political prisoners at the University of Washington in Seattle, and after the speech I'm being flown to San Francisco for a press conference. "I didn't imagine I would be seeing you again so soon, lady, isn't it wonderful?" I'd crowed at her. "That's what I wanted to talk to you about," she said. That must be it. My stomach panics, she is going to say she will have to be gone the twenty-first, when I'm in town. That I can't see her. I'll go where she is then, I think, picking up the extension phone at the other end of the loft, sitting down on the rug, trying to light a cigarette.

"I have something to tell you. I'm in love." "In love?" "Yes." I am still thinking of the weekend, the twenty-first, I'll see her. She can't take that away. In love—it's so pretentious I would like to laugh. To scream. To tear the machine out of the wall. But I only shake, completely unable to light the cigarette, strike the match, hold on to the receiver. Which has just shot me dead with a word, a phrase. In love. "Well, I suppose I'm glad for you." Trying for the sublime in good will. Remembering we are friends; friends wish each other well. *Ti voglio bene.* Even trying for a chuckle. "It's a nice thing to be in love, you couldn't wish anyone better luck than that." Thinking, All right, let her be in love. I won't be back till January, I can be in love any number of times before then myself. Wishing to God she hadn't told me. I wouldn't mind not knowing just for once.

"I could have fallen in love last night at a party," I

say, "but I wouldn't call you up to bother you with it." "No, this is serious." And it is, her voice makes it so. "It's very painful for me to tell you, but it seems only fair." I am too beaten for any recriminations; I remain silent. "This is really it for me." "I see." The little hope is gone, leaked out into the rug like my strength, like my will to fight, to go there and capture her, confront whoever this is, win her back, struggle, argue, plead. "Who is it? Do I know this person?" "Well, what is there to say? He's thirty-five years old. He's from L.A. . . ." The little touch, the first thing she says about him is his age, younger than I by five years, younger than she by fifteen. And his sex, revealed by a pronoun. If it were a woman, I think, I would try. But a man, no, you can't beat a man with her—no, her voice alone presents this as the ultimate triumph, the real achievement. A young man. The glory of it. L.A. All those trips to Los Angeles. All the boring people whose houses she had to stay at, the husbands of university officials who wouldn't drive her to the airport in the morning, leaving her and her insufficient funds to cope with cab drivers. It all comes together as it falls apart. I'm coming to the West Coast and so she has to tell me she won't be home this weekend, she'll be in Los Angeles with him. She can't spare even a day to see me, has given him all her future. But it's more than that. She is calling to say goodbye. She will be living with him. "No more room in your life for illicit affairs in distant places?" "No, I'm afraid not. He insists on monogamy."

It is all done in a telephone call. There is no need even to write, none whatever to see me in person. She discards me. The young man is named Erik. He used to teach at Sacramento. But then he was married. Now he's getting unmarried. They have been "seeing each other" since last November. On her visits to Los Angeles. On his visits to San Francisco. They have corresponded and talked on the telephone. In those afternoon hours after work when she liked to be alone? It was all going on while I was there. While I was intent upon Neal, there was Erik. What a fool, I never guessed. She goes on, telling the story of their love, their meetings, their plans. "I want to share my life with him," I hear amid the ruin. "I won't bother you now with arrangements about getting your things"—this small mercy, that I do not have to move my papers and books and clothes this very night. "And of course if you're in the Bay area this weekend, although I won't be here, you are welcome to use the house. Maud is here. And Walter. They're having a little thing." The trivia of Maud and Walter and their little thing is too much to bother with; I brush them aside without troubling to register. "No, I'll just cancel the trip to San Francisco. I've promised to speak in Seattle, but afterward I'll just come straight back home." "I'm sorry it worked out this way." "Sure, so am I."

The second is approaching when she will hang up, when it will all be permanently and entirely finished. Her voice winds toward that pause, picks up, but then changes: "You know, for what it's worth to you, whether you believe it or not, and without knowing just what it means now—I still love you." "Yes, I do too. Always." Wanting to say, And if . . . But not saying it. "Goodbye." "Goodbye." And then the line dead.

I do not know yet that I am free.

I go on then. Wanting to recapture her. Having lost her, wanting to recapture that time, and, against the future and its emptiness, to have some copy. Like the photographs we never took. Like the Sita in a long gown in the old movie still, the lawn and skirts of her afternoon, her broad straw brim, her wide-mouthed smile, young and a beauty and in a film. Sita in another life, one I never knew but was favored to catch a glimpse of. Because John Ford came to the little town where she was a waitress and she got to be an extra. Because the hand of time stopped for a moment, was suspended, in an act of art that would last forever, so far beyond its subject. Like the slides she found once at the farm, nude photographs of Ruth I'd taken one day at Provincetown when I got tired of drawing

and out of whim and pique and foolery grabbed the
camera and said, "This does it quicker and without
mistakes." So we made a game of it, photographed
each other, composing the frames, heaping a crimson
coverlet around her great Olympian white skin. "Like
Velázquez," I said, "very classical," the whole thing
half in mockery, half in earnest. Naughtiness, experiment, good times. But how to explain these pictures
to Sita, who was only jealous? And angry. I cursed
myself for not having put them away where she would
not come upon them.

All evidence of life. All the pictures, even these, the
life we had out there, the house, its hours and light,
its glasses of wine, its dinners and bedtimes. Its dull-
ness, its interest, its anguish or mellowness. But away
and beyond now and always, some Sita anywhere and
everywhere: the way her back would move walking
down a street in Rome, the lovely ellipsis of her hips,
the way her leg might pause on a corner in New York,
the lame one with the long cut on its knee, the sight
of her walking out from the foam at Santa Cruz the
weekend we were there two years ago and I was
aghast watching her come out of the water in her
orange bikini, brown and slender and belonging so to
water and ocean. Marina—one of her so numerous
middle names, and she was of the water, loved it in a
way nearly ominous. Because it said California and
the Coast and no other place. She would never live
away from it now. Now that she was free of husbands
and the desert where one husband or another had
made her waste seven years. But coming out of that
water she was her own woman, her head up, listening
to her own echoes only. I was on the beach and her
companion, but I had vanished, become invisible.

And if I could succeed, it would be in honor of that
Sita, the one who doesn't even know me, the Sita who
would go on walking in streets that are mysteries to
me, to eat dinners in restaurants I'll never see, visit
towns I've never heard of, sleep in beds with others
I'll never meet, the pure essence of herself. All that she
has gained or achieved or fought for in her struggle to
be free, to come to independence out of all the obe-

dience she was bred to, trained by circumstance or
necessity, children or husbands or privation.

No, beyond that. Surely the essence is not even in
this created self, deliberate and consciously formed,
but in the unconscious grace of her movements
and her character, the loveliness of her body and its
gestures, the kindness and sympathy, the amazing ingenuity of her attentions, her delicate favors and re-
membrances, the very tenderness of her consideration.
Almost as if a child very much in love permitted its
imagination to work in the placing of a flower by a
plate, a note scribbled where you would find it by surprise. Sita as lover, the eroticism of thoughtfulness or
of wit or of mischief. Or worldliness. Sophistication,
toughness, my slum queen Chiquita, my Sally Jean,
my countess, that delight in all things sensual, the most
inventive hedonism. Behind it the memory of suffering, war, rape, poverty, humiliation. The mixture
of these together producing the woman, the lover, the
companion. That she had suffered much and had
learned how to live. And taught me some of that,
honored me in knowing her. Sita.

NEW FROM BALLANTINE!

FALCONER, John Cheever   27300 $2.25
The unforgettable story of a substantial, middle-class man and the passions that propel him into murder, prison, and an undreamed-of liberation. "CHEEVER'S TRIUMPH . . . A GREAT AMERICAN NOVEL."—*Newsweek*

GOODBYE, W. H. Manville   27118 $2.25
What happens when a woman turns a sexual fantasy into a fatal reality? The erotic thriller of the year! "Powerful."—*Village Voice*. "Hypnotic."—*Cosmopolitan*.

THE CAMERA NEVER BLINKS, Dan Rather with Mickey Herskowitz   27423 $2.25
In this candid book, the co-editor of "60 Minutes" sketches vivid portraits of numerous personalities including JFK, LBJ and Nixon, and discusses his famous colleagues.

THE DRAGONS OF EDEN, Carl Sagan 26031 $2.25
An exciting and witty exploration of mankind's intelligence from pre-recorded time to the fantasy of a future race, by America's most appealing scientific spokesman.

VALENTINA, Fern Michaels   26011 $1.95
Sold into slavery in the Third Crusade, Valentina becomes a queen, only to find herself a slave to love.

THE BLACK DEATH, Gwyneth Cravens and John S. Marr   27155 $2.50
A totally plausible novel of the panic that strikes when the bubonic plague devastates New York.

THE FLOWER OF THE STORM, Beatrice Coogan   27368 $2.50
Love, pride and high drama set against the turbulent background of 19th century Ireland as a beautiful young woman fights for her inheritance and the man she loves.

THE JUDGMENT OF DEKE HUNTER, George V. Higgins   25862 $1.95
Tough, dirty, shrewd, telling! "The best novel Higgins has written. Deke Hunter should have as many friends as Eddie Coyle."—*Kirkus Reviews*